From a Sheffield Childhood to a St Ives Artist

The Memoirs of Victor Bramley

Acknowledgements

Thank you to Chris Keeling of Arc Publishing for his guidance and patience.

Thank you to the numerous friends for their invaluable support, advice, encouragement, and proof reading.

Victor was an emotional man. He would be touched if he were aware of the continued love and regard that his friends and family have for him.

Bernadette Contrino 2021

Published by Arc Publishing and Print
166 Knowle Lane
Sheffield
S11 9SJ

Telephone: 07809 172872
e-mail: chris@arcbooks.co.uk
www.sheffieldbooks.co.uk

Contents

List of Illustrations

From a Sheffield Childhood to a St Ives Artist

Victor Bramley

Preface

I didn't set out to write a book and I'm not sure whether this aspires to be one. It was written in the spirit of self gratification and, in a sense, to purge the memory of accumulated images. These tended to emerge when I was at the easel painting. It was as if some free wheeling clockwork mechanism somewhere in the brain had been tripped whilst concentrating, often a meditative approach to my work. The images became more insistent over the years and I attempted many times to start the story. These early attempts rapidly ended in failure but I found that I couldn't gainsay the ghosts that were prodding me and, successful as literature or not, I am at last relieved to have exorcised some of the memories of my early life. The reader may find that they are of little interest but I would suggest that every life is different, unique, and therefore, has an importance.

I began to realise as I wrote that I was building up not only a picture of people that belonged to me, but a description of a particular place at a particular time that will never be repeated. This may not be a historical document but it has, I hope, a validity. When young one thinks that all things will remain but a return only convinces one of the truth - everything changes.

This is an on-going story. My desire is to write the whole of my life as I remember it. The problem is that I am living faster than I can write and can never hope to finish it. This isn't important. To have travelled is important.

My name was formerly Victor Oliver but when I arrived in St Ives in 1959, to take up the career of an artist, I took my mother's maiden name, Bramley. I suspect that my father wasn't too pleased about this but he never complained to me.

I was born in 1933, so the story really begins in the decade leading up to the Second World War and ends with my passing the Eleven Plus exam and gaining a place at Firth Park Grammar School, of which I have also written.

These writings are dedicated to my father, my mother, and my brother Ernest, with the love that I should have given them when they were alive.

My Beginnings

According to my birth certificate I was born in a rather unprepossessing part of Sheffield (and there were many) called Darnall. Nidd Road to be exact. To be honest though it was more believable to me that I had dropped from the sky or crawled from a rabbit burrow. Not until my Grammar School days did I begin to think that I might just possibly belong to this world in some positive way or another.

Apparently my father took my brother, already five years old, to the Pictures, whilst I put in an appearance. My father said that I cried little and I would spend hours playing with a piece of string that hung from the hood of my pram. A friend of the family happened to be somewhat misaligned or you might say- simple. Dad said that he was "a sissy", whatever that was. When I was born he looked at me in my cot.

"What's his name?" he enquired.

"Victor," announced Father.

"God's gift victorious," he said, beaming from ear to ear.

Considering his own condition his sentiment came as quite a surprise, but so far, he has not been proved a prophet.

Surprisingly although my brother was named Ernest after my father, I was named apparently with a film star in mind: a rough, tough, hombre of the thirties and forties silver screen called Victor McLaglen, (or so my father said - he could have been joking.) There the similarity ended; I was never to be either rough or tough. A curious fact however was that everyone thought that I was named after another famous person of that era called, as I was, Vic Oliver. Star of stage, screen and radio, noted for his whimsical wisecracks and his abuse of his own virtuosity on the violin. He eventually became even more famous by marrying Winston Churchill's daughter. I was not very impressed by all this and really wanted to be my own man so I changed my name as soon as I was able. By then most people had forgotten about Vic Oliver, bit snobbish perhaps: it wasn't a name that I wanted to see appearing on the bottom of my canvases. I didn't suffer as a result of this at school as you might think, and I was never ragged about it, but the truth was I didn't like sharing my name.

The fact that my brother was five years older than me didn't seem to be the real reason for our different attitudes and sensibilities and it was difficult to find anything in which we displayed any similarities whatsoever, so much so that at times I began to doubt my own parentage. I only ever came across one small photo reputing to be of me as a baby whereas Ernest had a huge one of him in place of honour over the front room mantelpiece. The only early photo of us taken together, I suppose when I was about three years old, was a studio picture and shows me with my fringed platinum blonde hair, angelic features and innocent blue eyes gazing into a far off space standing in front of my brother. He, with his hand on my shoulder, bright cheeky face capped with dark hair brushed back and neatly parted, looks out onto his world, not mine.

My parents were always, one had to say, fairly but not desperately poor. Nidd Road was about as poor as one could get though but Father being the fighter that he was managed to upgrade to Gleadless, one of the better parts of Sheffield at the time, being quite modern, open to the wind and away from the industrial smog. Unfortunately he couldn't sustain the increase in rent for more than a year. That's when I was transported to Firvale. Not quite the pastoral paradise that the name suggests but a pleasant enough place, where trees and space could be experienced.

The wrought iron gates of the Workhouse even gave it some sort of regard.

It was called the Workhouse but I was never that sure what the quite magnificent house that could be glimpsed through the high railings actually was. The chain of inmates (often holding hands) that could sometimes be seen filing into what seemed to be idyllic surroundings didn't appear to be fit for any sort of work. On enquiring to my mother, I was only prompted not to stare at them.

The highlight of the tram ride from the City Centre of Sheffield, or the 'Town' as it was always known, was the sudden stoop down Barnsley Hill to Firvale Bottom, heightened as it was by one's elevated position. This was frighteningly steep and if no one wanted the request stop half way down the hill the shaking vehicle would gain such momentum that it always seemed likely that it might leave the tracks - and sometimes it did! The wall at the bottom of the hill was demolished on more than one occasion by a maverick tram travelling at full tilt.
I lived at the bottom of the hill for my first twenty years.
The screech and rattle of the trams negotiating the gradient and clanging their way past the shops along the Front formed a backdrop to my childhood and adolescence.

My very earliest memories are of course rather scarce. I seem to remember wearing soft leggings with many buttons up the side. I can see my mother doing them up one by one. I remember being pushed in a pram up to the pond at Firth Park and looking through the railings at the ducks and swans. I remember seeing the clock tower where the library stands and buying ice cream there. This was before World War Two and there seemed to be an air of gentility about everything. I think my maternal grandmother must have wheeled me there sometimes. She was my link with an age already flown. It all appears in a soft glow like an old sepia photograph with a gentle presence surrounding me. The rhythms of my mother's work around the home would be my next memory: her punching the washing in the metal tub and then the rubbing of it on the washboard with her ring catching the metal ribs; the squeak of the carpet cleaner before the electric Hoover arrived; the noisy mangling of the washing; the soapy water pouring into the tub; and perhaps more than anything, the beat of the flat iron on the mangle top and the particular scent of it all.

1. At the age of nine

The House

Although designated a road Skinnerthorpe was definitely a street outstanding only by dint of its unusual name and the fact that it had a splendid Picture Palace at the top end flanked by a four square mansion known as Cannon Hall. I always regretted that the cannons had been removed long before my time there, according to the legend anyway. Alas we didn't live in the impressive Cannon Hall, quite the opposite, and our house was, one had to say – well, dingy would be a fair word.

2. An early drawing by the author looking across Hodgson's wall. It shows Cannon Hall coach house after it was turned into a laundry - hence the huge extractor. The side of the Sunbeam Picture Palace appears on the right.

We lived in the only house in the street in whose living room you wouldn't have been able to swing the proverbial cat around. In fact if you simultaneously opened the back door to the yard and the interior door to the stairs you only had room to go outside, sit down on either of the two chairs, or perch on top of the mangle (this with its top down doubled as the table on which we all ate our meals - though not all at once.)

With the cat dominating the hearth the only place left to stand was either astride the cat with your bottom roasting on the little iron fire grate, or at the stone sink in the corner by the yard window, or in front of the pantry door that gave on to the cellar steps.

Apart from heating the oven the fire did a far better job of heating the doors of the toy, boot and pot cupboards when these were accidentally left open. The green paint blistered beautifully and my brother and I took great delight in popping them. This activity was always severely frowned upon as it did leave nasty scars on the doors, but blister popping was never neglected on our part.

Between the pantry door and the stair door there was just enough room to house an old wireless set on a small cupboard.

Fortunately at this time we were all very small in stature. My parents being only around five feet and two inches, my brother Ernest and I only exceeded this in our adolescence. The trick was either never to all be indoors at once, or for two to sit down whilst the other two stood very still, or sat on the floor with the cat. The one benefit of this familial congestion was that it kept us warm and anyway, as luck would have it, my brother was a complete extrovert and as Mum always said,

"Our Ernie only comes home to sleep or when he's hungry."

The 'Front' room or 'Best' room overlooked the street and was more of a normal size however it was only used on Sundays or when we had visitors, usually at Christmas. It sported a modern table with the latest pull out leaves. The top was highly polished and rarely saw the light of day being covered as it was by a felt mat. A three piece suite with polished wooden arms, which we were warned not to mark, completed the ensemble, together with an old dresser whose drawers and cupboards contained most of my parents' few worldly possessions.

In later years my parents revealed that the previous occupants had held séances there. I think this may have had some bearing on some small events; but I would not be at all sure.

Early every Sunday morning Father went through the ritual of lighting the Front room fire and the rest of the family waited for the smoke to clear. The room usually became habitable by about 2 p.m. but only achieved a reasonable mean temperature if the doors and windows were closed. One had the option of choking or freezing. If the wind was in the wrong quarter we suffered the smoke billowing out into the room periodically for the rest of the day.

Upstairs there was no problem like this as there was no choice. The only form of heating was the bodily kind and for long winter months we shivered. The cat came in handy and he would be smuggled up to bed whenever possible.

The stairs were very steep and, when descending, they seemed to be only a few degrees from verticality. This was due to the curious shape of the house. An underground stream ran between the houses and so couldn't be built upon; consequently ours was the only yard in the street that had a wide passageway access. This entry was used by cars to approach three garages that were situated in a line behind our diminutive raised garden.

The small bedroom where my brother and I slept together overlooked the little garden and the equally small gardens of our neighbours and it was only when you raised your eyes to the trees at the end of the garage area that vistas began to open up. The trees in fact were in the grounds of Cannon Hall which, with its lawns, gardens, coach house, huge greenhouse, chicken run, small orchard and pond covered an area large enough to swallow up the rest of the street.

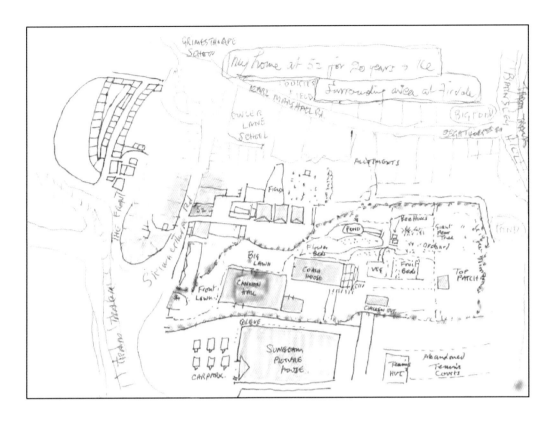

3. My home at 52 Skinnerthorpe Road.

Surrounding all this were acres of allotments on two sides and, on the other side, abandoned dirt tennis courts together with a large decaying wooden clubhouse. This overlooked the back of the Sunbeam Picture Palace. All of this was our playground; an area in which to burst from the tiny house, go wild and be anything you wanted to be; from Tarzan to Biggles, any other hero, or an English International sports star at any game that you could dream up.

But back to the house. Across the top of the stairs from our room was our parents' bedroom. When I was very ill I would be transported into my parents' bed and the doctor would be called, otherwise this was a no go area. The short landing outside our room led onto an even smaller room known to us later as Ernie's room as this was where in later years he had to sleep when we were no longer infants. This room was built over the outside passageway. There was no electric light in this room or on the landing. The old gas brackets were still there but no longer of any use. These then were places of dark shadows and they always made me very nervous. This was somewhere where ghosts probably lived, especially behind the curtain in the corner of Ernie's room - the Bunghole. My brother was not in the least bit worried about sleeping there and treated my fear as a huge joke often adding to it by telling ghost stories, pulling devilish faces or making weird noises whilst hiding behind the curtain with the domestic rejects. How he could actually sleep there on his own was a complete mystery to me and I avoided the place like the plague, never feeling comfortable there even in later life. However there was a worse place even than that. Opposite his door a small bare staircase wound up to a very large attic that was dimly illuminated by only one small dirty skylight. This attic stretched the whole length of the house and was by far the largest room. Dusty and empty it was never used. This surely had to be the breeding ground of all ghostly things. I knew that to go up there alone was to risk coming face to face with something unspeakable.

The cellar was more interesting, but I was rather nervous about that too. At least it had a light and one could practice chopping sticks and shovelling coal into the approved bucket. Also down there, Mother kept her home made beetroot wine which she amply strengthened with stout. I can taste it now. She would stand at the top of the steps and count the bags of coal as the black-faced coalman emptied them down the cellar grate, just to make sure he wasn't cheating. Unfortunately numbers were never her strongpoint and she would invariably loose count anyway. Always forgetful she would also sometimes lock herself out of the house, and my brother, and later, myself, would be called in to squeeze through the grate and stumble across the cellar to the light switch, being careful not to knock over the precious wine in the process.

4.   The Bramleys   1933

Lily, Freddie (Sonny), Grandad, Mabel, Nelly, Grandma and Billy.

Sonny died in his 20's from a brain tumour. Nelly lived out her life in Canada.
I am in my mother's belly.

11

My Parents

5. My mother and father in 1926

Father was a butcher.

"I'm not a butcher - I'm a butcher's cutter. We're all butchers' cutters. It's only your grandfather who's a butcher. He's a Master Butcher." There was no pride in his voice.

"Why is he a master butcher?" "'Cos he owns the business and we all work for him."

By 'we all' he was referring to himself and several of his brothers, my uncles. Altogether, he had eight brothers, all butchers, and five sisters, and even some of the sisters knew quite a bit about butchering meat. A large Edwardian family, they were a hearty lot; reared and very well known in that exceptional part of Sheffield called Attercliffe. Father pointed out that in fact they were the original Teddy Boys and the trend that happened after the War was a bit out of its time and not as unique as we thought. Needless to say, I didn't subscribe to it.

My father always liked to claim that they were responsible for feeding the steelworkers of Sheffield as they held the prime position in the heart of the steelworks - and there was much truth in that.

Father left school to work for his father at twelve years old. At this tender age he was told to take himself up to the Wicker Arches, some two miles away, where he would find a group of cattle which were due for slaughter.

"Put your hand on the head of the biggest beast and walk it back to the shop. The rest will follow it", commanded Grandpa. Attercliffe Road in those days, somewhere around 1920, would not have been full of speeding cars but it must still have been a nightmare job for a diminutive little lad just out of school.

Father was very short in stature. He had to strut to get anywhere fast. I would sometimes walk the two hundred yards to meet him as he alighted from the bus that carried the workers from Attercliffe. He would be striding out along the Front, one hand clutching his case and the other typically clenched into a fist. With his greasy grey trilby pulled over his eyes like some Chicago gangster, dull grey flannels and jacket, raincoat over his arm and stubble starting from his stubborn chin, it's an image that stays with me still. His words to me were always few. I knew that he could speak at great length with logic and passion, especially when embroiled in some political or business debate with his brothers. He just wasn't much good at kid's talk.

"Ah do. Aureyt ah' tha'? Bin' t'ut school? Good lad." -and that would be it - sometimes for the evening. Often he would stand over the fire ruminating, not choosing to share his thoughts with anyone, and indulging in his curious habit of making popping noises with his bottom lip- probably something to do with his very bad teeth. This wasn't the only affliction from which he suffered. He had psoriasis. This appeared as very large scabs on his elbows and down the back of his forearms. "It's not catching," he would declare. He also had it on his knees, though I never saw this - shorts were definitely not his fashion. He wasn't one for showing off his body, fortunately for us. He would often be unable to resist the temptation of having a good scratch usually in front of the kitchen fire. Pip, the cat, would often be the uncomplaining recipient of the product of both his skin problems, the other being recurring dandruff. Mother would continually reprimand Father but he would sometimes scratch until he bled. Pip however didn't mind Dad's effrontery, as he was always the first to receive bounty from Dad's case on his return from work. A bloody paper full of 'lights' would be slapped onto the lino and the cat would lift the offal with its talons, giving it some animation, and then 'kill' it with a swift grinding bite from the side of its jaws; at the same time emitting an unnerving primeval sound that belied the fact that this was a domestic animal. I quickly learnt that only blood-red meat brought forth this reaction and bits of bread and jam or potted meat dropped surreptitiously under the table at meal times would be ignored with a disdainful glance or consumed in silence.

"Never touch 'im when he's eytin' t'meyt." I didn't need telling twice.

6. My father with his brothers at Freestone Place in Attercliffe, where they grew up.
Harry, Edwin, Alf, Harold, my father, George, Ted the eldest, Herbert. A gap was left
in the middle as Dick, the youngest, was away serving with the Armed Forces.

The family had several butchers' shops at Attercliffe which were run with great efficiency, cleanliness and, above all, a great display of northern humour - particularly important in the War years. They were all brought up in a large Victorian house that had once been a vicarage. It stood solid and dark by the old graveyard that formed the cul-de-sac of Freestone Place. Along the other side of the grimy graveyard with its blackened tombstones ran the main Sheffield to Rotherham road, part of it being Attercliffe Common-or simply, the Common. This noisy teeming thoroughfare was the main artery of the steelworks and had the reputation of being the dirtiest place in England. This claim to infamy was, I felt, well merited as it was a safe bet that no one could walk the length of it, a mile or so, without getting an eye full of grit and dirty feet.

"Where there's muck, there's money" was an oft quoted maxim and certainly some of my uncles seemed to have done very well with splendid cars and desirable houses but, alas, not us. The family appeared to span a wide range from well off to hard up and unfortunately we seemed to be at the wrong end of that spectrum. However being in this trade meant that food, at least, wasn't as hard to come by as many other people found, especially in the War period, when almost everything was rationed and some things impossible to get. I was fed on all manner of meat and from an early age I was no stranger to the product of the cow, pig and sheep. Brains, tripe, sweetbreads, udder, heart, liver and kidneys were consumed with equal sanguinity, though tripe was certainly not my favourite dish. I wasn't told what I was eating until it was too late to make a difference; by then I had realised that some of it was quite delicious.

"What's this, Dad?" I would query, eyeing the contents of my plate suspiciously. "That'll do ye' good. Eyt' it up" I would only draw the line at fat and this in any form I would stolidly refuse to eat even though I would often see it consumed avidly, and often noisily, by my father and my uncles on social occasions. On Sundays we would sometimes have a joint of meat that Dad would ceremoniously carve, after first sharpening the long knife with deft strokes of the butcher's 'steel', a performance he was proud of and always performed at high speed and with professional gusto. Ernest and I would vie for the rich hot juices that flowed into the bottom

7. My mother

of the dish. Sometimes, if the eggs ran to it, Mother would bake a cake in the old oven that ran its erratic course by the tiny coal fire that serviced it. She was never hysterical but the unpredictability of her cooking facilities often drove her to the limits of her patience. Cakes and bread would magically deflate in the interior of this iron box and many culinary tragedies would emerge from its somewhat murky insides. To me, the legend of King Alfred seemed to have quite a predictable and a not surprising end. Of course the cakes were burnt - weren't they always?

My mother was a quiet person, as genteel as her upbringing would allow and there's no doubt that I took after her in looks and demeanour. As a young girl she worked for Viners, the famous Sheffield cutlers. Her job was to line the presentation boxes that held the better quality cutlery. This was factory work, but I think that she enjoyed the company of her fellow workers.

Her delight was to dance, and as her father happened to be the very smartly turned-out master of ceremonies at the local dance hall, I imagine she was never short of aspiring beaux. Old photos show how very pretty she was. Father was quite a dapper chappie too; Granny Oliver called him 'the particular bugger' as he was so fastidious. Being about equal in height, my parents would have been well suited, especially as they were both excellent ballroom dancers and I assume that they met on the dance floor.

It wasn't usual for women to work after marriage, especially if they were bringing up children and Mother was no exception to this.

I think that my brother and I were enough to cope with.

All I have of my maternal grandfather is a couple of old photos, one so smart in his official ballroom dress. He died of cancer before I was born.

The other sadness in my mother's life was the loss of her younger brother Freddie, affectionately known as Sonny. He died aged around twenty from a brain tumour, an affliction that eventually took away my own brother at the age of fifty-eight.

Young Friends

For me life centred on the house and the yard until I was trusted to cross the street on my own. In truth, cars were so rare it could be many an hour before one would appear. At the tender age of, I suppose, four, I did have one little friend who lived across the street. She was called Patti Farrell. I remember she had dark brown curls and a temper. For a while we just used to look at each other from across the street, that great divide, but eventually in our childish way we became friends and indulged our imaginations. I was never as keen on her after she had bitten my little finger. I don't know - it may have been passion. An idiosyncrasy that one of us had concocted was that instead of waving goodbye we would salute each other in military fashion and shout "God save the King!" After a while I began to feel quite embarrassed about this and always made sure that I was well up the 'entry' and out of sight of any passersby. One week she failed to put in an appearance and, on enquiring why, I was told that her father had died and she and her mother had moved away. Later on I learnt that he had, in fact, been pierced in the abdomen by a white-hot steel bar whilst at his job in the steelworks. I toyed with this gruesome vision as a child and never quite came to terms with it. Years later I was to work in the steelworks myself.

Shortly after that Gordon Parsons came to live in that same house. Another blue eyed blond, he looked even more fragile than I did. I suppose that we were undernourished and this was shortly to become exacerbated as World War Two began to become a very relevant factor in our lives. For the moment I recognised him as a survivor and probably more resilient than he looked. He was certainly important to me for the time being. I was allowed to play over at his house, ours not being big enough. Although naturally curious of other people, I always felt very self-conscious and uncomfortable away from home. Gord's mother was a very outspoken large lady and I quickly learnt that not everyone was as gentle and soft-spoken as my mother. His father was as thin as she was fat and he appeared to be rather old to be Gord's dad. As Gord had a much older brother who only rarely put in an appearance, I assumed that he had been married before. He walked with a stick and had to strut along stiffly with one leg held out at an angle. I thought his stiff leg could be made of wood but my natural good manners forbade me to ask. Despite this very obvious handicap and, looking a very ill matched couple, they were always very cheerful and friendly and that meant a lot to me. They seemed even poorer than we were.

He was the local cobbler, the front of the house being one of the shops that lined the shopping area that we called the Front. I would see him sitting there in the large window, high up to catch all the available light. He had a great view of everyone passing by and if you caught his twinkling eye he would grin and give a cheery wave. With his hobbing foot in his lap, nails would appear from between his thin lips at regular intervals as he tick-tacked away at one of the rows of shoes that surrounded him. The shop was called Coombs and I couldn't understand why he was called Parsons. After all my dad was called Oliver and it said Oliver on the front of the shop where he worked. When Mr.Parsons finished work he would often sit with his wife

15

and Gordon in their gloomy sitting room and with the aid of his one good leg he would play the small organ that stood against the wall and they would all sing, usually hymns. This was all very strange to me and I was quite happy to be an observer. When someone spoke to me I was usually quite tongue-tied and would blush deeply. He would also tell Gord rude jokes which were then relayed to me and this didn't help much either. This unfortunate shackle stayed with me for many years and only failed to afflict me when I was with my closest friends. Up to that point Gord was the only one I had. Although younger and even frailer than me, he perhaps had a bit more inner strength and independence as a consequence of the closeness and outspokenness that seemed to exist in the family. It wasn't long before he was put to work as a delivery boy and helper to the small butchers' shop across the tramlines and seemed quite content doing it. Later, whilst our Saturdays would be spent playing football or lounging in the park, he would be earning some money, although, to my credit, I did do a paper round for a while.

Ernie

The one big bonus about having an older, popular and outgoing brother was that he would often return home, after one of his frequent sorties, with arms full of comics, a prize of one of his bartering ventures, and I would fall on these with great excitement. All the unusual adventures that I found therein were fascinating; even though I had plenty of trouble relating them to my own small world. A cowboy, with a huge bristly jaw who ate cow pie; an ostrich that ate absolutely everything; a cat that talked and had more friends than I could imagine; and philosophical tramps that somehow always finished up being presented with plates of mashed potatoes with sausages sticking up, and usually sitting outside the Ritz! All very peculiar. By far the strangest characters were Pip, Squeak and Wilfred. These were very odd creatures indeed and, rather than entertain me, they made me feel very uneasy, seeming as they did, to live in a claustrophobic world of a rather menacing nature. Odd bods indeed. Eventually these copies of the Beano, Dandy, Funny Wonder, Radio Fun etc. were whisked away to be swapped off, only to be replaced by even more. Later on American comics hit the scene.

8. With my brother, Ernest.

Most of the days I never knew as to where my brother had disappeared. He seemed to exist on another planet, one that certainly wasn't circling in my particular universe. Nevertheless, he did have some brotherly duties to perform. If it was already dark he would be told to accompany me across the yard, sometimes in the snow, to the outdoor toilet.

This onerous task was alleviated by his being allowed to take a lighted candle as there was no light in there. As he was fond of playing with lit candles this was no chore. He would delight in seeking out spiders in the niches of the whitewashed walls whilst I was earnestly doing my best.

Spider hunting, in fact, became one of the 'sports' that we could share. The old stone wall up the yard was the arena for this. Some of the monsters were very big and looked, to my eyes, pretty evil. He would either tease them to come out with a bit of grass or, even better, go on a fly catching expedition first and deliver up the victims to be paralysed and silk-balled. It all seemed a bit fiendish to me but I couldn't deny the fascination and shock at seeing these nightmarish creatures rush menacingly from their dark holes in the wall. I would squirm with the adrenaline shooting up my legs. Later on I would become an expert fly catcher as, on hot summer days, they would pour into the kitchen from the allotments and the two sticky paper ribbons that Mother hung up soon filled. I quickly learnt that flies didn't see as well from the side as they did from above and a swift swipe across the wall would usually arrest them. At least drowning them in a bowl of water seemed a bit more humane than offering them up for live sacrifice! However it did seem to take a long time as they carried their own bubble of air with them! It was early bio-research work of a serious nature. Fly sprays hadn't been invented of course. To be honest it wasn't easy without a bathroom or even a decent place to get washed. Friday nights tended to be bath night and in the early days Ernest and I would share the zinc bath in front of the fire. Mother having to top up with hot water from the kettle on the hob. Ernest would play, squirting little fountains of soapy water from between clenched hands or making the soap jump up.

I noticed that he was playing with something else.

'What's that?' I enquired.

'Look! It's a torpedo!' Proudly.

'Mum, he's gorra' torpedo - I want one.'

'Don't be silly - you've got one as well.' Extremely puzzled I was searching under the water. 'There, ducky, there'. She pointed. Oh - that! I never realised. Well, well, well. 'But his is bigger!'

'That's 'cos he's older. Yours'll get bigger'. I settled for that and tried to make the soap jump. Having been thoroughly soaped and sponged by Mother- me yelping if the soap got in my eyes- and then dried off, the bath would be lifted, carefully so as not to cause a tidal wave, and taken into the yard for the water to be poured away down the grate. I think Father went to the public baths on the Common which of course, were not just for swimming but had bathtubs in rows of cubicles.

The differences between my brother and I were total. Being so much older he had his own circle of friends and, later on, I had mine. Rarely did we mix comfortably and usually not at all. Many would be the times that he would be off on some adventure and refusing to take me with him despite my mother's protestations. You can't argue with someone who's already left! Sometimes I almost forgot that I had a brother.

He was a superior being. He was handsome, strong, with fine teeth and an open, optimistic nature. He was never ill, feared nothing and was never phased. I, on the other hand, was frail, had poor teeth, fell sick easily and was often frightened by my own shadow. At least I had my mother's shoulder to cry on when necessary.

Yet there were the occasional wonderful times when I was allowed to accompany him past the confines of the yard and make the exciting trip into the land of Cannon Hall, the home of his friend, Bobby Allen. To my young eyes it seemed to be a place of magic where anything might happen. It was a fantasy land of jungle, canals, glass palaces, haunted rooms, trenches, battlefields, gardens hung with fruit and flowers, voracious cacti and encounters with insects, animals and people. To a small undeveloped mind it was looking into an age past and a life to come - but somehow I knew, for me, one never to be acquired. I could only be an onlooker.

Bobby

The Prince, the Tarzan, the Genghis Khan of this sequestered world was Bobby. Slightly older than my brother, he was already well educated and experienced in affairs that to me were not yet even dreamt of. Forthright, unafraid, expressive and, wherever possible, anarchistic: he ruled the roost. Fair, tall and athletic, he was the archetypal schoolboy hero. With classic good looks, his finely chiselled nose fell straight from his brow and this together with his close set unwavering gaze gave him the aspect of the hawk. The whole family was rather grand. To me, his mother seemed like the Queen. Kindly and beautifully spoken she went about her gardens, sunhat shading her rounded form, gracefully cropping flowers into her large wicker basket.
As she was small and round, so her husband Mr. Allen or properly, Mr. Hope-Allen, was very tall and straight. Standing around six feet, four inches, or maybe even more, he was a very imposing figure. His countenance was stern and uncompromising with a silent manner and a wire appearing from an appliance in his ear, he had a truly overpowering presence.
He kept bees in his orchard in three hives and, from the safety of my bedroom, I could watch him appear, garbed all in white, from the yard at the rear of the Hall. A huge straw hat from which dropped the mysterious veil of the apiarist, added to his impressive height. Large leather gauntlets covered his arms and hands, one of which held a curiously shaped canister that emitted a thin plume of white smoke. Stalking down the lawn in front of his house he looked like some latter day Don Quixote out to do battle, or even a space man ready to zap some monster lurking in his orchard. I never really got used to this bizarre sight and would always endeavour not to cross his path if I happened to be in his domain. Bobby had an older sister, Joan, and an older brother, Jack. Jack was a professional soldier and a Captain in the Army. We often heard tell of brother Jack but only rarely caught sight of him on his infrequent visits home. He was a romantic figure in his smart immaculate uniform and he sported a large ginger moustache to complete the ensemble. Joan on the other hand was always around and lived in one of the back rooms of the Hall with her new husband Lawrence. He was in the Air Force and always appeared to be studying for some exam or other when he was home.
Joan was a redhead and a very friendly person and I always hoped that if I bumped into anyone in the dark passages of the house, it would be her.
Granny Allen was still very much in evidence and she was the most vociferous of the bunch. Bobby adored her and would hang around her skirts. He seemed to be more like Granny in his manner than anyone else. She would direct operations from the depth of one of the huge armchairs in the large front living room. If it was a fine sunny day the family would take up residence at the top of the lawn, in front of the French windows, and she would sit there dressed in black with a shawl around her looking very much like Queen Victoria. I was afraid of her too, and I would always try to do my 'keep invisible' act whilst in her presence. She would rarely allow me to do this however, and would attempt to draw me into speaking. I would then offer one or two words and blush deeply.
"Look at him blushing! He's a mummy's boy, he is." And, of course, I was.
Although such remarks would evoke a strong desire to run off down the cinder path I would be too fascinated to do so. I found the whole family absolutely riveting. Although they perhaps had a dilettante image, surrounded as they were by working class folk, it had to be said that

they were the aristocracy of our small province of Firvale and, in retrospect, I was fortunate to be associated with them mainly because they definitely expanded my view of things.

Unless I was with my brother or Bobby I wasn't expected to wander at will in the grounds, but I did have free access to the lower areas that were out of sight of the house. A small fence had to be negotiated. This marked the boundary of the garage area with its concrete apron - that and a six foot brick wall leading to the allotments. If you gave the fence a smart kick, earwigs would fall out. The sight of these strange creatures would make my flesh creep and the shape of their scissor-like ends and the possible usage didn't escape my attention. I was always careful not to get any down my socks and certainly not near my ears!

The pond was just around the corner from the high sloping flowerbeds that hung heavy with the scent of dahlias, gladioli and many other flowers. Girt around with trees, it was a secret place.

The irresistible fascination with water could never be denied and the little pond was the centre of activities. Bobby had a collection of interesting toys that far surpassed our few cheap, battered ones and, on special occasions, a steamer or an unsinkable papier mâché lifeboat would be ceremoniously launched down the side of the pond. A few yards away a small stream appeared from a tunnel that, Jules Verne-like, seemed to go back into the bowels of the earth. This then formed a small canal that held minute fish and other aquatic wonders such as fresh-water shrimps.

Sometimes Bobby would build a clay dam across the neck of the canal and after waiting for a build-up of water this would be breached, usually with a short speech. Everyone present, shouting and whooping, would rush up the bank at the back of the pond in order to get a good view of the tidal wave as it surged across and down another tunnel on the other side. This of course was the stream that continued underground and flowed beneath our yard and under our passageway. It wasn't seen again until it emerged far away in Upwell Street, well named, in a culvert and continued on its way to join the great River Don.

One such dam project was fairly memorable for me as Bobby, carried away with his usual enthusiasm, ran down the bank and inadvertently- at least I think it was inadvertent- pushed me into the pond. My brother quickly retrieved me and tried to inveigle me into not telling, but on this occasion as I was wringing wet, I didn't have much choice other than to slop homewards leaving a wet trail behind me.

Ernie knew that it would mean a good telling off, if not a smart cuff from Mother and this is probably why he didn't really want me there in the first place. Bobby on the other hand couldn't have cared less and I was just as likely to be knocked in the next time.

He was still my God. Gods were blameless. A law unto themselves.

Near the pond a bull rope hung from the branches of a sycamore: a tree whose leaves, incidentally, were the first I came to recognise. I always stood well back as they did their Tarzan act, Bobby hanging upside down and giving out the famous yodel. Once in typical derring do fashion he tried to defy gravity altogether, lost his grip and fell headlong into the canal with a mighty splash. Considering that the canal flowed between narrow stone walls, I thought it a brilliant piece of aiming and all part of his Johnny Weismuller impression. His dramatic ability, or affliction, was undeniable and most things were usually exploited to that end. In my own shy way I tried to conform to this ethic in order to get his praise.

One day, having been taken prisoner, he volunteered to be tied to a tree in the orchard. This wasn't any hardship to him and wasn't an uncommon occurrence. So far no one had been able to secure him successfully. My brother left me to guard whilst he went on some mission. On noting that he was yet again about to break loose, I took the chance to impress him with my acting ability. Withdrawing my tiny battered mother of pearl handled fruit knife- one of my brother's cast-offs- I gently prodded him in the belly. For once surprise was on my side but the effect of this effrontery was even more surprising. "Ye Gods!" He cried. "Ernest, Ernest! This infidel has mortally wounded me. I think I'm dying!"

I was quite pleased to be called an infidel although I didn't know what it meant. At least it gave me some sort of stature.

My brother appeared running down the Top Path as fast as he could. "Wh - what?", gasping for breath.

"He's stabbed me several times with his kukri. I'm done for."

By this time he was on his knees clutching at his belly and looking at his hands for signs of blood. Superb acting - probably Errol Flynn.

"Banish him! Banish him from these lands!"

Cripes! Things were getting a bit volatile. I'd brought the King to his knees.

"He - he was trying to escape" Panicking as I realised that I was indeed to be banished - whatever that meant. My brother whispered in my ear.

"Ye'd better go 'ome until he's calmed down."

I thought this very unfair. Having achieved a major victory I was loath to go - but go I must. Trudging home once more with hands deep in my pockets, tears welled up from somewhere inside me. I was banished. I gave the little fence a vicious kick and squashed three earwigs with my foot. Justice had to be seen to be done. It was the Law. Bobby's Law.

The next time would see me trying to get into the act once again, but truly, the great adventures were not yet for me. I would often be left crying by the little fence as my brother ran up the lawn to join Bobby and his comrades. They would run shouting up the back steps in the Hall yard and I would hear them making their way across the Top Patch, across the abandoned tennis courts and into an unknown distance.

"Come in and stay with me." Mother would say. "Come and draw me a picture." I would sit at the mangle that doubled as a table and draw a picture of aeroplanes, as tears plopped onto the page of my exercise book.

Christmas

On Christmas morning early - sometimes before sunrise- Ernest would shake me awake.

"He's been! - Father Christmas! Look! Look!"

The glare from the bare bulb in the ceiling, hurting my eyes, would reveal two bulging pillowcases hanging off the end of the bed.

"Get yours - on t'other side!" excitedly hauling his onto the bed. I struggled awake, feverishly groping inside the sack. What's this? An apple, an orange, a box of Rowntree's Fruit Pastilles, a painting book, some toffees, and - a red chocolate vending machine, like on Victoria Station - with tablets of real chocolate in it.

"I can't get them out, Ernie," I exclaimed, exasperated.

"You need a penny. There's one." A golden penny - all new and bright. Another one and a shiny sixpence and a threepenny bit- all neat corners.

"Put yer penny in - ye' can gerrit back afterwards." It worked. A chocolate in bright shiny paper fell from the tiny drawer.

Fantastic things there were not but it was all special. A jigsaw could be pondered over for the whole of Christmas and the fact that Dad joined in made it all very special indeed. We played cards with a pack that, for my benefit, didn't have spots but colour pictures of funny people:

nevertheless they still made houses and skyscrapers and garages for Dinky toys of which we had one or two: until Ernie, true to form, would create an earthquake by shaking the table and I would cry again.

Colouring books and crayons were my favourite. I liked the smell of the wax crayons - all new in a smart carton with a window. They would soon be worn away or broken into bits and carelessly trod into the carpet.

"Look - I'll kill you - you little bugger." She didn't mean it. Ernest got all the clips around the ear - with the thick wedding ring. He was old enough to know better, whatever it was. He did, it must be said, have a penchant for upsetting me, mainly because the age difference of five years precluded him from getting over fascinated with any games that I liked to play. I suppose I was his best toy.

He would set me off with great enthusiasm.

"Let's play Indians! You Crazy Horse. Me Sitting Bull." He would hang a bed sheet to the hook on the back of the door and tie the ends to the bedposts. Squatting cross-legged in our wigwam in our pyjamas, we would wobble our index fingers in our mouths in the traditional manner and wait for Custer to arrive. Unfortunately I never met Custer, as Ernest would get rapidly bored and jumping up with a 'whoop' would run off down the stairs and leave me wailing inconsolably. Most of our mutual projects ended thus. Sometimes, in frustration, I would attack him furiously with both fists and feet flying, but he would invariably catch my hands in a vice-like grip that would infuriate me even more and I would be driven to rages of futile kicking and head butting whilst he, laughing, effectively held me at arm's length.

He would be the recipient of all the pent-up spleen that my tender years could muster until, finally being let loose, I would be left alone to turn anger into abject misery. His presence always excited me but he never failed to desert me; to his credit though, he never hit me. This was my brother.

The activity that seemed to cause most ructions and which my mother hated the most of all, was the cooking of the Christmas turkey. Father's work at the shop was always very hard but at Christmas it was increased manifold. Turkeys and chickens by the score would have to be killed, beheaded, plucked, drawn, dressed and then sold over the counter or delivered in the old Commer vans with Uncle Dick, Edwin or Harold at the wheel. As Christmas drew near Father would arrive home later and later, so much so that Mother would complain bitterly that she hardly ever got to see him as, being so tired, he would have to go straight to bed. He would arrive home with feathers still sticking to his clothes, and worse - fleas!

"They're not human fleas - they'll drop off." We all suspected that they dropped off onto the cat, where they took up happy residence.

We would await our turkey, Mother with great trepidation. It was always due on the last day of work as, of course, we didn't have a fridge. Once, I remember, it was too big to go into the oven and Father had to cook it next door; on another occasion, it was already high and smelt fairly awful.

"All those bloody turkeys and we have to have this stinker", Mother spat.

"Well it's fo' nowt'. It'll be alreyt' when it's cooked."

"Aye we know! Bloody fools we are; always get t'rubbish wot's left."

"It's not rubbish. It'll be alreyt I said." Father would admonish, she would complain, and the row would simmer on, sometimes longer than the turkey did.

Mother worried too much. Father was overbearing. Ernest would just grin and I would feel like crying and often did. It was hard for them but we kids didn't know any better anyway. We were happy enough. His wages were poor. The rent was eight shillings and sixpence a week.

HERBERT TED ALF HAROLD EVELYN (IN CANADA) DAD GEORGE EDWIN HARRY

EDNA LYDIA GRANDMA OLIVER DICK GRANDPA OLIVER LILY GLADYS

9. A Family Gathering

A Rather Large Family

The vicarage at Freestone Place was where my Uncle George and his family lived after my grandparents had moved out and gone to live in the safer haven of Brampton-en le Morthern. It would often see a huge family gathering especially at Christmas and again at other special times. There would be singsongs, games such as Monopoly and cards, and sometimes events that were perhaps rather more radical. Food and drink were always on the menu. Mother would always rile at being winkled out of her comfort zone and generally this is what would engender the rows that they sometimes had. Father always wanted to bring the family together but Mother always had to do battle with her shyness and inferiority complex, as did I. It was easy to see where I got mine. However, I did quite enjoy seeing all my uncles, aunties and cousins: Uncle George had eight children, carrying on the tradition. Pretty soon the argument would be over; my hair slicked back with a drop of water -or Corporation Hair Oil as Ernie called it-, the best of my clothes put on, and we would be off to Attercliffe, sometimes having to walk if the trams were on holiday too. The walk through the steelworks area would be strangely quiet and mysterious - something I enjoyed – perhaps with the muffled sound of a lone hammer doing a bit of overtime. Ernest would be down there already, attached to his cousins with a family umbilical cord, often sleeping over. I think that this facility also gave him easy access, together with his cousins, to all the Attercliffe girls. The vicarage would be full of people, many unknown to me. Uncle George would be directing operations and Aunt Ethel would be making Mother feel comfortable: Mum liked Aunt Ethel - she wasn't "stuck-up". "Fat? Tastiest part of the beast - that's a fact!" A red-faced uncle would declare as he sliced away at a joint of meat. A huge sandwich with doubtful looking strata hanging from the sides would be thrust upon me by a grinning cousin. "'Eyt that up, Vic lad!" "Oh! Thanks, Terry".

Inspection would prove out my worst fears, and I would surreptitiously convey the fatty contents of the sandwich to the living room fire. It was all very well intended but I failed to become one of the robust, friendly crowd into whose family bosom I had found myself born. Grown up games would be staged and uncles would take the floor and tell risqué jokes. I was usually an embarrassed onlooker.

High jinks were not just for Christmas. Many were the stories related of the doings of the Oliver Brothers of Attercliffe. Some of them, no doubt due to their dubious nature, were withheld from my as yet undeveloped psyche.

As well as feeding the people of Attercliffe, my uncles felt that they also had a duty to cheer them up in times of war and tribulation. Customers would often pop into the shop just to be entertained.

One story passed down to me by my cousin Eveline was related to a particular day of celebration and alluded to military honour and sacrifice - probably a Remembrance Day. Having given respect and acknowledgement to the customers who had fought a war and wished to prove it by wearing their medals, my uncles quickly realised that they hardly had a medal between them, even though some had seen service. Not to be outdone, a visit to the bins in the yard and a few minutes with a pair of tin snips produced a splendid array of 'medals' made from corn beef tins and bottle tops etc. Continuing to serve in the shop with dead-pan faces and said array of 'medals' on the chest, customers were suitably impressed by the fact that all the brothers, as they appeared from the recesses of the shop, seemed to have been well decorated. On being questioned, they were well capable of giving graphic descriptions of the battles in which they had fought. They didn't mean any disrespect - it was all part of the passing show.

They spent a great part of their lives cutting up animals, after all, and delicate natures had no part in the workplace. They were clean and first class at their jobs, even though the occasional headless chicken would accidentally wander into the shop from the back working area where it had been decapitated; the initial act in providing food for those who had enough coupons saved up in order to afford such a luxury.

The masters of bizarre humour were probably the three younger brothers, Harold, Dick and Edwin. Granny Oliver in her time at Freestone Place liked to keep a bit of livestock in the outhouses. She kept chickens in the yard and also had two tiny piglets on which she lavished attention, even affection. She fed and cared for them as if they were children and took great pride in seeing them so happy and healthy.

One dark night, the boys quietly exchanged them for two full grown pigs. The next morning Granny was seen, bending over the half-door, scratching her head and looking very puzzled.

My uncles' shops -and eventually there were about seven of them- often acted as help zones. Apart from outrageously flirting with the Attercliffe lasses, the brothers were there to offer advice, sympathy, practical help and humour to anyone who crossed the threshold, or even sometimes paying call at the back door. They also had little compunction or sentiment over swift justice or quick solutions. It was a hard life - there was not time to finesse.

A customer opened the back gate, crossed the yard and knocked on the back door. My father answered it. Could he please take a kitten off her hands, as she really could not manage to look after yet another one. Always happy to oblige, Father took the kitten and deftly despatched it behind the door, breaking its neck with a flick of his strong fingers. It was just another solution to another problem.

The family had a semblance of a benign mafia about them and some of their associates seemed like characters out of a Damon Runyan novel. 'Toughie' Wooton - young, handsome, charismatic, dark hair swept back: he worked with my father who regarded him as "just a bit lazy". Despite being somewhat hampered with what was then termed as a club foot - something that in these days of advanced remedial surgery is not very often seen- the local girls were not slow in dating him: in fact it may have even acted as a sort of catalyst. The party gatherings were usually supplemented with Charlie 'Fingers' who could knock out tunes on the upright piano, without faltering, for most of the evening. Or, if not available, there was always Johnny 'Squeezebox' with his beautiful accordion - dapper, smart and professional. I think he would have had to be paid! The Common was littered with characters, from the barber to the garage man, from the Swap Shop to the Pawnbrokers.

Winter

Winter brought its own delights and agonies. Sometimes it was excruciatingly cold. In the mornings I would grudgingly climb from a warm bed. The bedroom would be rigid with cold. We never wore underpants in those days, at least not in the working class families that I knew. Underpants were one of the privileges of being a better class child. The giveaway was the tell tale loops around the braces and if ever we noticed them the wearer was usually classed by us street kids as a sissy- whatever that was. No! Keeping your privates warm? That's what shirt laps were for! We would joke that we had to soften our shorts with a hammer before we could get them on in the mornings. Tough? We had to be, or perish, and there were times when I thought I might just do that. I wasn't so tough. The windows would be iced on the inside as well as on the outside and I would stand in my pyjamas- at least we had them- marvelling at the intricate designs etched onto the window panes.
"Why does it go like this, Ernie?" I would query, fingering the delicate cold tracery.
"It's 'cos it's freezin'. Jack Frost's done it in the night." "Who's he?" - totally bewildered.
"He's the bloke wot's done it - I just said."
I had to be satisfied with this characteristic piece of logic or find myself with another round of questions falling on deaf ears. Our breath would vaporise into steamy clouds as we tried to thaw holes in the rimy surface until at last we could rub hard with the heel of our hands and look out onto a changed, silent world.
"Crikey! It's snowed int' night. Flippin 'eck! Lookarit! It's deep!"
Gone were the blackened bricks, the privet hedges, and the garage roofs. It was all transformed into a strange world of pure white beauty; for the moment only disturbed by the footprints of our cat betraying where he had stealthily stalked the sparrows in the early morning.
"C'mon - snowballs!" and he was gone.
"Wait for me! Wait! - WAIT!" And I would tear myself away from the wondrous spectacle of the trees around the distant pond and even further, all transfixed in a twinkling silver frieze of indescribable beauty.
Father had already gone to work. If there were no buses, he would walk the mile. He was hard and would never stay off work. He always left at about eight o'clock. Mother would be making yet another cup of tea. Dickie Walters, the old gentleman next door, would already be starting to scrape away at the snow.
"Put your wellies on and your balaclava" -she always knitted our balaclavas- "and jacket and keep wrapped up - and don't bring any in here!" I could hardly get everything on fast enough.

Ernest was already aiming snowballs at any available targets: the cat, the sparrows, pinnacles of snow tipping the ornamental points of the garages, or the windows of the small greenhouse up the yard where Dickie grew his tomatoes. You could throw snowballs at windows without breaking them. Look! Bang! One hit the kitchen window. "Hey! - you little bugger! I'm getting washed here!" Mother at the only sink in the house. We were always told not to look when she washed her breasts. Cripes! How could you not look? "It was him!"

"No it wasn't-it was him!"

Sometimes the snow was so thick that you could only get up the yard with great difficulty - or down the street - or even go to school! This was great! What an adventure! No trams running yet. All muffled and strangely quiet. Out would come the shovels and a narrow trench would be dug from door to door all the way down the street.

"Clear your front, Missus? Only a shilling!" It was nearly as lucrative as carol singing. The cars and trams had to wait for the bulldozer which usually shunted the snow down Barnsley Hill and then backed it up into a great mountain at the top of our street.

This grand edifice would last until all the other snow had long since disappeared, successfully isolating our street from traffic.

As Dr.Pringle was just about the only person in the street who owned a car- his garage was on our street- this would have been a big problem for him but not for anyone else.

As the snow melted it was important to keep a close watch on the roofs to see where the snow was on the point of sliding off, as there was a real danger of being crushed. We became experts. Sections would fall with an almighty crash. Suburban avalanches. Like the silence that you hear when a familiar clock stops ticking, the snow brought a new awareness of our landscape. In due time we would make a track to the pond and Bobby would already be there, daringly walking on the ice before breaking it: "To let the fish breathe", he explained. It never occurred to me that fish might want to breathe.

Later, in the street, other big lads would turn up for a snowball fight. Harold Brookfield, who lived directly opposite us, would be there. Everyone called him 'Fats' although he really wasn't. Then Ray Siddaway- as flash as his name- with his dark hair all slicked back with Brilliantine, and clever with it. Then Gerry from Cannon Hall Road, "up the hill" -Barnsley Hill of course.

Snowballs would fly thick and fast. Bobby's- always the hardest and thrown with the most accuracy- were designed to hurt. I couldn't keep away but I always attempted to keep well out of range.

But the best of it was the sledging. One thing we did have was a superb sledge. I don't know how we came to have such a superior machine. It rode high on strong looping runners and would manage the bumpiest of courses with great élan, and being high we didn't get a build-up of snow or slush in our laps, or in our faces when belly-flopping.

Ernie would take me up to Cookie's field behind the school. This was the wildest course around, and kids would trek distances in order to have a go at mastering its ferocity. It was very steep at the top and sported a double bump at the bottom. If you weren't in control this would tend to pitch you over a short wall and deposit you in Earl Marshall Road, unharmed if you were lucky.

As big a trial for me was climbing the hill in the first place, and once having struggled to the top I would stand there rigid and afraid to move lest I be pitched downwards minus the sledge. Our wellies would nervously search for a grip on the already impacted snow as our breath burst upon the freezing air to form rings of rime on our balaclavas.

"Let me do't steering. Keep yer' feet well up or it'll slow us darn". I would sit behind him and hang on for dear life. The speed was incredible - the runners slicing through the snow with a sssss--sssss - sssss. My cheeks smarted as icy needles whipped up into my face; and we would race steeply down, flashing past more tardy sledges, until, hitting the notorious bumps we would be airborne for a brief heart stopping moment; and then land with a jolt violent enough to expel the air from our lungs. Only a twist to the left or right would prevent us from being precipitated over the wall into the awaiting snowdrift.

10. Me at the age of three with Dickie's dog 'Peter'

Sometimes, to add variety, Ernest would belly flop onto the sledge and I would be encouraged to lay or sit on top of him in the traditional double-decker. It was easier to steer with feet trailing and the streamlined prone position created less wind resistance, culminating in even faster speeds, and, on my part, even greater fear. Although I was scared stiff and, indeed, frozen stiff, I always had confidence that Ernie's escapades would be matched by his skill and street knowledge. Certainly having an older brother had its advantages at times like these.

He would be tempted to go for the 'leap over the wall'. Strictly for the aficionado, or the foolish, this demanded a high degree of expertise and steering ability, not to mention nerve, as the sledge was aimed at the gap between the rough stones that stood up like battlements in the low wall. The consequence of being emasculated didn't seem to enter into the equation although it might possibly have been the outcome of any last second course deviation due to the double bump or change of mind. I would often be left standing shivering on the hilltop, exposed to the elements and wishing that I was home sitting in front of the fire.

Night would fall early and hectic sledging would continue by the light of the street lamps and the torches flashing up and down the hill in crazy semaphores. It was certainly a great chance to indulge one's fascination with torches - that's if you were lucky enough to have one.

The frosty night air would ring with shouts as mates and brothers tried to keep in contact in the dark until, finally, the cold wind whistling around chapped knees and hands could be endured no longer.

We would plod back along Earl Marshall Road with the sledge dragging behind, down through the dark allotments with the tops of our wellies rubbing bright red rings around our legs: scrambling over the six foot brick wall: trying to suck life back into our fingers and, finally, into the sanctuary of our tiny warm kitchen.

"Don't get too near the fire - you'll get chilblains.", Mother warned, and tickled the fire with the metal poker.

Neighbours

Our neighbour Dickie and his deaf wife shared our little yard. One of my earliest photos shows me posing on the windowsill with their black dog Peter. The dog's kennel seemed to me to present a place of great security, and I well remember having to be discouraged in taking up residence inside it. Dickie was an ever present personality in my early life. He was a retired postman, and when he collected his pension at the Post Office on the Front, he would often come back with a tube of fruit gums for me- an act that today would perhaps be frowned on with some suspicion. He liked to call this my pension. If he forgot, I reminded him. Although Dickie showed moments of humour and high joviality, his life seemed clouded by the trouble he had connecting with his wife. She had an early form of hearing aid but she often left it switched off. He would have to shout very loudly in her ear, pulling her shoulder down as she was very tall. This didn't make for much chance of a private or intimate conversation. He would complain to my mother that his wife had no affection for him, and at times, this made him a rather sad and frustrated figure. They were both getting well on in years but, apart from her deafness, had no apparent disability, and he had certainly plenty of virility left in him.

11. With Dad and Ernest in Dickie's garden

He often turned out in his thick Post Office trousers and black waistcoat complete with watch, chain and fob. His highly polished boots seemed to receive daily attention from his polishing kit and this special ritual was always performed in the yard, often under my curious scrutiny. At the time I only had a pair of sandals. When I came out to watch he would often break into a clopping heel and toe dance in order to entertain me. This was often accompanied by a syncopated rhythm rattled out on the knees, elbows and head with the metal dish that he used to weigh out vegetables and fertilizer - he was in charge of the communal allotment hut.

He belonged to a Glee Club and had a fine basso profundo voice and he would often finish off with a song, leaving his deepest, longest note for the end. This would be delivered straight at me on a pipe tobacco tainted breath from beneath his thick walrus moustache. A tiny figure in those days, I would be rooted to the spot and probably with my eyes popping out. Apart from that, I couldn't have been a very great audience as I was so shy and usually mute, but my indulgence seemed to please him and I could always be sure of a repeat performance the next time that he came out to polish his boots. He watched me grow up.

Dickie cultivated one of the allotments, of which there were many, stretching along the back gardens of Skinnerthorpe Road, up to Earl Marshall Road and down to my first school at Owler Lane.

This was an area that was to become an adventurous playground for me and my friends later on.

He also worked for Mrs.Allen in the gardens of Cannon Hall - often with her.

Even at this early age I couldn't help feeling for the old man, particularly when later my parents talked about his bitter disappointment and incredulity over the behaviour of one of his sons towards a sibling.

His eldest son was born severely crippled, one leg shorter and turned over the other: again, the sort of affliction that isn't so common now in an advanced age of treatment. He could only move on crutches. He was married. He and his wife had a Morris 8, a bit of a status symbol, as not many people could afford a car. She drove him around in this. When they came to visit, he would always take his stance on Dickie's neat little lawn next to our garden. Father would always chat with him and often I would stand and listen. He was a very nice man. On one particular occasion, Father found him crying. I was told to go indoors.

The story was that Cyril - or was it Arnold? I'm not sure - Dickie's son in the National Fire Service, seemingly had had enough of his wife, Vera, even though she was still young and quite attractive. Somewhere along the line, he had become romantically involved with his crippled brother's wife. She was older and I always thought that she was a bit of a miserable crow as she never spoke to me. They were now quite openly having some sort of relationship. It was Cyril (or Arnold) who was now sliding into the front seat of the Morris 8 beside her. Much went on that I wasn't party to at my tender age but this episode was so overt that even I could fathom out that something was dreadfully wrong. I felt sorry for my friend Dickie. He had such dignity, and equally strong feelings, that it was he that was now crying on Father's shoulder. I'd never seen men cry before and this moved me considerably.

Life continued. Dickie always spread his affections in our direction. As he was particularly fond of my mother, she would sometimes have difficulty fending him off: so much so, that I remember on one occasion Father had to speak to him about it. He liked to drop in articles from the newspaper that he had found particularly interesting, but I was still struggling with the Beano, and Mother didn't list reading as one of her best activities; consequently they were rarely read. Athletics had been a passion of his at one time: he particularly knew all about the logistics of walking. This was the kind that employed the classic heel and toe action, with the arms swinging rhythmically across the chest and the hips swivelling. It took place at stadiums but was most spectacular as a road sport. It was exceedingly big in Sheffield and the Star Walk, promoted by the Sheffield Star newspaper, took place every year, was open to anybody, and was avidly watched by huge crowds lining the route throughout the City. Competitors ranged from wizened old men having trouble keeping their shorts up, to young fit aspirants who wiggled their way up Barnsley Hill as if it wasn't there. On a hot day some of the less fit didn't seem as if they would make it to the top and we were always ready with a glass of water. In recent times my account of it was published in Malcolm Ayton's book on the subject and I append it here.

The 'Star' Walk passed the top of Skinnerthorpe Road, Firvale. This was the street where I lived from 1933 to 1956. I was known as Vic Oliver in those days. An old diary records me being there for this annual event on Bank Holiday Monday the 26th. May 1952 but I watched it on more than one occasion.

This was a most popular event throughout Sheffield and the circuitous route from Town and back would be lined with cheering, clapping people. Most of our street would turn out. The weather would often smile benignly but this was of no matter anyway. These were very determined participants. A downpour of rain would see them waddling along, often soaked to the skin, with their race numbers threatening to come adrift. I say waddling because this word adequately described the action of some of the less elegant contenders - and there were many.

The more fit and serious athletes were a joy to watch as the required heel and toe action set the whole body into a rather fascinating rhythm. This was before the introduction of trainer shoes. The course had to be negotiated with hard, heavy shoes which, although extremely blistering, did help to swing the feet along. A part of the feet, as I understand, had to be seen to be in contact with the ground at all times and this rule brought forth the classic, once seen never forgotten, movement of the body. Of course this was not a local invention - in fact it was an event in the Olympic Games: there is fascinating newsreel footage of a small Italian athlete in a state of complete exhaustion, staggering towards the finishing line, being willed on, and helped, by cloth-capped countrymen - I think maybe illegally. He certainly was not heel and toe-ing; maybe it was the marathon.

The main contenders in the Star Walk would appear early, whipping smartly along Firvale Bottom; elegant, muscles rippling, hips swivelling and taking the formidable Barnsley Hill unflinchingly in their stride. Style was inherent in the form and aficionados of the sport took great delight in pointing out the finer points of the action. As the race wore on however, the field would start to straggle and there would be plenty of walkers who looked pretty exhausted and had thrown style to the wind, especially when they saw the incredibly steep hill rearing up in front of them. Sometimes they would throw away the rules altogether, show a little spirit and break into a little run. This in an attempt to catch up with ever diminishing figures on their way to Pitsmoor. It was a tough trial but many entered for it year after year and familiar figures would be recognised and given an extra cheer. Water would be offered and gladly accepted. Sometimes a figure would appear, sweating profusely, past the traffic lights, bald pate shining in the sun, and desperately hoiking up shorts as they threatened to succumb to gravity and all the hip swivelling that was going on. There would be some hilarious moments. Some would stop, have a laugh and a joke and then carry on. It was all taken in the best of spirits.

A real family treat, especially after the time of the intense hardship of the War.

One young aspirant and serious contender was Alfie Lowe who occasionally played for the football team that, to my credit, I had created. We called it Vale Rovers. Alfie was a very sound player and our loss was his dedication to running, being a member of one of Sheffield's athletic teams. He put football on the back burner and spent many hours in training. I don't think that he ever won the Star walk, but he always did very well in it. Our little group would wait for him -"Come on Alfie!"

But back to Dickie.

"In icy conditions, Victor - a flat foot and a firm thigh.". He would intone truisms at me in his deep, rich voice. "The best thing for a dry mouth when walking is a squidge of grape skins. If you don't swallow them, they'll last you the race."

I think that he hoped that one day I would enter the Star Walk at least, but I knew my limitations and I was never tempted. Dickie had been a masseur at one time and when I took up playing football he would always offer his services - but I was always too shy for that! Our toilets were housed outside in two small brick add-ons, attached to the back of their kitchen along with the dustbins. I was always not a little disturbed when our visits coincided, as he would always try to strike up a conversation through the dividing wall. This may seem highly irregular now, but we were only just coming out of the era of the communal twoseaters; and in some of the poor areas, around Attercliffe for instance, they still existed. "Oh. Just ignore him," Mother would advise. Not easy when you're on the john!

The Hodgsons

The Hodgsons lived on the other side of the yard and were, perhaps wisely, partitioned off from us by a trellis separator. They couldn't have been more different from the Walters and us. Life in their house was acutely controlled. They had both been in service, and although long retired, the influence of their life's work was plain to see. Mr. Hodgson didn't say much at all. When I was invited in from time to time, he would usually be seen sitting upright in a straight backed chair behind the living room door reading the morning paper. He would always be immaculately dressed in a black suit, waistcoat, collar, and tie. The newspaper would probably have been ironed first and, although he was quite portly, he always looked as if he too had been well ironed. I never saw Mrs. Hodgson sitting down, eating or standing doing nothing. The woman seemed to be cleaning continually; the house smelt of polish and shone like a new pin. She always wore a grey apron and often a grey cap, gathered in puckers around her thinning grey hair. She seemed to have positioned her husband where he wouldn't get in the way of her activities: one could well see them in some grand house, sitting below stairs, waiting to be summoned by bells, and looking pretty much the same as they did now. Despite this apparent rigidity, they were always kind towards me and would often spend time talking to my parents.

Outside, a couple of steps planted you on a neat lawn with flowerbed surround where not a blade of grass would dare to be out of place or a flower droop its little head. Everything had to be up early and shining brightly. Mr. Hodgson also had a grey apron and he would sometimes don this and shine his boots standing by the window ledge; boots, because shoes were not that common amongst the working class. Apart from being harder wearing, boots were considered workmanlike, whereas shoes were perhaps a little pretentious and relaxed or even louche - something that a spiv might wear - and might, therefore, even have the power to corrupt the wearer! I certainly never had a pair of shoes until I was about twelve and I remember my father even then trying to dissuade me.

The boot cleaning activities of our neighbours influenced me so much that I never had to be told to clean and polish my own - it went without saying. Years later, my shoes would be kicked to bits playing football in the street, in the schoolyard, and on the playing field, but it would have been undreamt of to go back to boots for preference. Later on, when I became a young working man with the Forestry Commission, and then the Sheffield Parks Department as a tree feller, I had to, but in between that were the teenage years of the be-bop era: suede shoes or brogues with thick crepe soles termed "brothel creepers" were the order of the day, and, for best, I even had a pair of shoes with gold chains! Cool!

At times my father must have thought that I wasn't 'all there', as they say, particularly as my brother was nothing of a stylist and was already working as a butcher by the time he was fourteen.

But back to the Hodgsons. They had a budgie that, to my delight, often spoke. My pleasure was to go into the small field behind the garages and collect a handful of a certain seedy grass that the bird liked to feed on. For this, I would receive a handsome sixpence. That budgie never wanted for seed!

A large sycamore belonging to Cannon Hall overhung their house and Mother swore that, in the autumn, Mrs. H. would watch from her window waiting for any leaf to fall. Sure enough, if a wind-propelled interloper invaded her territory, she would pounce on it with the yard broom, muttering under her breath- but not, of course, any swear words, as they were quite religious and went to church every Sunday.

They had a son, Bill, who was tall and had a very loud, bluff delivery of speech; we were always aware of his visits- his loud voice booming in the passage. I must say though that his overbearing voice came in useful on the tannoy at the Atlas & Norfolk Works Sports Day. This was a popular event when the thronging crowds would be given a non-stop commentary on the sports by day, and the fireworks by night. I think that he could have done it without the tannoy.

He had a son, Michael, much younger than me, who also had a propensity to talk too loudly. He often sought my attention but I only grew to value him when, later, my pals and I were willing to put up with him and co-opt him into our football games in Firth Park. He lived just across the road and had one rare and valuable asset - a football. You can't play good football without one! This profound truism was best made evident when the only thing we had to kick were our heels!

The genteel side of the Hodgsons family was personified in the rather elegant form of their daughter who was married and lived somewhere in the environs of Barnsley. They had a son, Bernard, who was quite different to Michael. He was a few years older than I was and already well educated, though not in street ways. Tall and upright with dark, wavy hair like his parents, he should have totally eclipsed me but to my never-ending surprise, this he failed to do. I suppose that I was already a street kid whereas he was rather cosseted and at best would certainly have been labelled an 'anorak' and, at worst perhaps - a wimp. He spoke with a slight lisp and called Mrs.H. - 'Gramma', and - couldn't I see loops around his braces?

I enjoyed his visits greatly, however, as up to the age of nine, the only friends that I had were Tony (more of him later) and Gord. As I wasn't encouraged to wander too far, I only saw Tony at school - for the moment.

Bernard brought his own culture with him. Barnsley was only about ten miles away. For me, it might as well have been on the moon. I think they were quite well off. They had a fine car, one of the few to park in the street - no yellow lines then, and they dressed far better than anyone I had seen before.

Mrs.H. liked to keep a close eye on Bernard when he was left in her care for holidays, and I was always asked in to play. We were very pleased to see each other; being so different we had so much to give.

He liked to play with plasticine and whilst my own lump had been pulped into a hard, grey mass long ago, his was all new and laid out in boxes of rainbow hues. He would often get irritated with me or go mardy as we called it in our neck of the woods. I seemed to be able to make more animated figures than he could and, later on, I could beat him at draughts. After he had shown me the rudiments of chess, I began to beat him at that too. I remember he once made his own rules up in order to try to win.

"I think Bernard's cheating, Mrs Hodgson."

"Now, now. You must play properly or not at all," she admonished. "Play fair now," bowing to my protestations. He hated me beating him. After all, he went to a posh school. He would bring books with him: I would avidly pounce on these. He also possessed an early example of a Biro pen, which, to me, was a true wonder.

Marbles was my game - I could beat him at that too. It goes without saying that he had a better collection than my motley selection. Unfortunately, he wouldn't play for keeps and so they always remained his. He kept them in a drawstring bag, which came in useful one day in the yard, as he saw it, to swat a wasp which had settled on my elbow. My cries of anguish quickly brought Mrs.H. from her cloistered lair where she found me almost on my knees and in acute agony. "I only meant to brush it off, Gramma," he explained.

"Really Bernard, you must be more careful -you should know better than to do that". "It was going to sting him," he protested. I would have preferred the sting.

"I think you should apologise anyway."

He apologised but I couldn't help thinking that he was just getting his own back for all the times I had beaten him at draughts.

At the time there was also a craze for French knitting and French cricket. It's a fair bet that the French did neither. The knitting comprised of a bobbin with nails around the top on which strands of leftover wool were wound. After much labour, a multi-coloured woollen snake would appear. This was quite useless unless you made enough to coil it into a circle, thereby fashioning a mat to stand a teapot on. If you were really clever, you could even make a tea cosy!

Although we did play French cricket up the yard, it was always more fun with a few more pals. At this time, we only had Gord living nearby and so it was always a bit limited. Briefly, the batter's legs acted as stumps and these had to be defended at all angles. Two or three fielders could, in effect, have him playing piggy-in-the-middle, as the ball was passed from side to side.

Needless to say we didn't play it with a hard cricket ball -even if we had had one! It was more fun on the rare occasions when Father joined in. He in fact had introduced us to it. He was quite clever with bat and ball and later when more friends became available, we would sometimes have a full blown game of real cricket going on up the yard. He was proud of the fact that he could bat right or left-handed - 'dolly-posh' or 'widdershins' as he called it. Unfortunately he was somewhat restricted by the fact that he had double hernias, eventually, on both sides, caused by carrying sides of beef from vans in the street into the shop. Okay for his big brothers to do, but not for him. Despite that he was still a mean spin bowler. In effect, there was a culture exchange going on here. In Barnsley they had a game called Knur and Spell, which was quite alien to us. Bernard showed me how to play this up back by the garages. There was a concrete square there that served as an excellent wicket for French or Real cricket, and K&S: naturally he had a real cricket bat. This was the way it was played: a fair-sized piece of wood was whittled down to the shape of a bullet: this was called the dolly. It was laid on a brick, hit on the end so that it shot vertically into the air and then given an almighty whack. Distance won but how Dickie's greenhouse windows survived remained a mystery.

Knowing Bernard who, as I said, was quite a bit older than I was, helped broaden my world somewhat. We would get permission to go to the bottom end of the street, cross the road via the small traffic island and pay a visit to the herbalist's shop that was owned by the father of one of my school chums, Geoffrey Scholey. I had by then started at Owler Lane Infants. Geoff was a bright, cheery lad. His father was established and well respected as the local dentist, though we always had our teeth seen to at school. He was also a herbalist. Needless to say we didn't go there to sample his packets of herbs; what attracted us was the sarsaparilla for which we acquired quite a passion! Bernard's presence meant that I could indulge in this wondrous beverage whenever we managed to avail ourselves of a silver sixpence - usually at the expense and kindness of his grandma. The shop, although very small, was magical. It had a few glass topped tables and a highly polished counter that sported handles, like a pub, for pulling the drinks. Bottles of herbs lined the back wall. The smell was sublime. On the walls were framed displays of cigarette cards of butterflies, sportsmen, and flowers. We could buy a big glass of sarsaparilla for five pence or a whole pint for six pence. There were also hot drinks of Vimto or orange, and we would opt for one of these if it happened to be a cold winter's day. Old men would spend time there yarning and I think that they always thought it a bit of a novelty when we walked in. They would be amused by our presence and talk to us, and we, sitting there with our pints, would feel tolerably grown-up.

Quite often they would be waiting for the Firth Park Hotel to open, which wasn't at Firth Park but just across the main road from my Owler Lane School and hardly a stone's throw away from the shop.

This was Dickie's favourite haunt and if I saw him going down the street, I knew that he was heading either there or for the Allotment Hut.

As time passed, I saw less and less of Bernard; I imagine that he went on to an even higher education. Dear Bernard.

Not At All Well

Illness followed me around like a hungry dog waiting for scraps. I was easy prey to the numerous diseases that went the rounds and I finally finished up with a spectacular rarity in my teens. At times I found that I had to resolutely turn a thin pale figure to the world as I found myself hanging on for dear life.

Measles laid me particularly low and I had periods when my sight and speech were affected. On one of these occasions I was duly transported into my parents' bed, which always meant that I was really ill. I remember lying there in a delirious state watching the walls take on a curious palpitating texture that threatened to overwhelm me completely. I also remember moving the objects on Mother's dresser in order, apparently, to try to stop them moving around willy-nilly. Having been told by Dr. Pringle that my ramblings were 'delirium tremens', my mother ever afterwards referred to them as 'trimmings', the nearest that she could get to the Latin.

"Our Vic's got trimmings again, Dad"

Father would come up the stairs and studiously lay his hand on my brow.

"Tha'll be oreight. Just lay there an' get better," he would say as if his very words would provide a cure.

One of my constant afflictions was catarrh and I would spend periods at the kitchen table leaning over a jug of steaming Friar's Balsam with a towel draped over my head. This would almost kill me by asphyxiation. My father suffered from the same complaint and I was very pleased when he decided to take on the treatment for himself.

"Good stuff this!" He ducked under and I ducked out.

Eventually, catarrh and nosebleeds became so bad that I was escorted off to the Royal Hospital where I had part of my nasal bone taken away. It seemed to work, though it still proves to be an irritating area even to this day. There was a humorous side to the proceedings as I wasn't the only one having such an operation. Father thought it rather funny to see me and other patients basting our noses with what looked rather like a huge lollipop. For some time after I observed that I could feel stitches up my nose. Father thought this quite absurd, but of course, it wasn't - one day I must have duly blown away the remnants.

My mother was hardly ever ill and always looked the picture of glowing health. My brother with his wiry frame was never around long enough for germs to catch up with him. His only complaint was something on the side of his neck that had been removed before I was born and which showed as a scar. However, he did have periodic outbreaks of monstrous boils on the back of his neck. Father called them carbuncles. He would have Ernest kneel on a chair holding the back of it and biting on a towel. He would then proceed to apply considerable pressure to these volcanoes of pus. I would watch horror-stricken. Ernest would grimace at me and then give me a wry wink. I would do the crying for him and then, when I could stand it no longer, plead with my father to leave off. This would never have any effect and he would pursue his quest to the painful end.

"That's gorrit! That's the core!" he would boast. I always wondered why he didn't take him to the doctor's - but then, perhaps he did. Generally I was kept in the dark about family events, I suppose as a protection, but I don't think this did me much good. It tended to alienate me and ultimately forced me into taking a 'couldn't care less anyway' attitude.

Father was always loath to go to the doctors. It seemed to be a point of honour not to have any time off work and go on the 'panel' as he called it. Quite often he would arrive home from work with a finger roughly bound in a bloodstained bandage having suffered a deep cut, usually from a knife skidding off a bone; or even more often, from the sharp edge of the bone itself.

Dr.Pringle had his surgery on the Front, sandwiched between shops: a tall Victorian house made of black bricks. In Sheffield, all bricks were black.

Many times I would have to sit with my mother in the waiting room listening to all the gossip and complaints of the other patients as they talked amongst themselves.

It was here that I acquired a taste for rather sophisticated humour, reading the back numbers of Punch. From time to time we would hear the back door of his inner sanctum open as he ejected a patient with a few appropriate words. We knew then that it was time for his head to appear around the connecting door. His head was massive. I was never again to see such an impressive head.

"No wonder he's a doctor," I used to think - "look at all his brains!" He was so tall that he had developed a permanent stoop in order not to hit his head on the lintels. His voice was heavily accented - I think he was a Scot. Heaving his large frame into his swivel chair, he would revolve around and confront me with a daunting look as my mother gently pushed me forward.

"And now what seems to be the trouble today? Hmmm?"

Mother would try to explain the symptoms as well as she was able. She was very nervous and not a little awe-struck in his presence, but she also had great faith in him. He was one of the few authorities in our lives with whom we actually came face to face. Gentleman that he was, he would put her at ease with some kind remark and she would stumble on more easily. I was usually rendered speechless. His huge white-haired head would nod up and down and a smile would flit across his face.

"Open wide - aaahhh" - in would go a wooden spatula. "Up with your shirt - deep breath." He would probe me with a cold stethoscope, then swivelling around would write out some prescription in cryptic hand.

"Humph - humph. Well, it's nothing too bad. Keep him warm. Tablets three times a day. He'll be fine. A week off school eh? Laddie?" His words were strong medicine and as equally as important as any tablets.

A picture above his desk, meanwhile, had caught my eye. This wasn't just a surgery it was part of his home. It was a scene of a backyard in Holland and probably by Pieter de Hooch, although at that time, of course, I didn't know that. I opened my mouth to speak.

He saw me looking.

"You like that - hmmm?"

"It's a painting," I managed to blurt out.

"Well not exactly. It's what you would call a print of a painting," he corrected. "It's by a Dutchman."

"Th… the bricks are … red," I stammered almost inaudibly.

"Indeed they are - and do you paint?" I had swallowed any words I might have had and I could feel my cheeks beginning to burn. Mother came to the rescue.

"Oh! He's always drawing."

12. Mother at Skinnerthorpe Road

"Well done! And now away wi' ye' and be a good boy for your mummy. And goodbye to you, Mrs. Oliver." And so we were summarily dismissed. He turned the heavy brass knob and we were outside into the cold winter air.

"Well - that wasn't too bad, was it?" said Mother heaving a sigh of relief. She gave my hand a comforting squeeze as we headed along the Front, the trams rattling past.

Later, in my teenage years, I became ill with a lung affliction that still harasses me occasionally even now. Dr. Pringle was always there to alleviate our fears and also, incidentally, pass judgement on my increasing interest in painting.

Prescriptions were always duly delivered to Mr.Firth the chemist, just past the cobblers. Mother liked him. Quite young and good-looking, dapper in a pin-stripe suit, hair neatly combed and parted in the middle, he was always pleasant and welcoming. Both my mother and I had far less trouble talking to him than with Dr. Pringle, and my father would prefer to pay him a visit for any medical advice that he might need.

He always had our respect and finished well up on my list of grown-ups that I really liked-maybe because he would always drop a couple of sweets into my hand, even if they were usually medicated ones. Dr. Pringle, I suppose, represented authority, culture and intellect, and all that was a bit frightening.

School

My mother was a simple loving person. When the time came for me to start school, I am sure that she was as worried about it as much as I was. My brother offered little hope of protection as he had already passed on to the Intermediate School that was situated next to the Infants on Owler Lane where I was to commence my education. Being wrenched from the womb of 52 Skinnerthorpe Road was a real re-birth and filled me with a great fear. This was barely calmed by Mother's assurances that all would be well. A happy-go-lucky smiling boy I was not.

The great day came and I found myself hanging up my raincoat in the cloakroom and being ushered into the large hall. I exchanged my mother's hand for the teacher's, only after I had been promised that when I next saw the double doors by the cloakroom, she would be there waiting for me to take me home for my dinner. Unfortunately, I didn't understand about playtime and so when we were all released from Miss Allen's classroom, my mother's round freckled face was not to be seen beaming through the glass of the double doors as I expected. I was utterly distraught. Standing in the great hall weeping furiously, I was eventually rescued by the biggest girl in the school. She squeezed me to her budding bosom as if she had at last found a real baby with which she could appease her maternal instincts. For my part, I was quite happy to be squeezed by her and the novelty of it soon abated my tears, especially after she had explained that it wasn't in fact dinnertime. I quickly dried my tears with a freshly ironed hanky pulled from my little pocket and walked off holding the hand of my new protector.

After that, I persuaded my mother to come at playtime too. Fortunately the school was only a long stone's throw away from the end of our road. She wasn't allowed into the school so I was fed a piece of chocolate or a sweet or two through the bars of the iron gate of the top playground, like an animal at the zoo. It made me happier.

Although the teachers were very kind and I soon fell in love with Miss Allen, nothing could replace seeing my mother and I must have imposed this regime on her for many a long day.

Eventually my brother would bring me home at dinnertime and he would also be waiting for me at the bottom gate at home time. It was always a great relief to see him but for him I fear it was a chore accepted under the pain of terrible consequences should anything untoward befall me.

I was excruciatingly shy and totally reserved with everyone. Dr. Pringle said that I had an inferiority complex and that I would grow out of it! My God, Doc! It took another thirty-odd years!

The other children seemed to have an innate knowledge of what to do whereas, most of the time I was utterly bewildered.

I remember being drawn to the display of numbers on the classroom wall, shown as 1 - 9. What baffled me was that each number was shown as the appropriate amount of big, brightly-coloured spots. Thus I assumed that, for instance, four was always blue and nine was always yellow etc. I was unable to resolve the problem and it left me confused about numbers and colours - not what was intended. I think my perception of logic may have been running ahead of the rest of my development. I was nervous of most situations and seemed to be unable to operate on a simple level, as a child should. The boxes of toys that were brought out at certain periods seemed not to be for me, and I was usually content with watching others play with them. Any suggestion that I might want to lie down on the camp-bed provided to rest tired little heads was quickly rejected. I wasn't a baby! I was a grown-up in disguise!

Playground activities in the form of competitive games, usually with coloured sashes around the shoulders, found me trying to be as inconspicuous as possible and in fear of being picked to lead anything. I was the only one in the school who found the simple, natural act of skipping along to music impossible, and so was unable to join in the communal dancing. This was mirrored later on at Grammar School, when I realised that I was almost the only person in the form who couldn't swim! It's not that I was ill-coordinated - I went on to become an adequate football and tennis player; - it was more as if I was some sort of alien life form, helplessly trying to conform to events that, by and large, I didn't understand.

Even so, the teachers were kind to me and my angelic looks continued to attract girls.

My imagination was fuelled by the benevolent and portly figure of Miss Collins who, in instalments, had read us 'Wind in the Willows'. I sat in the front row of desks, and she would deliver these delicious forays into the world of Toady and his friends, actually sitting on my desk and almost squashing me with her soft, fat body. I found this quite encouraging and reading soon became, together with painting and drawing, a favourite lesson.

I began to make friends, avoid enemies, and make my own way home. One character who fell into the 'enemy' category was Ronnie Gaden who seemed to take a fiendish delight in snatching off my cap and flinging it into the trees that fringed the lower playground. One day my brother caught him doing just that and gave him a clip around the ear, which curbed such further activities on his part.

My first sweetheart was rosy cheeked Ann Butler. She was obviously enamoured by my angelic features and probably by my mother's hand-knitted jerseys. I thought her very pretty but I didn't understand her intentions. She would search me out in the playground and whilst I stood there, rooted to the spot and tongue-tied, she would kiss me on the cheek and occasionally squeeze a square of Rowntree's jelly into my hand. Although I was always completely nonplussed by these actions, I never failed to devour the offering. The Freudian symbolism was, of course, completely lost on me but I am sure that watching me chew this wobbly morsel had the desired effect on her fast growing libido especially in the light of my later knowledge of her. She eventually grew into a great beauty, with an even greater reputation locally as a very desirable sweetheart . Of course, I was far too shy to take advantage of the fact that we had once shared jelly, and my appreciation of her had to remain mute and distant.

My best pal emerged from the crowd. His name was Tony. At that time a crinkly-haired, chubby, energetic lad, he had a propensity for telling stories, most of which seemed to be embroidered beyond the bounds of truth. I think he probably liked me because I always took the trouble to listen and seemed to be intelligent enough to get the essence of his already highly developed raconteurism. Over the years, his wide-ranging interests and his ability to express them opened up my horizons and the awareness of the possibilities in our little lives.

The other important school diversion that took place on rare occasions was a trip to the local pond, above Earl Marshall Road. (Who he?) These trips were arranged imaginatively, and, I must say, bravely, by one of the younger teachers whom we all loved. In fact there were two ponds but the top one was larger and, of the two, far more interesting. They lay beneath the watershed of Osgathorpe, beyond the no man's land of the abandoned tennis courts, and as I had never seen them, they were still the stuff of legends as far as I was concerned.

All the children were very excited at the prospect of escaping from the confines of the classroom, and I became intrigued as we set off on safari and chattered our way up through the privet-hedged, ash-strewn tracks that defined the allotments of Earl Marshall Road.

The ponds had formed in abandoned clay pits - clay being the sub-strata of the area. The banks of the top pond had been flattened by numerous small feet and were a pleasure to run around. A large fallen tree, half sunk in the pond, provided a balancing act challenge for the more adventurous. The teacher proved to be a mine of information about water boatmen, skaters, and all the other beetly things that were diving and swimming around. There was also quite a large colony of frogs and the occasional toad, together with their tadpoles and spawn. The rarest find would be the newt, and we held a sort of reverence for this magical creature. The only fish were sticklebacks and minnows. We usually had no compunction in netting these and plopping them into awaiting jam jars. Having culled our harvest, we would then march back to school proudly carrying specimens for the school tank.

Occasionally, at the school we had parties, when parents would bring food, and the classrooms would be decorated with our homemade paper chains and other trimmings; but this is where I would slip back into my protective shell again and become a mere observer of events. There were also the usual Nativity plays and suchlike, and I was always careful not to be considered as a participant. I might have looked an angel but I didn't particularly want to be dressed as one.

Tony, on the other hand, was expressing himself in all sorts of ways - not the least sexually. Although only about seven, I suppose, he was already beginning to notice the opposite sex as being - well - sexually opposite, as you might say. Pointing out in appreciative tones the curvaceous posterior of one young female dancer, he exclaimed, "I say! What a figure!" He was definitely in advance of his years. I wouldn't say that I was unaware, but it all seemed unmentionable and secret, whereas for Tony it was already becoming something of a pursuit. His parents, unlike mine, were both large, loud and dominating, and were not above giving him a clip around the ear. This was something that I never had to suffer - although I'm sure that he needed controlling far more than I did. I think that the testosterone had begun to flow very early for him and I know it was already beginning to lead him a merry dance. As for me, it was still all a mystery. Despite the difference, our friendship lasted to the end of our teenage years.

Even so, I was attracted to one Brenda Dawson, even though she wore spectacles and apparently suffered badly from adenoids. I think it may have been her self-assured demeanour and better class accent that impressed me - that and her silky blonde hair. I remember that I happened to be walking behind her on the way to school one day and burning to speak to her, but, of course, not doing so. It was only later that I happened to come across her at the top of Firth Park, by the long wall. I can't remember how I happened to be there, but I was already beginning to wander and explore on my own. She was standing in the long grass, catching tiny white moths in her hands. Her body swayed, her thin dress fanned out around her, and with the soft clapping of her hands formed a kind of a dance. I was utterly charmed and, shyly, at her beckoning, joined in. It must have looked like some rather badly choreographed fandango. That concluded my intimate moment with Brenda. She was the only pupil to be allowed to use the school scissors. A superior girl.

Another person who stood out in my early school life was Peter Swain. We were to remain acquainted through this school and the next two, although he was so centred on himself that one could never call him a friend. I saw him as some sort of artistic genius and I admired his work enormously. He was an inspiration but he could also be a pain in the butt: I'm sure that he knew this and even played up to it. He would paint in an excited way, living the work, and often jumping out of his desk to see what everyone else was doing. This was allowed, and ideas were reciprocated, even though most of the other children's ideas and efforts were comparatively- well- childish. He always worked feverishly and very quickly, often with his tongue sticking out. For a period, I thought that this last trick of his might be the secret, and a prerequisite to good work, so for a short time I copied the habit. He seemed to be able to create the most interesting and exciting stuff without, apparently, having to stop to think, and with great facility. He was my first encounter with the artistic muse. We were quickly attracted to each other's work, but I soon realised that he eclipsed me in imagination and skill and also in the ability to scale his work up to mural size. He was, without doubt, a prodigy. Bright and undisciplined, he talked incessantly despite the fact that he had a very bad stammer. He came from a good family and his parents encouraged his talents by buying him all manner of materials - pencils and paints the like of which I hadn't yet come across. They, too, were housed in poor conditions, in Upwell Street.

I didn't lack imagination but I certainly couldn't keep up with Peter's effortless fluency. Most of the other children, meanwhile, were still painting lollipop trees.

My interactive painting, where armies would do battle on the page, had already been transcended. That was kid's stuff. My efforts were more considered and much slower and seemed to be the result of a much more painful process of trying to visualise, in a detailed and realistic way, something that I had already encountered. This became a problem when at the next school, for instance, we were asked to paint "Life at the bottom of the Sea"- especially as we were many miles away from it and I couldn't swim! This is where I had to borrow from the imaginations of Bobby and Ernest who would often talk about curious animals and such things, octopus being a favourite! In fact, Bobby had a toy diver that actually submerged and made its way along the bottom of his pond!

Two other figures stand out from this period at Owler Lane: one predictably being the school bully. The other one, everybody- especially the teachers- perceived to be a real headache. Fortunately the school bully lived on the same street as me. This, plus the fact that he knew that I had a big brother who had big friends, gave me an edge over other possible victims. In fact, we even developed a mutual respect and a sneaking affection for each other, especially as I began to realise that he was more of an 'agent provocateur' than a real bully. His reign of terror stemmed more from an uncontrollable urge to dominate and disrupt the status quo, than anything of a malicious nature although I did once catch him rubbing a grass sod into the face of Geoffrey Scholey, another schoolmate who happened to be as cheeky as John, but naive enough to try and outwit him. A lesson I learnt about bullies: remain invisible whenever possible. John, unlike Geoffrey, came from an extremely poor background and this probably had a lot to do with his attitudes. His best mate, Billy Parkinson, lived just around the end of our street on Bagley Road: funny that - being called a road - it was so short that you could throw a stone the length of it- and he seemed to be even poorer. Billy always seemed to have the potential, with his obvious body weight and strength, to crush into oblivion anyone he didn't like. I had a theory that my weakness and their strength was probably due to their having to eat their crusts whereas I was allowed to leave mine on the plate.

Dressed in unclean ragged clothes and clogs and smelling somewhat- there were no bathrooms- they presented a formidable pair, although to his credit, I never heard of Billy harming anyone. It was all threat and somewhat bovine. In a sense, they were the victims.

Later on, when I grew a little stronger and confident, I would accept John's challenge to a friendly wrestle in the playground and we would roll around in the leaves under the school wall, subtly testing each other's strength. This probably earnt me more respect from the other children than I deserved. Violence of some kind never seemed to be far away and quite a bit of school life seemed to be a matter of avoiding it. Although all the teachers at Owler Lane were very benign, I later learnt that it wasn't just school bullies that could dish it out. Teachers could be just as vicious and irrational. Often violence wasn't intentional, such as the occasion when I was inadvertently knocked down by a madly careering older girl and suffered a wildly bleeding nose; and another frightful incident when, stooping over the brass water tap in the yard, the queue shunted and I lost two front teeth at a stroke, together with much lachrymose spirit. Fortunately they were my milk teeth. The same large girl came to my rescue.

The most disturbed person at the school and thereby the most disturbing was Annie. She had a big problem. Her behaviour was totally irrational and quite often took the form of explosions of violent temper that left us gentle souls looking on with uncomprehending minds and gaping mouths. She was totally disobedient and if any kind of restraint was imposed on her, it would bring forth fits of shouting and screaming necessitating her being dragged off from the classroom by some distraught teacher in an effort to maintain some sense of sanity in the class.

The War

A greater war than Annie's, however, had now been declared, and this brought a bigger upheaval to the status quo than even she could inflict. The War was to affect everyone's lives. It was soon apparent that Hitler meant serious business and shelters were rapidly constructed in brick, concrete and sandbags, to protect us from the impending air raids. At the school we would have to undergo shelter drill and we would file into the gloomy dank passages built into the fabric of the school itself. Although this brought its own particular brand of excitement, sitting squeezed up on wooden benches, it was also shot through with a great angst. We were aware enough to realise that we could die down there. Gas masks had been issued to each of us and we had to get used to wearing these sitting in our subterranean labyrinth. We would all don these strange affairs with their smelly rubber surrounds and transparent screens.
"It's mica" Tony said, "Mica"! He seemed to know an awful lot, I thought. We would sit there listening to our breath going in and out through the metal canisters hanging off the end of our faces.
"It's full of charcoal," Tony revealed. Later I learnt that he also had an older brother - much older and therefore perhaps a stepbrother- who was already in the RAF and probably the source of this wonderful knowledge. Tony soon discovered that if you blew out of the side of your mouth you could set the rubber vibrating, which gave a pretty accurate rendering of a fart. Pretty soon everyone at our end of the shelter had mastered the art and was busy rubber - farting away. Meanwhile Annie had decided that she was never going to wear a gas mask - ever. Her screams echoed along the ill-lit passages with a frightening intensity. We all fell silent. Annie's screams struck a chord in all our souls. Life from now on would be deeply coloured by the looming enemy across the Channel. Our gas masks had to be in their cardboard boxes on a string around our necks wherever we went, and we all quickly learnt what we were expected to do should we hear that dreaded wail of the sirens and find ourselves under attack. My education was about to take a downturn. Up to now it had been quite well adjusted, despite the efforts of the Luftwaffe. Occasionally the bombers would arrive by day and, perhaps fearing that the bombs might hit the school and put an end to the junior population of the area, classes were, for a time, dispersed into private houses. I remember sitting in someone's front room at a nearby area called Page Hall trying to do lessons in comfortable but distracting surroundings. These home lessons didn't last long, and we were soon back at school. I suspect that some of the teachers found it difficult to get to work after being up all night and coping with air raid conditions.
Due no doubt to this, on one occasion my class was crowded in with the senior class. The desks were pushed together and the senior master took charge. I can't say that I had actually noticed him before, or his image may have just slipped into that great void called memory loss. Anyway we were issued with pencil and paper and ordered to draw a tree. This was right up my street. I carefully articulated my best tree.
"Now do one with your gasmasks on," he intoned. I couldn't think why we would have to be drawing a tree if we were being gassed, but nevertheless, we scuffled into our cardboard boxes, always at hand, donned the necessary, and proceeded. He squeezed between the desks and examined the results.

13. At the age of six with my gas mask.

"This young laddie can draw a tree better with his gasmask on than the rest of you can with them off!" he declaimed in a derisory voice. I was just turning around to see who the genius was when I felt his hand on my shoulder and realised that he was talking about me! I glowed inside my gasmask.

In later years when I took up Art as a profession, I would cite this example as being my first encounter with praise for my work, and I suppose- Art criticism! I liked it but my moment of glory was very brief.

Naturally, the pastime- it couldn't be called a lesson- that I enjoyed the most was drawing and painting, coupled with making things, such as, spills, for example, which were supposed to be an aid to lighting the fire.

Duly painted in gay colours in a matching holder they were proudly presented to my mother, and they would be lodged by the fireplace, much to my delight. When I saw my father actually lighting the fire with one, I suddenly felt very useful. There were also my coloured paper chains at Christmas, of course.

Peter's precocious talent was given full reign when the school made a hall display relating to the War. I was thrilled when my drawing of an 'E' boat was added to it - albeit in the corner.

War had the effect of uniting everyone in a common effort and people would speak where perhaps no word had passed before. There was a call by the government for any available pots and pans to be deposited at collecting points. Ours happened to be the school playground and I set off one morning proudly clutching one of our old pans that had already been repaired with a metal washer sticking to its bottom. They'll be pleased with this one, I thought: it'll look fine bolted to the wing of a Spitfire. On reaching the school I couldn't believe my eyes; a veritable mountain of pots and pans had appeared in the yard, as if impelled there by some giant magnet. At this moment I realised that powerful forces indeed were at work. A few decades later I read that all this domestic contribution was of little material use and most of it was never used. If this is true, I can't help thinking that there would still have been some valuable life left in that old pan.

Lorries drove down the street dropping off lengths of wavy metal on our side of the street.

"What's these for, Dad?" I asked excitedly.

"Well, this weekend we are all going to build a shelter in the garden so that if Hitler comes and drops any bombs we shall all be safe inside it."

Hitler-Hitler, everyone was talking about Hitler all the time.

I asked my brother.

"Who is Hitler?"

He stretched up and took his comb from the mantelpiece. Eyeing himself in the mirror by the sink, he stroked forward his dark hair, split it over his right eye, held his comb under his nose, erected his arm and clicking his heels snapped to smart attention.

"He is der Fuhrer. Zieg Heil! - He's a big Jerry."

"What does Zieg Heil mean?"

"It means - Go to Hell!" and he goose-stepped out into the yard.

Once I had got the message about Hitler, it was Ernie's delight to deride me in my fits of temper.

"You're a little 'Natsy', that's what you are", he would taunt, grinning. This was the ultimate insult, coupling me with Hitler's bunch of thugs and it didn't make me feel any better at all!

Though our narrow strip of garden measured only a few feet by even less feet wide, it was my father's pride and joy. My mother said that he knew every weed that popped its head up and he spent what little spare time he had there, often just standing: a small stocky figure holding a mug of strong tea often laced with whisky, waiting for things to grow, and probably worrying about work and the war.

The following weekend the War came to his beloved patch of ground.

It was hot. One of those heavy summer days when everything seemed to be well forever. My brother quickly stripped to the waist and very soon all the plants that my father had so lovingly reared were carefully taken up and placed to the side.

"Save 'em all Ernie. We'll plant 'em back on t' top o't shelter."

Soon an enormous hole began to appear, which together with its attendant mound of earth occupied what had latterly been a garden. My brother and Father gradually sank from view. It was an exercise in toil and good humour, which at times took on the atmosphere of an archaeological dig as odd unknown things were excavated.

Ernie's head would pop up.

"Ere, look at this Vic - a Roman coin wi' Caesar's 'ed on it". He tossed me a bit of rusty metal.

"Save it. It'll be worth summat." I never believed much of what my brother said.

The neighbours on each side watched with interest and not a little sense of incredulity. They were older and much more staid. If they were to be bombed, they would die in their beds, thanks very much.

"Shall we dig yours fo' ye?" Father enquired, knowing full well the answer.

"No thanks Ernest, we'll manage." Their pristine little plots of flowers enclosing their small, neat, bright green lawns would not be dug up for Nazis or anyone else.

Mr.Barker, a benign old gent who lived down the street, was one of the few people who had access to the six foot brick wall at the top of the yard, past the garages. This provided him with a short cut to his allotment. Sometimes I would be allowed to go with him and he would show me all the vegetables that he had grown and what they were called. Then we would go and sit by the stove in his little hut and he would tell me stories about the other War. The Old War. I would usually go back home with a couple of lettuces, or a cabbage, or my favourite, rhubarb.

"What's up 'ere then?" he queried, eyeing the pile of earth as he jammed his thumbs into the pockets of his waistcoat.

A voice from the hole.

"We're off to Australia before t' Jerrys ger 'ere."

"Well good luck then and send us a postcard!"

Mother would supply a constant flow of tea to the excavators and, as it was Sunday, our special treat of a cup of Camp coffee made with milk. I was always intrigued by the label on the bottle that depicted an officer of the British Raj being waited on by a turbaned aide-de-camp. What was that all about? We would have a break and Ernie, clutching a silver sixpence, would run across the tram tracks, almost unused on a Sunday, and return with a bottle of Tizer bought from the Creamery- a reward for his labours. Even though I wasn't allowed to do any work I made sure that I drank as much as he did.

Being jealous of my brother was a total affliction.

In due time the hole was finished and the metal sheets were lowered in and bolted together. A week later, around came the lorries again and dropped off wooden bunks with tinned metal lattice and these were duly fitted in.

It was fun, it was novel, and it was just a bit frightening.

Father had piled up all the earth back on top of the shelter and re-set all his plants. "Sum'll grow, sum'll die - just like us I suppose." I had a good idea what he meant but I didn't like to think about it.

There were always moments of humour however. On one such occasion Father, from his newly found observation post on the top of his garden shelter, had spied that Dickie, whilst on the pretext of doctoring the lawn at Cannon Hall, was actually doing his best to get the best view that he could of Mrs. Allen's bloomers - and here, I don't mean flowers; she being busy bending over tending her flower beds. It was something out of a McGill postcard. It was a sunny summer day and, mischievously, my father called out Mrs. Walters and my mother in order to watch Dickie's antics as he kept manoeuvring into better viewing positions; and then his acute embarrassment as Father shouted out his revelations to him and to Mrs. Allen. In truth, it didn't seem to worry her one jot and, after a further riposte, she carried on, still bending over, whilst Dickie, in his embarrassment, worked his way, head down, to a bit of the lawn where he couldn't be seen by any of us.

There was no room left now for a path between the shelter and the neat privet hedges that bounded the little garden. The low wall stopped it falling into the driveway that delivered the few cars up to the tiny garages. In order to overcome this problem, Father had built a few steps of old bricks by the shelter entrance so that he could carry on tending his beloved plants. There was something just a little bizarre watching him apply such passionate intensity to his charges, now bedded in a mere foot or so of soil atop this hole in the ground - a hole that just might be instrumental in saving our lives. Mr Barker, the old gardener, would again stop and chat, pulling at his braces.

"That looks better, Ernest."

"Aye, they'll be allreyt as long as t'bombs don't come and blow 'em out agen."

"Well, they might not get 'ere tha' knows."

"Well, it's not looking too good is it? I reckon we shan't gerr'away wi' it much longer."

"'Appen you're right. We're bound to be on that little bugger's list bein't steelwucks an' all."

His braces expanded dramatically.

It all sounded very important.

I learnt that some people had a special table under which to hide. These were called Morrison, named after, I think, a man in the Government.

Ours was called Anderson- I didn't know who he was. Some people couldn't have an Anderson because they didn't have a garden; this included all the people on the other side of the street. High walls formed the boundaries of the shop properties on the Front and cut off their yards into small areas. If one had neither of these sheltering options, or you happened to be caught outside as bombs were falling, then there was only one place to go - the cellars of Cannon Hall.

They had been specially strengthened and fitted out. Bobby took Ernie and me down on a private view and proudly showed us around the sandbags and new brickwork that led into the cellars.

"Will ye come darn 'ere when t'bombs go off?" I enquired carefully.

"Not us", he said with a disdainful air. "We shall stay in bed. Bollocks to Hitler!" He spat on the floor. We explored the cold, dank areas.

"Berra gerrof nah, Vic" commanded my brother, always protective. "Mam will be looking for yah."

I ran down the front patch, hardly a lawn this one, scrambled roughly over the wall by the solitary sycamore tree, and dropped into Skinnerthorpe Road by the row of wooden garages that graced this end of the street. I waited until I had reached our entry, then running up, I gave the Hitler salute.

"Bollocks!" I said and spat on the floor with as much venom as my tender years could muster. Mam was washing the pots at the little stone sink in the corner.

"And where have you been?" she enquired looking over her shoulder.

"Lookin' at Bob's shelter", breathless as I slumped into the chair by the door. I picked up the Dandy where I had left it under the chair and with my finger, I traced out the words that came ballooning out from the mouth of Korky the Kat. I looked at our jet black cat, Pip, lying sleeping on the hearth. If only he could talk.

I asked Father why he was called Pip and he replied that he had found him as a kitten sitting on an orange pip. I was quite happy to accept this explanation and pursued the conversation no further.

But shelters were not the only things issued to the people to help defend against the ravages of war. Certain houses were equipped with useful items that might be needed in case of incendiary bomb attacks. Letters were stencilled on the end of the designated houses so that interested parties would know where to run and collect whatever was thought to be necessary to ensure their survival.

We were issued with a stirrup pump and duly had SP emblazoned on the wall facing the street. I thought that quite important.

Dad gave a quiet laugh.

"Ey - that wain't put much out burr'it's just wot I want to water me plants wi'". And that thankfully was the only time it was ever used.

It became a bit of street cred amongst the local kids as to who had what.

"We've gorra ladder! Me dad cleans winders wi' it."

"We got two red buckets fo't watter"

"Way - way - we - we got sum - er - sandbags."

"Way - ye won't be able to get near t'bombs wi' them. Ye'll get burnt alive!"

" Me Dad's strong - 'ee can throw 'em." Knowing his dad well enough, we thought this might not be possible, but we didn't want to upset him.

Indoors we were advised to put sticky tape to criss-cross the window in case of bomb blast. Father rigged a gismo that switched off the lights when we opened the back door - the only door actually, as the front door, which was in the passage, never opened.

And so it went on.

More of Bobby

I was bored and went to stand on the shelter, thinking that it might come in useful as a hideout, except that I didn't have anyone to hide from.

At that moment I spotted Bobby walking down to the pond carrying a bucket.

"Shan't be long, Mam. Just going to see Bobby."

"Allreyt but don't be late fo' yer' tea," she said, drying her hands.

On arriving at the pond I was amazed to see that the water had been diverted into the tunnel, leaving the stone basin quite empty.

"Hiya Bobby - where's Ernie?" I knew that he would be more likely to know than I would.

"Dunno".

"What are ye doin'?" I enquired cheerily, eyeing the bucket balanced on the parapet.

"Mind your own business," he groaned. He never looked particularly pleased to see me. Bucking up as much courage as I could muster, I stepped nearer.

"Er - can I watch?"

"You are doing aren't you?" By now he was sitting on the bottom of the dried up pond, plastering some sloppy stuff from the bucket into the crevices between the stones. I always marvelled at the interesting things he found to do but then I slowly began to understand that they were usually at the command of his imperious father. He slapped on more stuff with an extravagant gesture, some of it landing perilously close to my new grey flannel shorts. I took a step back.

After a while of slapping and smoothing over he sat back and took out a small paper packet of W.D. & H.O. Wills cigarettes.

"Nip along the Top Path and see if the old man's around." This was real danger. Mr. Allen was a man of mystery who worked for the Admiralty, which had offices in Attercliffe. I never got to know what his job actually was but when the War started I liked to imagine him as some sort of boffin inventing weird, devilish devices that squashed hundreds of Germans at one go. If I got caught I might just end up in one of his scientific experiments.

But it was an Indian Chief giving orders to his best brave and I had to obey or suffer torture and banishment from the tribe. Again.

I crouched down and scuttled around - carefully now past the beehives (I'd already been stung and it hurt) - then down into the lupin beds - good cover - from where I could see the large greenhouse that leaned up against the coach house. This was where the enemy usually lurked, tending his vast collection of cacti and exotic plants. A tall dark figure moved inside. I ducked behind the dahlias. Sure enough, it was none other than the Head of the United States Cavalry - probably preparing an ambush. Wriggling back to the path, I jumped onto my faithful palomino- which always came at a whistle- and galloped furiously but silently down the canyon, Starlight's hooves being muffled with sacking. Spanking my right buttock hard, I swept along the edge of the Colorado River and, neighing (well, it was Starlight neighing actually, not me, that would be silly), reared to a halt in front of the Great Sitting Bull.

"He's in the greenhouse."

"Spiffing! He'll be there for ages." He took out a box of Swan Vestas from his top pocket and lit up. A long draw on the cigarette produced a couple of smoke rings that hung in the limpid air.

"Aha!" I thought. "Summoning up more of his lesser braves before he presents me with the coveted mountain leopard's eye-teeth."

"We're having goldfish in here," he said, eyeing me. "I've got to make sure that the water doesn't leak away.

"Why is that Bobby?" I asked, still thinking about the smoke rings.

"Because, you twerp, they'll die if it does." And he laughed. "Damn shitty job; that's all I know." And we laughed together.

The goldfish came and eventually went. I never found out what happened to them but they were certainly a constant source of wonder whilst they were there.

On rare occasions I would be allowed to accompany my brother into Cannon Hall itself.

The large stone-flagged kitchen was the easiest place to access as it lay directly behind the heavy wooden backyard door. To penetrate any further was always tempered by the thought that I might bump into Mr. Allen, especially in the spooky, dark corridor that connected the other rooms. I say spooky. Once my brother showed me one of the front rooms that wasn't used. All the furniture was covered in white sheets.

"Do ye' wanna look under the sheets?" I was already heading back to the kitchen - quick time. The kitchen had been left in a primitive state. It felt like a cave and this made it even more exciting to me. The walls were undecorated and the large windows over the sink at one end failed to let in much light as it was obstructed by the huge mass of the Sunbeam cinema. Quite ironic that - the Sunbeam!

Unfurnished, except for a couple of old chairs and a large wooden table, it was a cold, inhospitable sort of place. Despite this it was still a sanctuary, especially when the rain teemed down. On being allowed to enter, I felt that a certain privilege had been granted me.

The large trough-like sink was usually the centre of activity and was the venue for the water consuming contest that was always won, of course, by Bobby. He seemed to have the capacity to do everything better and bigger than anyone else, and usually with a swashbuckling bravura. Standing with his legs splayed apart beneath the naked light bulb that hung desolately from the cracked ceiling, he would lay a cider jar full of water over the crook of his arm, bend his head back, and quaff back a large quantity of the contents, only stopping to give off loud belches in the manner of some medieval king he had probably seen in the neighbouring cinema. My brother and I could only stand back and look on in admiration. When he was in the mood, he could bestow on us even greater privileges. Taking us across the yard, he would show us the old coach house and stables. Pulling at the crumbling plaster, he would reveal how the walls had been made with an inclusion of horsehair. The black hairs were there; it was undeniable. Recently equipped, the coach house had been rented out as a small private laundry and three or four girls were now employed there. Although somewhat older, they had already received Bobby's ardent attention but I wasn't allowed to have any information on such matters as it was generally considered that I would probably snitch to my mother. Really! Buttressed against the walls of the top side of the yard was a long ramshackle shed with windows down the whole length of it. I say windows but much of it didn't have any glass, or if it did, it was too dirty to see through. The bench inside was even dirtier but was piled high with all manner of tools and gadgets. Huge saws, files, hammers, and plenty of rusty objects that were completely strange to me. We would enquire after their usage.

Bobby would hold up old leather straps and brasses.

"These were for the horses - but as you can see we don't have any now - horses I mean." Other items would be picked up and either whacked or twanged against the bench sending up a cloud of dust. Their properties would be investigated. We would be asked if we would like to try out a real thumbscrew or even a more prosaic but formidable looking vice, with our own fingers being the object of the experiment. A passionate shake of the head would be met with a scornful look from his unwavering eye. There was a limit to hero worship even if it meant being labelled a coward. Certainly Bobby could be dangerous but this, of course, was part of his charisma.

Yes, events tended to be centred around the pond, in the orchard, or on the Top Patch. I quickly discovered that the bees weren't the only potential danger lurking in the orchard.

Although pears fell most welcomely from the spreading arms of the Giant Pear Tree, alas, this wasn't all that did. On an unlucky day, whilst picking up windfalls, you could theoretically - I stress the word - be the unwitting recipient of something rather nasty cascading from the top branches. Only one person could climb the Giant Pear Tree and it wasn't always easy to ascertain whether a silent watcher was waiting for you having baited a fruity trap beneath. To stand and peer into the leafy heights could be your undoing. The whole scenario had the smack of the White Hunter and the innocent buck come to drink at the water hole; the idea probably culled from certain Victorian books in Pop Allen's extensive library. I'm happy to say that my foraging never brought the ultimate penalty down on my head. Needless to say, any culled fruit was always scrupulously examined and washed in the pond!

The vacated pigeon hut on the Top Patch also had its lure - a ready made gang hut. However this also had to be viewed with some reservation as, having once foolishly volunteered to be tied to a bentwood chair covered in pigeon droppings, I failed to escape, and spent some of one Saturday morning wishing that I had never laid eyes on the place. Everyone else had forgotten about me and gone off to pursue some wild activity on the old tennis courts.

My lot, I have to say, was not always a happy one in those very early days.

More War

Soon we were all to suffer in more realistic terms.

Ours was an important City - a steel City. A place where high factory walls formed cobble-stoned canyons that sliced across the East End in long, straight perspectives that never seemed to terminate but only fade into grey atmospheres of ever increasing density. Ranks of tall chimneys etched on an opaque curtain of smoke of their own creation, belched forth sulphurous hues that merged into a backdrop of murky air that was palpable. An ever constant presence gritted the eyes red, settled into the corners of the mouth, invaded the linings of the nose and lungs, turned the feet black every day, and crept into the pores of the skin like some malevolent creature insidiously intent on suffocating its prey by enveloping the whole body.

Sheffield. The fields of sheaves remembered in the City's coat of arms; the names of a few pubs and in that of the River Sheaf, which gathered pollution unto itself on its way to join the River Don. All gave lie to the rural idyll that once lay in this natural bowl scooped out of the Pennine Hills in the very middle of England.

Now in its heyday of impassioned work, Sheffield was turning out millions of tons of raw steel, hammered and rolled into the stuff that would help combat the German bomb and bullet and turn an impending defeat into victory.

For the moment the image of storm troopers swarming over Britain was ever present as they blitzkrieged their way into France and the Low Countries.

The wail of the sirens heralded our time to face the appalling menace that threatened us. Conjecture gave way to a grim reality as we were at last driven into our shelters by an unremitting foe that came to us in darkness and taught us how to tremble with fear. Firvale is about a mile from the industrial part of Sheffield and, although we talked about the steelworks being an obvious target, we personally hoped that we might stand a chance of survival when the onslaught came- as we were convinced by now that it would. And if we did survive, might we then be saluting German soldiers as they marched down our street?

I always expected the bombs to arrive in the daytime when we were at school but day raids, in fact, were quite rare. No - it was usually suppertime or in the depths of the night that they came.

At first I suppose it must have been quite an embarrassment for my parents to go and sit in a hole in the ground for hours at a time but any such feelings must surely have been quickly overcome when the seriousness of the situation became more and more evident.

Our neighbours on either side of the yard, however, resolutely chose to ignore the moaning of the siren - that fearful sound that was only diminished in its intensity of message by the knowledge that it united us all.

My first sense of personal despair came when I realised that Hitler had secret information as to the timing of the attacks. They invariably arrived just as I was about to devour my second sausage, or my first bit of fish from the chip shop.

"Come on! -dah'n t'shelter," Father would command, grabbing the door key from the mantelpiece.

"Take yer' chips wi' ye'."

My brother and I would grab our plates of precious food and Mother would grab a rug and some coats and we would all rush across the yard in a mad balancing act of panic, desperately trying not to lose any chips, sausages or pickled onions on the way. Sometimes we heard the planes almost immediately, identified by the distinctive thrumming of the engines.

"That's a Jerry!" Then the anti-aircraft guns on Shirecliffe would open up with a 'cerack - cerack -cerack'.

Ernest would get very excited.

"Look at the searchlights, Vic." We would dare to poke our heads back out of the rough doorway in order to see the long tunnels of light flaring against the high clouds and sometimes crossing each other in an effort to pinpoint the Luftwaffe.

"Gerr' in 'ere before ye' get yer' 'eads blown off!" Father would drop the sacking that covered the entrance. We would sit on the bunks, often for long periods; anxiously waiting at first, sometimes hardly daring to speak above a whisper. As we got rather more used to this strange regimen, we began to indulge in simple amusements to pass the time, such as making shadowgraphs by the flickering light of the candles, or a game of 'I spy'- the latter becoming quickly exhausted as there really wasn't much to see.

We would hear the whistle of the bombs as they fell from the sky, and then await the awful seconds before detonation, and wondering how close they would be. 'Crump - crump!' Often they were far off, sounding like distant thunder, but sometimes, 'Bang-Bang-Bang' in quick succession, and very near. We would wince and cower. Dribbles of earth would fall from the seams of the metal plates and shrapnel would rattle down the slates of the houses. After an interminable time, it would grow quiet and we would doze off, until at last the 'All Clear' sounded. Ernest would run out and round up any bits of shrapnel he could find.

"Look'erit, Vic! A piece o' Jerry bomb -it's still hot!" Trophies for us - death for others. Walking around Sheffield in the light of a new day, we would gaze unbelieving at the gaps where familiar buildings had stood. Lives and bricks just blown away.

My grandparents lived in the very bull's eye of the target but were prevailed upon by the more influential uncles to leave Freestone Place and go and live in a cottage at a small village called Brampton-en-le-Morthern, some way outside the Sheffield area; this, after much cajoling, they agreed to do. They liked living in the country so much that they remained and died there, in their old age. Meanwhile George, one of the older brothers, took up residence at Freestone

Place with his wife Ethel and their eight children. If ever a house was well used it was this one.

One memorable night, acting on the rumour that Sheffield's date had come up in Hitler's diary and this was the night it was to be wiped off the map of England, my uncle Herbert- one of the younger brothers and fairly comfortable with his own butchering business- called late at night. I was already asleep.

"Hurry up - they're cumin'. They're on their way now. Leave that Mabel - get the kids in an' let's gerrof!"

We were all bundled into his car in quick time. I hadn't a clue as to where we were going and I was too tired to ask. I was wrapped in a blanket and whisked off into a starry night. With muted headlights hardly able to pick out the road ahead we eventually reached, after what seemed an interminable journey, some place near Hathersage - just over the Derbyshire - Yorkshire border. By this time I was beginning to wake up and getting somewhat excited in my childish way about the prospect of having a fine view from these high hills of something very sensational happening. After much imbibing of tea and watching from the patio, my brother and I were bedded down in a makeshift space under the stairs. Sleep had finally fled away and whilst the grownups talked of the possible consequences of a disastrous air raid, I lay there trying to come to terms with my somewhat strange environment. Then suddenly I was gripped with a cold terror. Beyond our feet in the black recesses of the cupboard, I could see that someone - some thing - was watching us with a gleaming red eye. Full of fear, but carefully so as not to be noticed, I pulled at my brother's arm whispering that we were being observed, possibly by a fierce Derbyshire animal that had somehow got in and crept under the stairs - or worse than that, it could be a ghost whose sole unblinking eye was fixed resolutely upon us.

"Don't be daft. Go to sleep," he mumbled sleepily.

I persisted. At least it wasn't moving yet - just biding its time and waiting to pounce. I slowly edged my knees towards my chin lest my feet be bitten off.

Ernest stirred and finally lifted his head.

"Wh - what are you doing?" Then he saw it.

"Cripes! What's that? Dad! Dad!"

Father's head appeared in the cubbyhole doorway. They were still talking.

"Eh? What's up?" Then he saw it. "Ey up! What the bloody 'ells that?"

Father's head was replaced by Uncle Herbert's. He gave a characteristic Oliver belly laugh.

"Ha -ha, haha! It's the electric meter!" Mother and Auntie Winnie's head poked in to see.

"Well! I've never noticed that before!" said Aunt Winnie.

"That's because ye've never 'ad to sleep in there. Yet!" chortled Uncle Herbert. I quickly fell asleep.

The next morning was one of rare beauty, not least because I hadn't often seen the dawn break. We all stood outside the house with mugs of fresh tea and watched the sun rise over the Derbyshire landscape. A vaporous mist hung mysteriously over the river far below and the long gritstone edges catching the first rays of gold were slowly transformed into medieval bastions of long lost cities. I was spellbound and utterly consumed.

The Luftwaffe didn't come to Sheffield that night but, as time wore on, the news became even more grave as cities such as Coventry and Plymouth were virtually razed to the ground and London suffered a continual battering.

We waited.

The Blitz

The film that we had been waiting to see at the Sunbeam, with not a little hype from my brother, was Geronimo. Finally it was here and the excitement, as we once again pushed back those curtains and walked into that palace of dreams, was hardly controllable. This was to be the best Western of all time when, at last, the much abused Red Indian was to play havoc with the lily faced US cavalry and, at last, the ubiquitous cowboy would take a back seat. Geronimo represented everything that was wild and free. Huddled in the dark, we waited with bated breath - and then - MY GOD! - there he was - suddenly thundering across the screen on his piebald steed and leading his band of screaming braves headlong towards a troop of bewildered cavalry. A close up showed the war scars and the war paint, swathed over a swarthy, savage countenance, all twisted in a handsome, devilish snarl. What a film this was going to be!

At this point, the screen went blank.

A hollow voice announced that an air raid was already in progress and that we must leave the cinema at once and seek shelter. A minor air raid would sometimes be ignored and the film continue: "We might as well die enjoyin' oursens," Father would say, sitting back and sucking at his quota of toffees (he still had very bad teeth) -but not on this occasion. This time it was different. The sirens had failed to sound and there were already serious explosions to be heard. It was one of those instant, unheralded raids. Suddenly they were upon us like Geronimo and his Apaches, and all hell was being let loose. The exit doors were flung open and people galloped down our street even faster than that brave Indian.

"Straight in te't' shelter, lads", as the Shirecliffe guns opened up.

We lay under our parents for an interminable time that night as they attempted to shelter us from possible catastrophe. My mother's body registered every bang and crash as she held me tight, her breath catching as bombs whistled down. "We're in for it this time," said Dad. He was never an optimist.

It was a long and frightful event and I thought that whatever death was, we were heading for it.

However, gradually, as the night wore on, the terrifying sounds subsided and died away. "I think we've gorr' away wi'it," breathed Dad, relaxing, "but the bastards might come back."

Near dawn the all clear finally sounded. Father stuck out his head.

"We've had it - the house is on fire:" There was no panic in his voice - just resignation. "No! Wait! Hang on - it's a reflection!" He emerged carefully and turned around. "It's Sheffield - it's all ablaze - Oh, look!" Despair in his voice.

We all gazed at the sky with disbelief. The clouds of the morning glowed red and angry, mirroring the destruction beneath and bearing witness to a shameful night.

Our neighbours, the Walters, had Vera, the wife of one of their sons, staying with them. I think that they may have spent the night huddled under the living room table - that is except Mother Walters who, as she was stone deaf and not able to hear anything, and never having heard a bomb drop, stubbornly refused to leave her bed.

We all congregated in the yard. The daughter-in-law, Vera, was very highly-strung, as they say, and began to scream hysterically when she realised the importance of what she was seeing in the sky. Her husband was in the National Fire Service (NFS), not being eligible for the Army for some reason, and so would have been on duty by now, probably in the City.

It was very unnerving, and Dickie, her father-in-law, didn't quite know what to do with her. So, my father in time honoured fashion stepped forward and gave her a smart slap across the face. That stopped her. He must have seen that done at the cinema, I thought - Cagney or Barbara Stanwick.

Up to this point, I had been clinging hard to my mother and managing not to cry. Then a works' siren sounded off. It had a weird cadence that I hadn't heard before. This was the last straw. I was convinced that the bombers were coming back. I broke from my mother's arms and ran back into the shelter and despite my brother's assurances refused to move. It wasn't until my father had managed to stem my flood of tears and calm me down and convince me that, for the moment, all was indeed well, did I dare venture forth.

Ernest by now had slipped away up the back and had been looking around the garages. "Hey Vic - look what I found!" He had a wicked looking piece of shrapnel in his hand. "Another one for the collection!"

Everything was at a stand still, but when the first trams were seen to be running again, Father and Ernest caught one bound for the City - as far as it would go, then walked the rest of the way. Their curiosity outweighed their good sense, as there would be plenty of danger about. Many areas, of course, were barred off as firemen, wardens and policemen struggled to contain fires, rescue the buried, and try to make safe the many stores that had been reduced to tottering towers of masonry. Marples Hotel, a grand edifice in Fitzalan Square, the very centre of Sheffield, had received a direct hit and had been reduced to a pile of rubble. Of the seventy seven people sheltering in the cellars only seven survived. The rest had been blown to pieces. Blood and remains plastered the walls. There was plenty more to tell but I wasn't allowed to hear. The main shopping area of the Moor, which ran downhill from the Town Hall, was cordoned off as the Luftwaffe had taken out almost all the properties on each side for its whole length. The legend was that they had mistaken this straight wide road as one of the major arteries of the steelworks, which consequently remained relatively unscathed. Another theory was that an enemy pilot had followed a train across the works area and into the main station at Pond Street and carried on his deadly work from there. Many pockets of devastation could be seen around the city years after the dust had settled and restrictions had been lifted.

The loudest bang that we had heard above all others and which seemed to be right on top of us was generally regarded as a very large land mine. It landed about a quarter of a mile away and took away a huge piece of Bolsover Road. We were not experts in such things but we were learning - the hard way. There was much awe struck gazing at piles of rubble and solitary house walls left standing with the contents of what had once been a home suddenly exposed to passersby like some giant doll's house. The scars on the city lasted for many, many years. In some people's minds they never healed. The Sheffield Blitz happened on the nights of the 12th and 15th of December 1940. I had just turned seven.

Living normally was totally out of the question. Ration books were a fact of life. There was some trade in coupons as almost everything was rationed, and this carried on for a period of time after the war had concluded.

Father did his bit of amateur black market as any that could, did. It was a matter of survival. Meat, of course, was relatively easy for us and this was traded with the Maypole grocers that happened to be next to Olivers' shop on the Common. Butter and eggs would periodically emerge from Father's small brown attaché case that went to work and back with him every day. I often wondered what everyone on the bus thought that he might be carrying in such a thing in these times, as it was very obvious that he wasn't a travelling salesman; but in all fairness it also carried an awful lot of bloodstained smocks and aprons that poor Mother had to wash in the copper boiler by the sink.

Father gritted what was left of his few remaining teeth - if Hitler was to conquer Britain, he would sooner or later have to deal with Dad.

We were hungry and I was painfully thin, but we were never starving. There was always a bowl of dripping to lape on some bread, to fill a gap at suppertime, if it wasn't chip night.

Teatime fare was usually jam sandwiches, rhubarb and custard, or biscuits, whilst avidly listening to Larry the Lamb and Dennis the Dachshund doing their thing in Toy Town. I was always a little worried about Dennis. He was constantly getting lost and falling foul of Mr.Policeman. He also spoke with a German accent - very suspicious. We were continually being told to watch out for spies. Sometimes, clustered around the ancient wireless set, we would hear the two Princesses, Elizabeth and Margaret, identifying themselves with us and the pickle that we were in. This wasn't difficult as they were almost the same ages as Ernest and me, and also hadn't been migrated to Canada. Life went on. People and communities became closer. Next to our school a street name was replaced with one saying 'Keep Smiling'. We liked that.

In those days of continual threat from the Fuhrer and his forces, we would keep an ear permanently cocked to the News coming from the wireless. I could never understand why it was called the wireless as on the many occasions that my father and brother had seen fit to probe its inner recesses in order to keep it going, I could plainly see that it did indeed have wires. My questions on this point would fail to bring any satisfactory response and be met only with a flashing smile from my brother and a grunt from my father. I didn't understand too much about the News either, except the gloom that would descend when some of it was bad, such as when gallant vessels like the Ark Royal were sunk; or jubilation when successes were scored over the Bismarck or the Tirpitz and so on. When Monte Casino was violently destroyed, the tragedy of the event didn't register with me at all. I remember being fascinated by the sound of the words, so much so that I went around the house chanting them - until I was told to "Put a sock in it". Later, at Grammar School, I was to do well in Italian (and French) and I regarded this early meeting with the language as an indication of some natural feeling for it. Obviously no one appreciated that at the time and I didn't realise the importance of it. A similar thing happened with classical music, which no one in the whole huge family listened to. On occasionally accidentally tuning in to a concert, I would immediately start to be absorbed, only to be rudely shaken from my reverie by Dad turning the dial to Itma or Much-Binding-in-the Marsh! I was never to play an instrument but I developed a life-long passion for the classics.

For the moment I had to settle for my brother who would do swaps for copies of the War magazine, which had all the latest drawings and photos of Allied and Enemy armament etc. Looking at these made things a little clearer about the War although I couldn't yet read properly and my drawings of aeroplanes and tanks looked nothing like the illustrations in the magazines.

"Why has this aeroplane not got any wings, Ernie?"

This was his field. I got an answer.

"It's side on. Ye' can only see the ends o't wings."

"Why do they draw it like that? It won't be able ter' fly."

"It's a scale drawing."

"What's a scale ……?"

But it was too late. He'd already disappeared down the passage with a jam sandwich, leaving me to ponder on the logic of grown-up drawings. I never got into scale drawings. For me it was all interactive stuff: bullets and bombs flying all over the page and, with the battle at its fiercest, the pencil tearing into the paper. For the record though, I did pre date Star Wars by mounting some of my 'planes on legs so that they couldn't be shot down. Father actually showed an interest in this but after a short conversation, he failed to appreciate the visionary insight of my invention. It could have won the war for us a lot more quickly.

The war ground on. We would sometimes see squads of soldiers marching past the top of the road with army lorries in attendance - somehow reflecting our more peaceful marching activities. I had eventually joined the Life Boys.

Occasionally a tank would crunch past and we would watch in awe and with great excitement. After its departure we would examine where the huge tracks had ripped up the surface of the road. Up to that point the only similarity had been the wrecking of pennies that had been laid in the tramlines on Barnsley Hill. Sometimes the soldiers would fall-out and find the space in front of the wooden garages in the street an ideal resting place. In exchange for mashing their tea, my brother would sometimes be successful in cadging a badge or some other souvenir. He was always a great cadger! The big cities were still being plastered with bombs - likewise by our RAF in Germany. The history books tell the tale but at the time we just didn't know what was going to happen to us. My father and most of my uncles were already too old to be conscripted , but his two youngest brothers had been at Dunkirk and were now army drivers - Dick handling a DUKW on D-Day- a sort of amphibious barge for carrying troops from ship to shore. Uncle Herbert was in the Fleet Air Arm, which gave him a good slice of charisma, and cousin Eveline was a WREN. She later married Bill who was on minesweepers in the Navy. Eric, married to cousin Irene in Nottingham, was in the RAF.

Dad was obliged to join the Home Guard. He absolutely hated it. Playing soldiers was really not in his make up. He was usually worn out by the time he had finished working at the shop in Attercliffe - cutting up and serving meat all day. The last thing that he wanted to do was to sleep under a tarpaulin or spend the night on a draughty billet room floor. The billet was housed somewhere at Pitsmoor, beyond Barnsley Hill and he would groan and complain when he was ordered to attend. He thought it was all a bit of a farce- he enjoyed rather more his night duties as an ARP warden. He felt that shouting "Put that light out!" at lit windows in the street had rather more immediate usefulness as the bombers droned overhead. I think that he also liked giving orders rather than receiving them. The Home Guard turned him into a reluctant machine gunner. This meant that he had to spend weekends at the Totley shooting range on the outskirts of Sheffield - often in the rain, draped in a cape. I was proud - I had a machine gunner for a Dad.

Eventually he caught pneumonia - well, double pneumonia he said - he never did anything by halves; double hernias, double handed, you name it. He blamed the Home Guard for it, but I think the fact that he sometimes had a fag didn't help. He never smoked after that. Later on, after the war, he survived a heart attack. He died at 82, feeling that he had had enough anyway.

The 'Flicks'

As there was yet no television for us, our most graphic source of war information was the Gaumont British or Pathe News at the cinema. This, of course, was highly propagandised, but we didn't care about that - as long as we were seen to be winning. Father was a one-cinema man basically and that was the Sunbeam, mainly because it took only about two minutes to walk there. Situated almost next door, it provided a weekly escape from the world of hard work and an entrée for us into a great fantasy world. There was always a frisson of excitement when you brushed aside those dark, heavy curtains and followed that sweeping torchlight to awaiting seats.

Twice a week, usually Mondays and Fridays, when the programme had changed, we would all forget the climate of shortage and rationing that flavoured our daily lives and bask in the Hollywood glamour and the adventure of Ealing comedies or drama, or better

14. Queuing on a Bank Holiday for the Regent Cinema (later, the Gaumont). Mother to my left. Father is on the extreme left. He thought that the people surrounding us could have been a bit better looking!   The photo appeared in the 'Star'. 1946

still, a Walt Disney spectacular. We paid our sixpence admission fee. Upstairs it was nine pence and it was only on rare occasions, usually as a treat for Mother, that we would ascend the double staircase with its lavish décor and red carpet with golden stair rods. Saluted and ushered in by the uniformed door attendant, it all added to the illusion of, just for a moment, having a rather superior existence, and then, again, as we finally peered down onto the heads of lesser mortals.

Occasionally if the picture proved to be particularly popular, like Gone with the Wind, there would be a queue, not only on Saturday night which was normal, but on every night; and if you were late, you might find yourself shunted by the light-flashing usherette into the Pit or even to the very front row where there was little chance of reading the elongated images flickering in grotesque format way above your head. At the interval, when the girl with the tray of ice cream was highlighted in the side exit, there would be a mad scramble, not only for the ice-cream, but for the seats further back.

Such was the popularity of the Picture Palace at this time that we had a huge choice of film and venue each week and a penny tram ride would get you to most of them. The Star evening paper would always carry a whole page of cinema adverts.

It had to be something special for Father to say "Cum on. Get yer' best things on and comb yer' 'air." We're goin' tot' Regent - up town." That was posh. He was a great cynic of the Cinema - very iconoclastic; and I was never really sure that he enjoyed much of what he saw; or maybe he felt it some sort of weakness that he be involved emotionally and admit it. Certainly, I never saw a tear in his eye. In fact, Mum said that the only time she had seen him cry was when I was taken into hospital years later. He needed to keep a grip on life. He enjoyed a good laugh though, and I think that he was probably taken back to his youth when he watched Chaplin, or Laurel and Hardy and the like; though he was inclined to disparage our particular heroes, which I found quite a bit deflating. "Who's on? Bloody Bogie (Bogart) - Bloody Tarzan? Oh! Bloody 'ell!"

The performances always consisted of the main film, a B film, a cartoon, trailer, adverts, and the News. Anything less was frowned on and considered as being short-changed. At the end, everyone stood up to attention whilst the National Anthem would be played, together with a picture of the King. I quite enjoyed doing this, as I was very patriotic and felt that this would contribute in some way to the War Effort. On one occasion, as the last strains of the Anthem died away, I turned to my mother and asked her if God had indeed saved the King and what sort of trouble had he been in to warrant such attention. My mother trotted out this story for years afterwards at social occasions. Father didn't like this sort of ritual. It embarrassed him to stand in public gatherings unless it be at a cricket or football match; in fact, it wasn't unusual for us all to be dragged out of the cinema five minutes before the end, as the detective was still explaining the vagaries of the plot and revealing the villain; or lovers had at last been united. "To avoid the crush" was his reasoning but I didn't believe it. My life in the Thirties and the early Forties was consequently blighted by never having witnessed the end of many films!

Occasionally I was allowed to go with Ernest, he having been threatened with the usual dire consequences should any ill befall me. We would sometimes call for Bobby at Cannon Hall. This was a great thrill for me but any illusions I had about being 'one of the Gang' were quite false. I remember Bobby being as demonstrative in the cinema as he was outside, and there was always much whooping and shouting and stamping of feet as swashbuckling heroes such as Errol Flynn, Douglas Fairbanks and Tyrone Power dashed across the screen with rapier and cutlass whilst Tarzan swung from tree to tree with acrobatic skill. (Ernest incidentally, grew to look rather like Tyrone Power, and all the girls loved him). If it was such a programme, aimed at the young, the audience would consist of wild, effusive lads, and the noise at critical points would reach ear-splitting proportions; such as the sudden appearance of the disembodied head of Mickey Mouse or Donald Duck surrounded by psychedelic rays. The gangsters were all tough, adroit and smooth: Bogart, Mitchum, Cagney and Edward G. Robinson. We loved them.

They would manipulate their environment - something that we couldn't do; and the fact that they sometimes met a sticky end made them all the more plausible. The ones who never met sticky ends were the cowboys: Gene Autry, the Lone Ranger (and Tonto!), Roy Rogers and my favourite - Hopalong Cassidy! He didn't waste time singing as some of them did, and he always wore black - not some fancy white suit that never got dirty. His neckerchief was held with a pin shaped like the horns of a steer and he had pearl-handled shooters that flew from the hip. None of this modern two- handed, straight-armed stuff. He also had a droll laugh with which he concluded his films, having got his man with the help of his sidekicks: the admirable Lucky Jenkins and the endearing Gabby Hayes.

There was an infamous cinema in Upwell Street, a short walk in the direction of the steelworks. This held a Saturday performance for children only, called The Tuppeny Rush. The programme consisted of the usual cartoons but was especially renowned for running a serial featuring stars such as Flash Gordon. Unfortunately, I was considered too young to go, even with my brother, lest, I suspect, I be trampled underfoot.

We didn't like romantic films and we would groan if trailers forecasted stars such as Claudette Colbert, Bette Davis, Clark Gable, or Cary Grant. These films would undoubtedly include long scenes of boring dialogue and what we called "slop", which would find us fidgeting madly in our seats and desperately waiting for the appearance of the ice-cream girl. Mother loved them all - Father would pull faces; it was years before we were to appreciate the allure of Bacall and my favourite, Bergmann.

One special occasion for me was when my brother invited me to join him on a trip to the Coliseum. His mates must have been otherwise engaged at the time. The Coliseum however wasn't a Roman arena - just another cinema. It's major claim to fame was that it still contained double seats! Useful for courting couples.

The film was Scott of the Antarctic and this proved to be a bit of a benchmark for me. That's it! I was meant to be an explorer. At last, I had tasted my destiny! OK - so we all die - but what glory! The other thing that grabbed me was the music of Vaughan Williams - music with a wind machine? I loved it.

Grimesthorpe

And so it came to pass that we were due to leave Owler Lane and its sanctity and go forward to the Intermediate School at Grimesthorpe. We were growing up and Grimesthorpe, as the name suggests, was no place for infants. We soon realised that just past Cookie's Field was a very grim school in a very grim place. Surely, only a Dickens could have invented a more onomatopoeic name than the one that this school had.

I almost didn't go. People were getting even more anxious about a possible Nazi invasion from France, and the air raids were continuing. One of my mother's sisters, Nelly, had lived in Canada for some time, and it was proposed that my brother and I should be sent there. I didn't relish leaving home and my mother one little bit, even though we were already receiving parcels from there that spoke strongly of a better life in a better land. Miss Eaton was the Head at Owler Lane by that time, and my parents and I were called to her study to see the nurse, as a final check. It was the first time that I had been to her study. I liked her kind, friendly manner as she talked to my parents. I was given some sort of physical examination but the only thing that I can remember is Miss Eaton putting her hand down my shorts and patting me on the bare belly, saying, "He's absolutely fine." I was pleased that she thought that I was fine; as far as I knew, I had never been touched in an intimate way by a stranger before, and this surprised me not a little. Her warm hand gave me a definite new sensation that thrilled and puzzled me at the same time. So that's what Heads did. I liked her even more.

Anyway, it wasn't to be. Shortly after that, I was told that a U-boat had sank a ship full of passengers and evacuees - and so, like the King and Queen - we didn't go to Canada. Instead, I went to Grimesthorpe. A high Victorian building, it was something out of a Dickens novel.

Almost a Dotheboys Hall! It had been built up to the back of a small disused quarry with wasteland behind it and was surrounded by high stone walls that were blackened with soot. It looked more like a prison than a school. The streets of back-to-back houses fell away very steeply at the front and side, and the road tilted alarmingly. A police box leaned precariously on a small traffic island. This divided the road as one street went on to plunge down towards Brightside and on to the labyrinth of the steelworks area; the other dived in another direction to a little bridge, between the houses, that spanned the now fast flowing stream that disappeared at Bobby's pond. Across the bridge was Upwell Street where Peter Swain lived. Upwell Street was a dark, dismal thoroughfare on the way to the steelworks, where trams clattered past the brick houses, almost scraping the walls. A short distance further on, a works rail line crossed the tramlines; sometimes the trams had to give way to a small steam engine as it pulled across from the coke factory and into the yard opposite. Then the trams plunged steeply and darkly under the main line railway bridge with a screech and a shower of sparks as the lines turned down, veered sharply and did a quick ascent into the realm of the English Steel Corporation at Brightside Lane (although there was nothing "bright" about it.). Later when I worked in the steelworks, that dive under the bridge had to be negotiated on a bicycle, and although every Sheffield youth who owned a bike quickly learnt how to negotiate tramlines at speed, this particular hazard also had cobbles added to its ramifications. I have to say I did go over the handlebars on, at least, one occasion. This seemed a fairly normal event, repeated in other places, and later, on (or off!) motorbikes. In exceptionally heavy rain the dip under the bridge used to flood and we would be excommunicated for a time. With the coming of global warming and the New Millennia, the River Don gave up its watery load and flooded the whole area. But that's modern history.

I would often meet my pal Tony on the way to school as our routes coincided and I thanked the powers that be that we were still together. We would climb through the hoardings on the main road and then make our way along the quarry around the back of the school. Tony would recount his stories that stretched both our imaginations somewhat, or he would elaborate at great length on some film that he had just seen and somehow I had just missed. We were soon to master the art of reading and he became a great lover of books, Biggles being his favourite.

"Worrals is just as good, burr' it's a girl", he informed. Captain W.E.Johns would have approved. I suspect that the lure of the young ladies at Firth Park Library (which was excellent - the library, that is) might have had something to do with his literary ardour later on.

His optimistic cheerfulness helped me to face the trial of the early days in this depressing place that I was diligently forced to attend. It wasn't unusual for me to be ill and I must say I wasn't particularly sorry that I couldn't always be there. Lying in bed trying to read, and being fed on hot milk, with an egg beaten into it, and buttered arrowroot biscuits, always seemed to be a better option, of which I took full advantage. It also gave me time to read.

Suddenly we were under a new regime of learning and discipline, led by the two chief members of the staff - Mr. Briggs, the Head, and Miss Hanson, the senior teacher - both stern and unsmiling people - though I have to admit that Miss Hanson was an excellent teacher and 'Briggsy' had to run the school with a rod of iron or be trampled on.. The junior teachers were lenient and I enjoyed the lessons. One of the hardest things to accommodate were the school meals. Wartime being what it was, there was very little food available and hardly any variety. The meals were basic and awful. The smell of the over-cooked cabbage at dinnertime pervaded the place and put me off vegetables for years. I could see that some of the poorer pupils were actually glad to wolf it down as it was probably the only substantial meal that they had but, although painfully thin, I couldn't bring myself to eat much of it. I can't remember there being meat or fish; I think it was mainly boiled potatoes, carrots and cabbage. Product of 'Digging for Victory'.

The sweet was usually semolina with a prune. Fortunately there was no pressure to eat. Some of us who had a bit of pocket money would frequent the chip shop on the corner of the opposite street, and the baker on the other corner. A freshly baked, still warm loaf would cost one penny and three farthings. We would first greedily eat the centre and then fill it with the chips.

This school was a whole new ball game. The whistle blew and we formed lines in the yard as usual, but this time we had to be in order of seniority with older boys at the back. Absolute silence would have to be maintained as we marched down the fortified passageway and into the school, where our marching footsteps would be drowned by a stirring tune played on the clanging piano. Inside wasn't so bad; as I said, the junior teachers were quite nice. It was some of my school 'buddies' who were a bit of a culture shock. Running noses were the order of the day and the club members weren't fussy as to whose sleeve they wiped them on. Nits and fleas were common enough; swearing, bullying and spitting became part of my everyday existence. The school was the gathering ground for the kids in this downbeat area and many of then were extremely poor. The few pupils who had arrived with me from Owler Lane, namely: Tony, John Derek, Peter Swain and one or two more, were really aliens in a foreign culture, as all the other pupils seemed to be living within a stone's throw of the school. This was their school, not ours. But we had to integrate.

One lad in particular, called Terry, wore a coat shot through with grease, owing to the fact that his parents ran one of the many local chippies and he smelt accordingly. The wearing of clogs was not that unusual and clothes could be ragged.

The 'cock o' the roost' was Brown who, as it happened, was relatively neat, tidy and dapper but who also had a quiet, calculating evil air about him. His henchman, who never left his side, was called, oddly enough, Green! Quite the opposite in nature, although a bully through and through: he was longhaired, dirty and gobby. He also had a pair of clogs that were metal-shoed, like a horse - deadly weapons. Totally ignorant and uninterested in learning anything, his mission was to support Brown in everything he did- no matter what. One of their favourite pastimes was to compete in pissing over the lavatory wall that bordered the street, and failing this, to spray any lesser mortal who happened to step into the loos at the wrong time.

My basic survival skills were beginning to become quite well honed, and I kept out of the firing line by practising the art of becoming invisible at will.

Just how nasty these two could be was brought home to me when one day, from the darkness of the passageway, I saw them, in the empty playground, upturn John Derek and throw him to the floor in a cold sadistic fashion, banging his head on the asphalt with a sickening thud. They didn't tolerate competition. This was no playtime - it was my first sight of a hands-on, harsh and frightening violence. Also, I was no hero and I didn't want to see any more lest I be seen, so I melted into the darkness and slipped away. John had, at last, met his match.

I began to notice that I had been gifted with rather more intelligence than most of the other children, and this I found made a useful tool when it came to protecting myself. I often talked my way out of trouble when challenged, and I actually found favour with one group of local lads simply because I was able to spell their leader's name correctly. He was graced with the name of Osbaldiston and this, much to their amazement, presented me with no challenge at all.

I was becoming a little bolder; I even began to take a leaf out of Tony's book, soon discovering the delights of tickling one of the more attractive, plumper girls, when I was fortunate enough to find myself sitting in the same double desk. She liked it. I liked it.

My halo was starting to slip a little, but not much.

My reading was coming along in leaps and bounds and I quickly became a proficient reader thanks to all the comics that I had struggled through. My first real book, that my parents bought me at the age of ten, was Stevenson's classic Treasure Island. How that book thrilled me! It opened up new vistas.

At Grimesthorpe, -you have to admit now that you could not have invented a more appropriate name- the painting classes had become quite animated with our growing confidence; Peter Swain and Tony would jump up enthusiastically to compare their work and show it off. I was getting completely absorbed; I loved Peter's paintings- they seemed to appear rapidly out of nowhere without any effort. His skill and imagination flowed from him in a completely natural way that quite amazed me. Showing off was his thing and he was very mouthy with it. His stammer, as bad as it was, didn't seem to bother him. At times he would be absent from school in order to attend special therapy sessions which, when I questioned him, appeared to consist of time doing even more painting!

His parents held a birthday party for him and I, together with Tony, and some of his neighbourhood friends, were invited. The novelty was that there were girlfriends of his there. Really? Girlfriends? He had girlfriends? One beauty, whom I assumed to be from his therapy class, had taken elocution lessons and proceeded to stand up and intone a poem in the most wonderfully enunciated English that I had ever heard. I was gob-smacked; I realised at that moment how far I had to go, as I was still quite tongue-tied and shy in strange company. On the one occasion when I managed to say something, a swear word fell out. Utterly embarrassed.

In my defence, my father swore consistently, albeit it only 'bloody' and 'bugger', and the latter not in the sense that it may now be interpreted. Mother, exaggerating, said that every other word that fell from his lips was a swear word. To counteract this however, my father was a friendly, affable man and generous to a fault.

"He'll be givin' us away soon if we don't watch out". Mother would assert.

In a way Peter had taken over this part of Upwell Street. One could see, particularly from the top deck of a tram, how he had commandeered the brick walls in several people's yards in order to paint, in the name of The War Effort, large patriotic symbols, flags, slogans and pictures, including an excellent portrait of Churchill with his fat cigar. It was a real morale booster and brightened a very gloomy area. I was mightily impressed, full of admiration and proud to call him a friend even though, I suspect, he rather preferred admirers. Thanks to his liberal minded parents, he had been allowed to become a genius of the art of wall graffiti long before it became as common as it is now. At Grimesthorpe a high wall divided the girls' yard from the boys'; it was a risqué thing to be seen loitering by the connecting gate. "You don't like girls, do you?" Despite my infrequent tickling activities, girls were still a big mystery to me. For me and almost all the other boys in the school, playtime and dinnertime were taken up, not with chasing girls, but with something that was meant to pass as football. There was one lad who was much bigger and better orientated than anyone else - he also seemed to be a lot older, but I guess that he couldn't have been. Anyway, he dominated the proceedings. A swarm of boys would press from one side of the yard to the other, surrounding this giant of a lad. At first I was at a loss to see what we were actually doing but eventually I realised that we were all meant to be chasing an old tennis ball - the idea being, of course, to kick it! It didn't seem to matter which way.

This was my introduction to football but I have to say that in the years that I was there I can't remember coming in contact with the ball- it was quite common not to see it for long periods. I suppose it resembled the Eton Wall Game, hemmed in as we were by walls! It was nothing to hear screams as junior members were crushed in the melee. Certainly no holds were barred. In the daily skirmish that would ensue, it seemed to be a legitimate tactic- if you had the excuse to be anywhere near the ball- to kick someone on the shins out of sheer frustration. The main objectives seemed to be: not to get squashed up against the wall: not to be knocked down in the rush: and to avoid, like the plague, being kicked by the giant boy.

However, football grew large in my consciousness from here on in.

Miss Hanson's classes were held in strict discipline and were often quite frightening, especially when she announced that we were to have a test. This usually involved mental arithmetic, working on the basis that the twelve-times table, repeated in a singsong voice ad nauseum, had been fully and truly absorbed. I found that the worst concepts were sums involving people's ages and the times of day. There was certainly no tickling or giggling in Miss Hanson's class! She could get quite angry and was always stern faced. However, I think she was a good person.

Apart from the actions of Green and Brown, who happily weren't in my class, other events brought me nearer to a necessary state of self awareness in an awakening world where strange things could happen without warning. One day, a really nice girl called Joan suddenly fell out of her desk onto the floor and proceeded to throw violent convulsions. The other pupils immediately sprang up and gathered round in curious astonishment. Miss Hanson immediately took control.

"Stand back - give her air - she'll be alright."

I'd never seen anyone have a fit before and I found it very disturbing, especially as I liked Joan very much; I was glad that I had never tickled her.

Another event disturbed me. Having reached the senior year of ten I now found myself occupying the rear lines in the yard. I was deeply ensconced in finishing an extremely important game of conkers with another friend, Terry Wilson, as we were marched in. Unfortunately we had been spotted from an upstairs window by Briggsy. My blood ran cold as he beckoned us from the window. Once inside his study he proceeded to administer a good whack on each hand with his dreaded cane. I thought this quite shocking and savage. I was a good boy and so was Terry. We shamefacedly returned to the class whereon we were met by all faces turned towards us. As I sank into my seat at the side of John Derek, he whispered the secret antidote.

"Put ink on thi' 'ands - it'll tek' sting art' on' em." The master spoke and this we surreptitiously did, following knowledge gained through long experience. We had been welcomed into his elite club; thereafter he began to treat me almost as an equal. Needless to say it gave me a certain kudos with the other children, but I never forgave Briggsy for violating the sanctity of my childhood. Messrs. Brown and Green, of course, had been caned many times and this event had become quite familiar to them. Judging by the way they fought back the tears and squeezed their hands under their armpits on leaving the study, they certainly earnt plenty of strokes. It was part of their everyday existence. For different reasons we were all becoming one. The Top Guys.

Another regular candidate for Briggsy's leveller was Wheeler - the school joker.

Miss Dearnley, the young, nubile, shy teacher, fell to his whimsy in the PT lesson in the yard. Creeping behind her, he cleverly rolled over in order to look up her skirt, much to everyone's amusement. Unfortunately for 'Wee-Wee', Briggsy was also getting a good look at Miss Dearnley from the lower dining room windows and our clown prince paid the painful price.

It wasn't all doom and gloom. School plays were always fun and gave the show-offs an opportunity to excel. Swain was a master and he always took every opportunity to do his special thing. This usually took the form of an ad-lib charade involving his own hand-made props. He particularly liked to impress and build up a following with the most recent arrivals to the school; this went on right to the end of our long schooldays together. By that time we were sixteen and both at the same Grammar School. He became almost revered by the younger element- not for what I saw as his natural talent- but for his blatant outspokenness, cheek and audacity. John Derek, meanwhile, had found some hitherto undiscovered acting talent and was given the chance to shine. I was very pleased. One of the brightest aspects of the curriculum was the singing lesson where we found that we could let rip with some rousing lyrics from the songbook that often included little masterpieces by such composers as Vaughan Williams- now one of my favourites- although it was a great deal later that I discovered who he was. Tony would get very excited with any new song that came along, our favourite being The Blacksmith. Its rhythm echoed the stroke of the hammer on the anvil and we always gave it as much gusto as our high-pitched voices could manage.

Visits by the school nurse were always viewed with great suspicion and trepidation; she was, like the school dentist, not a popular figure. On one occasion we were all stunned into silence when one vociferous lad ran screaming from the adjacent room, having just had a boil lanced! Whatever that was! Flea nits in the scalp were a constant problem and I doubt that there was a single pupil who didn't suffer from them at one time or another. Mother usually blamed mine on the cat but I fancy that they were passed on from our more neglected and unwashed fellows. One project at school that fascinated me was the weather chart that was scrupulously maintained daily by one of the teachers, fostering my interest in nature. Alas there were no trips to the pond from Grimesthorpe, it probably being thought too much of a risk. It wasn't beyond probability that Brown and Green would have attempted to drown some unfortunate whilst the teacher's back was turned! - or even the teacher!

Eventually we were to make our own adventurous journeys to the ponds. Excited? You bet.

There were one or two boys from somewhat better class families at Grimesthorpe, and I found myself being attracted to these more genteel souls as friends. One, Brian Clarke by name, I found less likely to punch you on the nose than some, and another, Brian Kelk, actually played the violin! His parents prompted Miss Hanson to give him homework - unheard of at this school- which he duly presented the next morning in a leather-bound ledger. Although impressed, I thought it very masochistic - doing sums - gratuitously? I really didn't like sums! I also noticed that he had loops around his braces. By this time I had graduated to the more macho belt that usually fastened with a metal snake. Cool! Another of Ernie's cast-offs.

Both of these chums (and Swain) went to Firth Park Grammar School with me after passing the Eleven Plus; Kelk played for some of the football teams that I was happy to captain. A nice, steady lad but not a good footballer! Brian, although starting off as weak and shy, rather like me, put on a spurt in later teenage years and rapidly grew tall, becoming a good athlete and footballer. He played for the Boys' Brigade, as he came from a religious background- their excellent team being a well-knitted band of friends.

One of my best friends was a Cub, and certainly better class. Cubs were the Boy Scouts' juniors and rather grander than the Life Boys, although we never admitted it. They, I feel, had a much more interesting regime and, at times, I wished that I could have been one of them. It sometimes meant going away on camping expeditions; consequently it seemed to be only families who could afford it, let alone pay for the rather expensive looking uniform and other accoutrements.

Maxwell Harry Ernest Watson was my friend, although I was never quite comfortable with him as I was all too aware of the class difference. He was the only person that I knew who had more than one name. He was intelligent to a fault and had braces across his teeth- not very common in those days- which affected his speech somewhat. He was rather removed from the street life that I was already committed to, as he lived in a semi-detached house high up on Barnsley Hill where the backs of the houses were open to vistas across the same old tennis courts and allotments and all the area surrounding the ponds up to Osgathorpe. I enjoyed the better environment and the fact that they had a fair sized garden, and a garden shed, that I found quite fascinating. This is what houses should really be like. He lived at the top - I lived at the bottom, and I'm sure that he had loops around his braces - the braces on his trousers - not his teeth.

I borrowed his scouting books, read them avidly, and wished that I could get badges for lighting fires and running backwards. They had the most modern house that I had yet been in, and his charming mother always made me welcome. I saw little of his father as he worked for the BBC and was away a lot of the time. I was once invited to listen to him speak on the radio and afterwards Max and I were persuaded to recite a poem (that we had learnt at school) to the small group of followers that had collected in the front room. I remember it was called Puk Wudgies. I can remember that, but I've forgotten so many important things! What a strange thing is memory!

Most times we would play in the garden, usually at Max's favourite game, which was flicking cigarette cards against a wall and winning the ones that landed in a certain fashion. I did think this was a bit sissy (whatever that was) and tame; often I was quite glad to get back to having punching matches or a bit of sword-fencing using sticks, with Gord, or catching Tony at home for a quick game of 'popping-in' with a tennis ball.

My friendship with Gord took a downturn when he passed the Eleven Plus and went on to the King Edward School. This was often the time when childhood friends parted company. There was a feeling that 'King Ted's' was the best Grammar School in Sheffield. I also passed the Eleven Plus and made a preference for Firth Park as it was very near to home. This legend of superiority was soon dispelled on my arrival at my own beautiful school. Max was certainly better class and he too went on to King Ted's; Gord certainly wasn't of equal class, which says a lot for the Grammar School system at that time. Meanwhile, Gord carried on working in his spare time at the butcher's, and after he had accompanied me on one or two sorties to Firth park, he eventually decided our antics were not for him and he went on his own sweet way. Dear Gordon.

Later on, in his late teens, Max was hit by a car on Barnsley Hill whilst walking with his girlfriend and suffered a severe head injury. As we had not associated for years by then, I received this information second-hand, and never got to know the outcome of this dreadful incident. Dear Max.

Naughty Tony

Meanwhile, Tony was still busy exploring his burgeoning sex drive. One day whilst playing innocuously around the old abandoned tennis hut beyond Cannon Hall, two or three young girls joined us. Gord and I were busy sliding on our bottoms on the steep clay hills that backed onto the Working Men's Club on Barnsley Hill. Shouting us over, Tony said he had a surprise waiting for us back in the hut. On investigating, we discovered that, unbelievably, he had been crass enough to inveigle the girls to take off all their clothes whilst standing in a tall tennis equipment cupboard! As he swung back the cupboard doors, I had to admit that his prediction that I would be surprised was very accurate. I was definitely very surprised! In fact for a moment I thought I was seeing things! Three naked girls cavorted and giggled in front of us, seemingly enjoying their new found liberation. As I hadn't a sister, this was a completely new experience for me. I didn't know where to put my face as I blushed with embarrassment. Tony grabbed one of the girls and thrust her towards me.

"What do yer' think o' that, lad?"

To my horror, I realised that this particular girl was none other than a class mate's young sister, not yet fledged or sprouting breasts. What was I thinking Tony? I couldn't begin to express what I was thinking, but I immediately realised that someone was going to be in deep trouble and I didn't want it to be me. The hut had a big cellar that we were wont to drop into and explore. Suddenly, it seemed a good place to be and I rapidly disappeared through the hole in the floorboards. Tony you were a naughty boy!

I didn't ask for details, but John and his mate Billy were known to have applied certain unpleasant pressures on Tony's more wayward ambitions. I wasn't prepared to take any rap for Tony's folly and, although John knew that I had been present, it didn't affect our hard won mutual respect. Tony was a very good friend over a very long period, lasting into our late teens, but he could never master his over-ripe sexuality; I witnessed him getting into trouble on more than one occasion. I loved the guy but sometimes he made me cringe.

He grew tall and strong, his athleticism only being hindered by an inherent clumsiness, as if he had outgrown his strength - just a little bit.. He was at his best as a goalkeeper and he went on to play for Sheffield Boys - a great honour for a young lad, and one that I envied greatly - but I wished him well. But more about football later. He was a great favourite with my mother - being almost an antithesis of myself. He would knock loudly on the door when calling for me. Mother would answer it and be faced with a heavily sweating Tony who had just run all the way from his home, about half a mile away.

"How are you, Mrs. Oliver? Could I please have a large glass of water?" and he would rapidly quaff it on the doorstep. "May I please have another one?"

"Ooo! That Tony - he's a lad." He certainly was, and he continued his antics for the years that I knew him.

Tony's parents preferred him to go to Owler Lane Intermediate School where my brother had been, rather than to a Grammar School. I think that there was a good reason; I can't believe that he would have failed the Eleven Plus as he was very intelligent. He eventually became the Head Boy at that school and maybe this was his father's intention in aiming lower. Tony didn't have much chance to win a straight argument with his father, who was rather overbearing and headstrong though ambitious for him; he often tried, and on one occasion down at the prestigious Ecclesfield Football Club actually defied him when he insisted that Tony resign on account of his not being picked for the team. Well, I wasn't picked either, but later on Tony was. He used to do his homework at the Firth Park Library as he said that it was too noisy at home. This it probably was but we, his mates, thought that he probably had a hidden agenda in that he was probably fancying the female staff. He was never one to miss an opportunity or create one and we would often see him go whistling up Firth Park Road, shirt collar crisp and smartly turned up, books under his arm. Further up the road, having bunked off our homework, we would be nipping into the park for a quick game of footie before nightfall. Dear Tony.

Derbyshire

But there were times of release from a somewhat oppressive environment. My parents were great ramblers, and Father saw Derbyshire - essentially the Peak District - as his escape ground. This was fortunate, for it engendered in me a fascination and respect for the Great Outdoors that was to last a lifetime, and an interest and avid devotion that never left me.

Some Sundays would find us catching a tram and jolting our way through town and out to the terminus at Endcliffe Park. From there we could walk through the park and into the woods. I loved the trees and seeing different birds. This was my delight. My brother, always up to mischief, would find ants' nests and stir them up with a stick until they ran up our legs in protest.

Sometimes we would go even further afield and catch a bus to Fox House on the Derbyshire boundary, a mere eight miles away, or to the Roundhouse at Ringinglow where we would continue by walking over Burbage Moor. If I became tired, Father would hoist me onto his shoulders for a while and I remember seeing the tall, rocky outcrops of Carl Wark and Higgar Tor from this elevated position. It would fill me with a great elation and excitement to see such natural wonders. Even though very modest in mountain terms, they had an air of romance and adventure about them that appealed to me even at that early age; I have since then spent many hours exploring and writing of such places. I thank my father for presenting me with the gift of appreciating the beauty of natural surroundings and the freedom of spirit that it has brought me.

We would often take sandwiches and a flask, or a paper bag of 'spice' as he always called sweets (I wonder how that originated?). From time to time, a toffee would appear from his pocket. What could be better than this?

Well: independence.

For that, you had to have your own mate who was always there for you.

Ron And A Loss Of Innocence

At the tender age of nine, he appeared in the shape of Ron Clark. It was 1942 and I had two more years to do at Grimesthorpe School. We were still at war.

Ron was eleven, so two years older than I was, when he came to live in Skinnerthorpe Road. He, with his parents and younger brother Brian, had moved from the romantically named Tea Garden Terrace at Burngreave. In reality, it was a wretched little cul-de-sac very near to where two more of my friends-to-be from Firth Park Grammar School resided. On the edge of the City Centre, the whole area was dreary with little escape from the serried ranks of back-to-back houses, and only the tips from opencast mining and bombsites providing any play area. Firvale was a step up, being more open and farther from the industrial area. There were even trees galore to be seen in the nearby Workhouse grounds that bordered the part of Barnsley Road that left the tram route and made a very pleasant walk up to Firth Park by the back way. Kick up the leaves in autumn!

We fell in with each other, naturally, as kids do, without question; we were inseparable until the age of sixteen, when, as so often happens, we disputed over loyalties - or at least, I did. Ron grew into adolescence with far more confidence than I could muster, but at this time he still needed me to bolster up his large ego and back him in some of his rather risky doings.

Finding my own particular friend suddenly revolutionised my life. Unlike Gord, Tony, and Brian Clarke, he seemed to be relatively free and unrestrained by his parents, and was always ready for some adventure. This was not to say he didn't respect his parent's wishes, it was perhaps that they were a little more liberated and easy going than most. I think my father was a little suspicious of him but I am sure that he trusted me not to get into trouble. I was at last free from having to rely on my brother and his mates for exploring my surroundings. The five year difference between my brother and I had never been resolved in terms of companionship.

It was Ron who became my brother and in all the years that we were together, he never failed to put in an appearance when required.

He had passed the Eleven Plus for Firth Park Grammar School and this is what may have prompted his parents to move nearer to the school. Oddly enough, he didn't speak too much about the school; it was left for me to catch up in the next two years before I could understand what he was experiencing. One thing he was not was a braggart. Rather, he was somewhat secretive, which I respected. He was intelligent but I felt that he was rather a reluctant scholar. Weekends started to take on an air of wild freedom as we began to wander into new areas of existence.

Forays into the grounds of Cannon Hall took on a more surreptitious character. The fruit bushes were a painful, desirable attraction. Food of any kind was not easy to come by. As the seasons came around, it wasn't easy to resist the cherries, apples, pears, gooseberries, red currants (the black ones weren't nice!), strawberries and best of all, the loganberries, that grew, often profusely, in 'Pop' Allen's garden. Just about the only fruit that we could afford to buy (for one penny), would be a green cooking apple from Roses greengrocers on the Front, and this couldn't be guaranteed not to have a worm inside it (not uncommon).

Ron's presence always gave me more courage than I could ever muster on my own, and sometimes we would decide that raiding the orchard and the fruit garden would be worth the risk. The gooseberry bushes were well out of sight of 'Pop' Allen's greenhouse. He could often be seen there tending his extraordinary plants, (but by now I never imagined that he belonged to the U.S. cavalry!)

"Some can eat flesh!" Bobby had pointed out in one of his friendlier encounters referring to the cacti. I thought he meant fingers - the old adrenaline running up my legs again - but surely, on consideration, he only meant flies.

"In the Brazilian rain forest they eat men - alive!" He went on.

Now, did I not see that in a Tarzan film at the Sunbeam?

I was not convinced that his mysterious father didn't eat live flesh as well, so I was understandably nervous when, one day, Ron and I laid ourselves down under the gooseberry bushes, bent on a criminal escapade. It was an outrageous abuse of privilege and a total lack of respect, but the lure of the delicious fruit, together with the excitement and adventure, was too much of a heady cocktail to resist. Loganberries were lush and exotic, but chances had to be taken to acquire these delicacies as they actually grew in sight of the greenhouse - but perhaps just a sample from the end of the row? We were stupid enough not to realise that the passage of a previous raid had already probably been witnessed by the scars left when fruit had been avidly plucked and then quickly crammed between lips red with forbidden juices. This was probably our undoing as it would have been enough to alert the Great White Hunter himself. But what did we know?

We were mates, lying on our backs gorging on large hairy gooseberries; the smog had dispersed, the Luftwaffe was nowhere to be seen, Firvale was soaked in sunshine and everything was a dream. Nothing - but nothing- could be better than this.

Dreams, my friend, are there to be shattered.

A very long shadow fell across me and there peering down at me with a cold, frightening gaze on his austere countenance was 'Pop' himself. He had probably noticed the tops of the bushes responding to our fervent pluckings and had then crept along the path. It was an ambush, after all.

"Er - Ron - Ron"

"Eh? Waa? Shurrup - gerron wi' it before Pop sees us", his teeth gnashing a particularly large goosgog.

"Ron", urgently. "He's 'ere".

Choking. "Gerauggh. Oh shit!" He squirmed out from the bushes.

With hearts banging against our ribs, we shuffled, heads down, past the towering presence. He knew he had done enough and we would not be going back. We held our breath until we hit the steep bank that marked our escape onto the old tennis courts and no-man's land and ran to the clay hills where no grown person had ever trod.

Guilty - yes - but it didn't keep me away from Cannon Hall.

I eventually had to come face to face with Mrs. Allen - was there ever such a genteel, sweet lady?

"Eating my loganberries eh?" It was enough, as she swept past me down the dark corridor. When I bumped into 'Pop' again, it was as if it had never happened. Still preoccupied with the 'Jerries', I suppose.

We were not the only invaders of 'Pop's' privacy and tranquillity. Timmy, the beautiful cat that we had lately acquired (I know not from whence) had taken to sitting on the top of the laundry roof. We never discovered how he got up there, as it was so high. Unfortunately, he often liked to take the quick way down, which was to slither and then drop on to the panes of the greenhouse roof that butted up to the wall. This act of feline enterprise would startle the wits out of 'Pop' who would often be right underneath meditating with his plants. It was not difficult to predict that the obvious would one day happen and our cuddly moggie would crash through the ageing glass. 'Pop', with his enterprising and somewhat wayward son Bobby, and neighbours crashing in from all sides, certainly had some strife. Timmy had learnt his lesson. The shock of the episode behove him to take up his leisure residence on a less vulnerable structure, namely, the small wooden tarpaulin shed that Ernie and Father had fabricated behind the garden wall. Somewhere to keep Ernie's old bike, and a fair enough spot from which to pounce on unsuspecting sparrows.

Above the Top Patch was some rough ground that was too sloping to grow anything more useful than nettles, dock, golden rod, thistles and 'old man's beard'. A particular depression in the ground had been enlarged by Bobby to make what Ron thought could be a secret meeting place for his gang - not ours. Our gang by now, incidentally, consisted of Gord and all the little kids in the street that were now old enough to be released from their mothers' bosom. Bobby, and no doubt, my brother, and Fats, and Ray, and Gerry, had ripped off glued paper from the wooden hoardings on Barnsley Hill. Their purpose was to reveal what was showing at the local cinemas, of which there were six within walking distance, but Bobby had another use in mind. The paper always came away in thick layers and this proved to be an excellent waterproof roof for the trench. This was then camouflaged with branches and grass sods. Very nice!

My brother warned me not go near it. I was quite prepared to comply, thinking that Bobby probably had a mad dog tied up in there. Ron was not to be put off.

Doing the commando crawl we, one day, plucked up our courage and approached the hidden hump. We were not a little surprised when we heard muffled voices emerging, as it were, from the very ground itself. Peering into the makeshift entrance, we were met with the puzzling sight of Bobby pulling up his trousers and a certain grown-up girl from down the street, pulling up her knickers. This was revolutionary and revelatory stuff as far as we were concerned. We were completely taken aback, more so because we knew the tall girl, and always thought of her reputation as being impeccable, and certainly being the last person to indulge in such shenanigans. As such, the event came as a double exposure. In the feeble light filtering through the cracks in the paper canopy we were sure that we had had our first taste of 'I'll show you mine if.....' It appeared that all the other participants of the gang, which included my brother, were all happy onlookers. We had surprised them at their most vulnerable moment.

My brother quickly leaned forward, ever intent on preserving my innocence.

"Vic - go home. You shouldn't be here. Go away now!"

I was shocked and just a bit horrified that my brother was actually sitting there. We were happy to flee before Bobby could get his trousers on and wreak some sort of revenge.

Of course, we never looked on the girl with quite the same eye as we watched her pass demurely down the street. She was a sister of one of my younger friends and already working - a very 'nice', quiet girl. Suddenly she had popped up in the most surprising place imaginable. How could a thing like that happen? How could I be so wrong about someone that I liked? One could expect Bobby to do the unexpected but this I could not understand. She was completely out of context - a million light years away. I wasn't blind. I had no inkling that such a thing could occur right under my nose without my knowing. There was quite a bit of reassessing to be done here.

A short time later, whilst out shopping with Mother, I spilled the beans. Ernie had riled me over something and I thought it was an excellent way of getting back at him. I was peevish like that and I couldn't think of a good reason to protect him from any punishment that might be coming his way - even if I never got to know about it. I had felt just a little betrayed. 'Hecky thump!' What did I know about anything?

The cat was out of the trench and the cow had jumped over the moon.

The following week I was in shadowy but brave attendance at another gathering by the French windows.

Bobby whispered in Granny Allen's ear.

She eyed me.

"Oh! This is him is it? Tell-tale tit!"

That was it. No more - no less. I had done my bit for justice and the moral integrity of the neighbourhood. If they didn't like it - hard cheese.

Trench warfare? Tell me abaht it!

About this time, Father bought me a bicycle, maybe to stop me snooping on my brother. It was a long way from being new but that didn't matter. Ernie had a bike but I couldn't reach the pedals. My Hopper was exactly right. The good part was that I learnt to ride- mostly learning balance on the landing upstairs, and then along the passage wall. The bad part was that on my first sortie into the street, escorted by my brother on his old bike, and attempting my first turning movement -not enough room on the landing- I went straight over the handlebars. This was the start of a long career of flying over handlebars. My ego was more bruised than the palms of my hands. I was not allowed beyond the limits of the street with the bike, which proved to be a wise decision on my father's part as, a few weeks later, on braking hard, the front forks parted company with the rest of the bike and that was the end of my Hopper. It was a great day when I reached the pedals of our other bike! Almost as good as when I learnt how to tie my shoelaces and reach the tap over the sink - though not at the same time!

The Life Boys

One of my first forays into new territory was to join the Life Boys - something I certainly wouldn't have done without Ron's backing.

The junior section of the Boys Brigade was called The Life Boys and it was a requirement of membership that you went to Church or Chapel. This wasn't something that I particularly wanted to do but I did want to be a member of the LB. Brian Clarke helped me along with this one, as he was already a chapel goer. I found the Sunday morning ritual rather strange and not a little boring, whereas he, being accustomed to it, treated it as just another play area in which to fool around. I thought this very disrespectful and I was often embarrassed. If I had taken the trouble to go, then I wanted to try to understand what it was all about. Ron wasn't at all interested - he must have fiddled the LB membership card that had to be stamped!

The LB was held on Monday evenings at Firvale Church Hall and did a good service in helping to keep local lads out of mischief. We had very smart navy jerseys and even smarter navy-type hats. A white lanyard around the neck and the ubiquitous grey shorts completed the ensemble. We did lots of marching and counter-marching, played team games, and did group activities, often competing against each other. It did extend our physical and intellectual welfare and gave us a real sense of belonging. We also made new friends. Miss Wells was the bright, young, bespectacled lady who looked after us and with whom we all fell in love. She lived in our street and we would gather at her house to escort her when the time came: the Commodore surrounded by her little matelots. It was really all very peculiar, particularly as Sheffield is as far away from the sea as you can get in England, and I doubt that, at that time, any of us had seen, let alone been in, anything bigger than a rowing boat (and that not on the sea) - and we knew nothing about knots! Apart from at last successfully tying up Bobby, what good would they be?

The marching, apart from teaching us disciplined co-ordination and teamwork, was to prepare us for the Annual Whitsuntide Parade. This was a huge and major event in the Sheffield calendar, when all the different Churches and Trade Unions paraded across the City to their local parks, there to end up in mass community singing. Huge decorated banners would be brought out year after year to proclaim solidarity, and these would be held aloft flapping in the breeze, as we proudly marched along. We traditionally followed our own Boys Brigade seniors with their drums banging and their trumpets blaring. My brother was a member of the BB and played the trumpet, but I fear not very well! Everyone would turn out as we marched from our departure points and I would feel very grand and important as we passed the end of Skinnerthorpe Road where our parents would be waiting to give us a wave. The whole affair for us would end in Firth Park, where crowds would gather to sing to an accompanying brass band, and if fine, sit around on the grass. A surrealist touch would be the local barrage balloon usually trying to pull away from its moorings. On one occasion it did.

The LB was held on Mondays and this gave my parents a chance to go to the nearby Working Men's Club at Page Hall. Father loved to play cards and he had a group of friends there who were all addicts of Whist, Solo and Cribbage and the like. Mother would chat with the womenfolk and have a quiet drink. Neither of them ever got drunk fortunately for me.

I waited in Mrs Hodgson's, after the Life Boys, until they came home. There would always be a biscuit and a drink waiting for me and I would sit and listen to Ronnie Waldman's Monday Night at Eight. Then there were always Mrs. H's treasured picture books of the Royal Family, which I avidly devoured. Queen Mary and George V etc. seemed to be favoured, so I had to ask many questions.

Ron's parents also had their night out. I would be invited in to help pass the time whilst they went off to a club of their choice, probably the Firth Park Hotel. Their house was somewhat bigger than ours and much better appointed: consequently there was room to play table tennis and our version of shove-halfpenny, which was really a primitive version of Subbuteo. Ron by this time was into Pop music but in those days it didn't actually 'pop'. There were still no Beatles and we had to make do with Frank Sinatra or Frankie Lane and his Mule Train. A sortie to Cann's Music Shop near the town Haymarket could only produce a copy (shellac of course) of Nellie Lutcher singing "He's got a fine brown frame (honey, won't you tell me your name)". It was amazing that they had a gramophone that we could play it on. Well, as it was the only record of its kind that Ron ever managed to save up for, it would definitely, given the chance, have worn through to the B side (…'on that buzz, buzz, busy line'.) His little brother put paid to that by accidentally sitting on it. That was a sad Saturday night - no Nellie. After that it was increasing doses of Jack Jackson and Radio Luxembourg. This gradually became a solitary exercise as Ron's parents teamed up with relatives who had a daughter of Ron's age who was also stranded - with us. Girls really didn't figure on my agenda yet, but Ron (two years older, don't forget) had, I think, other things than shove-halfpenny on his mind, so every time she came, I went. I was hoping that Ron wasn't going to take a leaf out of Bobby's book and indulge in a bit of 'trench warfare'. At least, not yet.

Books

I have to say that books didn't figure greatly in our household and the only book that I can remember my father having (apart from a war-time economically produced edition of The History of England in ten volumes, that he would periodically attack) was Norman Mailer's The Quick and the Dead. I wasn't supposed to read it as it had 'rude' passages in it. I used to sneak it from his bedroom. He said he had read plenty of Westerns, notably Zane Grey.

It was at this time that I received my first book that could be classed as literature. This was R.L.Stevenson's Treasure Island. How that book inspired me! Sixty-five years later, I still have that treasured copy on my shelf. This set me off on a lifetime's voyage through books, most of them loaned from Firth Park Library or, when I got ill, fetched by my mother from the 3d. Lending library on the Front- Rider Haggard and Rudyard Kipling being favoured, as they didn't stock Biggles, William or Billy Bunter. Most of my serious reading seemed to have been done lying on my side in my sickbed.

When I was deemed to be mature enough to pick out a new book from a local shop, for a birthday perhaps, I went for The War's Best Photographs. This was approved. At a later date, I thought The World's Best Photographs would make an excellent companion addition to my library of, by now, about five books. Unfortunately, this book had a photograph of a statue of Orpheus in the Underworld in it, which showed, to my mother's consternation, that genitals need not be covered up in the underworld. It was duly returned to the shop to be swapped for a Rupert Bear album. Good old Rupert. He wouldn't be showing any naughty bits.

Lone forays to Firth Park Library opened up New Worlds. I could hardly believe that I now had free access to unlimited knowledge and the only boundaries were my own lack of awareness and just how much time I was prepared to give. It fascinated me that I could now uncover whole areas of experience that were completely new to me. Exploration in the deserts, mountains and forests of the world. Great sea journeys. Astronomy. Books about animals and insects and subjects that I had never even heard of. Yoga? What was that? I borrowed the book and found out. A hundred years later, I taught it!

I never recovered from the wonder that books evoked and as I write this I'm surrounded by about, I suppose - what? - 3000 books? All individually collected since those far off days, most of them second-hand at bargain prices, and all loved.

Holidays

Holidays were so brief that recollections of earlier years at the seaside have long slipped into the quick sands of memory.

They were always spent with parents. I say 'holidays', but Father only ever had one week's holiday a year. That was it, apart from Sundays, and the odd days at Whitsuntide, Easter and Christmas. It was always exciting when he was home, as I knew that he would come up with some idea involving a tram or bus ride to somewhere away from the immediate environment. Apart from family visits and get-togethers when my wayward hair would have to be plastered down with water and neatly parted, and my shoes polished, there would be the annual trip to the seaside when I would even be decked out in one or two items of new clothing. In the early years, my brother would be with us, but later on, it was just me. It gave me a chance to get closer to my father, and at places like Bridlington and Scarborough, I could usually get his full attention. There was never a problem with my mother. She smothered me with love.

Our first trips were to the modest resorts of Cleethorpes and then Skegness, or 'Skeggy' as he called it. These were humble enough places in those days, with military restrictions, barbed wire and concrete structures much in evidence. We always stayed in digs and fed ourselves - all this on Dad's weekly wage of £10. I suspect that he had to save really hard all the year to afford that.

We often set off from Victoria Station at the Wicker. I was frightened of the steam trains but excited at the same time. They made such an extreme noise and seemed to blow jets of potentially dangerous steam in all directions. I made my mind up that I never wanted to be a train driver. The journeys were long, tiring, and dirty, with the issue from the engine blowing in through the window, especially when we went through a tunnel. Father would jump up and yank at the leather strap that raised the window - a hinged strip of wood locking it into place. He was never slow to take charge of a situation and also ready to talk and make friends with anybody.

Fortunately, I liked books with puzzles and when I got bored with that and watching the countryside speed by, I would happily fall asleep to the noisy rhythm of the wheels. You could say that if you change puzzles into the Weekend Telegraph crossword and upgrade the train into a modern one and 'Skeggy' for Paris say, then not much has changed - I still fall asleep on trains!

My brother found it a hard exercise to channel his vital energies- he often found it difficult to contain his curiosity and excitement. I believe that this didn't alter much as he went on through life. The fact that he emigrated to Canada as a young adult, and still with more butchering to do, filled the position of a Fire Chief in Ontario, seems to bear this out. Now he did fancy himself as a train driver, I'm sure. He did like a blast!

As we neared the coast, he would stand on the carriage seat and wait to catch the first sight of the sea. I'm sure that from any particular geographical standpoint this couldn't be attained but details like that never worried Ernest.

Fitting into the spirit of things, I was happy enough to have a striped short sleeved vest with an anchor on the pocket but insisted that another vest underneath had long sleeves that were never rolled up- there is a photo to prove it! Shyness was me. There were sand castles to build and destroy - thanks Ernie - and rock pools to explore and the curious phenomena of the sea. It was big, it was wet and it was usually very cold. My feet sinking into the sand as the tide receded; how it tickled my toes; almost losing balance; the noise as it rattled the pebbles - and how people splashed me as they ran by in the surf. I wasn't at all sure. It made me feel vulnerable and I never strayed far from my parents: I kept my sleeves down. The ice cream I really enjoyed.

Father suddenly became munificent.

"Of course you can have an ice cream!"

"Er -sorry?"

His generosity spilled over when, in Bridlington, on the way to the digs, we happened to pass a house taken over as a billet for airmen. Some were hanging out of the ground floor window.

"Got any spare grub, mate?"

"Spare grub? Will this do?" He pulled a currant cake that Mother had recently baked, from the depths of one of the suitcases that we were carrying, and flung it into the waiting arms of the airmen.

"Bloody hell! Thanks Mate - smashing!"

He got a bit of stick from Mum as he had just given away our tea.

I enjoyed doing a bit of crabbing with my brother but he would soon get bored and, I suspect, go off on secretive missions trying to pick up girls. Soon I would be doing the same thing. There would be times when we would pal up with other families on holiday (not difficult for Dad) and do the Yorkshire thing and play cricket on the sands - sometimes with girls included! Scarborough soon became our favourite holiday place. It had a romantic ambience with the lighthouse and working harbour. Once there was a replica of the Hispaniola, rescued from the film and berthed there. We were allowed on board. I was delighted! My book was coming alive! "Stand back there, Jim lad, I'm taking over - where's Long John?" Furthermore, an ancient house of Richard III's that was reputed to be connected by secret passage to the fine castle on the hill above. And there was the grave of one of the Bronte girls. By the splendid bridge was the magnificent Grand Hotel that apparently housed Charles Laughton's brother, Frank, together with his important Art collection. Not bad for starters!

And so, time passed and eroded my childhood in the process, leaving me stranded in the shifting sands of my adolescence.

What was supposed to happen now? I really had no idea.

My Beautiful School

This is a labour of love. If ever I loved a place, it was this one. Firth Park Grammar School revolutionised my life; and I am sure that this sentiment would be held by many more of its former pupils. I didn't achieve any academic heights and my sporting prowess was a modest affair but the sense of belonging to something inestimably worthwhile became the most important consideration in my life as soon as I crossed that threshold.

I realised that I had arrived at an important crossroads, where opportunities were there to be taken and developed. In those few short - all too short - years, I was moulded by masters and pupils alike into a vehicle that could accept knowledge and use it - especially in the future. It's my regret that I didn't work and play harder, but it takes a special kind of person to be able to sort out all the desires, pressures and conflicts that youth has to do battle with and come out the winner. I wasn't a winner but I enjoyed taking part.

I owe a life's debt to the hand that pushed me into that school and I know that I would never have trod the same path if I had not gone there.

Here I must point out that my name at this time was Vic Oliver - a name I didn't cherish as it also belonged to a quite famous comedian of that era. I belonged to the well-known butchering family of Oliver & Sons who operated mainly in the Atttercliffe area of the City, but the last thing that I wanted to be was a butcher.

When I went to St Ives Cornwall in 1959, hoping to pursue an artistic career. I then changed my name to Victor Bramley.

These writings are dedicated to the Masters and pupils of Firth Park Grammar School.

"You've passed! - you've passed the Eleven Plus!"
Mother was shouting up the stairs. It was Saturday and I was still in bed.

I was allowed a choice of Grammar School but as Firth Park was only about a twenty minute walk or a tram ride away, it was a case of fait accompli. We didn't have a particular axe to grind so, like 'Albert's Mum', that was decided upon.

I was invited with my parents and all the other prospective beginners to the preview and we duly arrived, somewhat trepidatiously, at the school gates, having walked up Barnsley Road.

I should explain at this point that Barnsley Road is really in two parts and has completely different characteristics. In a sense, both start at Firvale Bottom where I lived. One tram-lined, and going very steeply up towards the complexity of the City, and the other- again steep and partway a bus route- went in the opposite direction and constituted a very pleasant walk. Shaded on one side by the trees in the City General Hospital grounds, and taking one right up to the school, it only relinquished its name on reaching the natural boundary of Hartley Brook and by that time you were on the northern edge of the Sheffield boundary itself, two or three miles away. The whole area, in fact, formed boundaries around most of the intimate parts of my life. Barnsley Road, Firth Park Road, and Bellhouse Road were the main arteries of my corporeal existence.

'The Brushes', as the school was called, was formerly the residence of the Booth family who were early Sheffield industrialists. Before that, it had a history as a farm going back to the 17th.century. The complexities of the house and grounds, not to mention the family, are well recorded in The Brushes Story by one of the teachers at the school - T.F. 'Spike' Johnson. According to 'Spike', it was re-built as a house in around 1780 and after several owners, finally sold to Sheffield Corporation in 1911. It was termed as Firth Park Secondary School in 1921 and changed to a Boys Grammar School in 1937. He also describes how on his appointment as History master in 1935, he was startled to discover on his arrival, an 'urban Balmoral'! Perhaps a bit of an overstatement, Spike, but we know what you meant. The castellated Tower and the stonework of the older buildings certainly added to the ambience and dignity of the edifice and made a wonderful focal point.

However, I am not an historian. I bow to Spike and people like Bryan Woodriff, one of my exact contemporaries at the school, who keep memories alive for us.

The house was always known as The Brushes and presumably referred to the fox's brush, as signalled in the weather vane in the shape of a fox, atop the school roof. It was, after all, a country mansion in those early days, and was surrounded by fields, open country, and woodland. Even in my day, there was a great sense of openness abounding, with some woodland still existing and three great parks, which were our lungs and our playgrounds. Up there, one could forget the dark, dense and dirty aspects of Sheffield that many of us had to tolerate.

As a Grammar School, the Brushes was known as the Redcap school, and I, for one, was proud to turn out in my uniform of red cap and blazer with gold badges bearing the school arms and motto, and a maroon and green tie - the school colours.

15. A painting of the tram that I caught to school and back every day. This one is standing at Page Hall and is on its way to Attercliffe. Some went on to the City Centre and I could jump off at Firvale.

I did also, like most boys of eleven years, have shorts on - of course! They were grey and later manifested as my first pair of long trousers in the second year at school. They soon lost their creases. We had all been kitted out with our uniforms at Coles, the main outfitters in the City. I sometimes think how difficult it must have been for my parents to have funded this, along with other requirements. It was a regulation that caps had to be worn when in uniform, with the threat of detention for disobedience, but as I always wore a cap anyway, this didn't trouble me.

The main means of conveyance for many of the 700 or so pupils was the ubiquitous tramcar and to ride in the front bay on the top deck of a Sheffield tramcar could at times be almost as exciting as the Big Dipper at Blackpool. As these mechanical monsters clattered their way across Sheffield, corners would be negotiated at speed and with great panache, passengers being often swung sideways or sliding along the leatherette seats in the bays. As it lurched around the corners, the front of the tram would move tangentially, only coming around into line at the last second. The prow seats were the place to experience the thrill of this and it was always exploited to the full in the company of one's pals from school. At ten minutes to four a whooping swarm of red-capped Grammar School boys would clamber aboard these friendly monsters, mount the metal staircase, and clutching satchels full of homework, squash as many bottoms onto the long bay seats as possible. Rocking too and fro as the tram careered down the track, any friendly conductor would be the recipient of cheeky remarks. If luck was in and it happened to be an attractive young woman then all eyes would be on her hoping that a good lurch might deposit her in your lap.

Our school motto, by the way, was "Each for all and all for each", which laudable sentiment was often corrupted to "All for me and none for you". We also had a great school song that we stentoriously sang out in Latin. This, I believe, was created by our effusive and well-loved music master Mr. Benoy (Beano).

Now come with me on a short tour of the school.

From the large front yard, a short flight of steps led into the small but splendid main entrance hall where the honours board displayed the names of former pupils who had achieved academic success. A heavy, polished wooden balustrade enhanced a sturdy flight of stairs up to the first floor. Here was the Headmaster's study, the office, lockers down the corridor and several classrooms. The old building was very much in evidence here with original woodwork to be seen. My favourite was Mr.Hartley's English room, which was actually in the Tower and looked out onto the quad that consisted of flowerbeds and a walkway around the large central lawn. From this first floor, a very narrow twisting staircase, only just wide enough to take two columns of boys going up and down, led to the top floor where my first classroom gave very airy views down to the lawn in the quad. This floor also had another attic classroom; the prefect's study, where summary punishment could be dealt out for matters too trivial for the Head to deal with -usually for being cheeky- and the stockroom.

Look down into the quad - on the right, you will see the chemistry and physics labs and lecture rooms and the popular diminutive tuck shop. These were built on the site of the old farm, which bordered Barnsley Road sometime between 1921 and 1927, as were all the new extensions; the Hall/Gym, the Gym wing, and the Craft workshops; all except the Library wing, which was built in 1936.

The music room, constituting the ground floor of the Tower, graced this covered entrance to the quad and the labs.

The Gym wing bounded the opposite side of the lawn (which, by the way, was inviolate!) and housed several classrooms each side of the ample corridor, with cloakrooms at each end. To reach this wing from the quad, one passed along what was affectionately called Moke's Alley. This referred to the Senior Master, Mr.Hipkins, whose classroom guarded the entrance to it. His subject was Latin; as my second language was Italian -French, being every pupils' first- I never had the privilege to attend his class. A left turn on reaching the Gym wing brought you immediately to the changing room and showers and then down to the Gym itself.

A right turn here would deposit you unceremoniously into the rear yard area, whereas a left turn revealed another entrance from the main yard where we started. But don't go out there - we haven't finished yet. Go left up another short flight of steps and back into the old building - past another chemistry lab (Mr.Hilton's); the teacher's rest room (they needed it), with the kitchen conveniently placed across the narrow corridor and staffed by a few nice ladies. This inter-connecting corridor held the all-important notice board and led you immediately back to the main entrance, where we started our little trip.

Passing through the main doors again, we can cross the front yard and go over to the Caretaker's cottage by the Main Gates. The caretaker was called Mr.Ironside, although he wasn't at all a hard man - not like some caretakers I met later in life! Funny though - Spike recounts how, in the Civil War, the Brushes farmhouse was seized by Roundheads! I wonder if 'old Tinribs' knew that!

This lower part of the yard also housed the main kitchens and the dining rooms, overlooked by the Wood and Metal Workshop, which like a ship at the wharf side, had somehow managed to slip rope and detach itself from the Gym at rather an odd angle - or so I thought. Then, by the bottom gates, the bike shed. Well, there were two reasons that you couldn't kiss a girl behind the bike sheds. First- there were no girls! - and second- as the sheds were attached to the wall - 'behind' would assume that you were standing in Horninglow Road! Sorry - this school was different. The one or two pupils who were errant enough to indulge in 'dragging on a fag' at break, had to make do with the toilets, which completed the structures on this side. To return: if you looked across the pristine half-acre of the quad lawn from the sanctuary of the old building, then your gaze would have to be lifted in order to confront the most modern part of the school i.e. the Library Wing. Elevated and two stories high, it was well built and cleanly designed. It had a stone staircase at each end that circled around, rather echoing the pattern of the Tower itself. Both floors had a row of classrooms; at one end of the wing sat the Library with the Art Room above it. The back windows looked out onto the quiet Tideswell Road that somehow came to represent freedom!

But the Brushes was never a prison. It became to me a release from ignorance and an escape into a new world of knowledge. It also gave me an attitude to life for which I have been forever grateful.

My parents were suitably impressed with what they saw and Father managed to speak to one or two teachers. He also pointed out where Brylcreamed heads had lolled against a classroom wall and left greasy marks. Trust him to notice that.

Then there was the Jewel in the Crown. The Field, as it was always referred to, was just across the road - so near that you didn't have to be the Victor Ludorum or First in the 'throwing the cricket ball' contest in order to be able to reach it with a well-aimed projectile. But it was far more than a field. It was a place where dreams could be dreamt. A place where a reputation could be made. A place where ignominious defeat would have to be absorbed gracefully. A place of glory and disappointment.

Installed in its vast acres were four football pitches, a cricket pitch, practice nets, changing rooms, sheds, and the groundsman's hut. It also served as a great piece of open landscape in which to evolve and interact with other pupils in non-educational situations. It seemed endlessly large; boundaries melted into interesting areas of rough ground, coppice, and notably wide vistas over Longley Park with its trees and estates -comfortably distanced. From the Field Gate, the landscape rose up at a steady level, leaving the highly manicured cricket pitch as the only flat piece of ground. This was the pride of the groundsman Mr.Tring and anyone seen fielding a coveted old tennis ball -escaped from an impromptu footie game at dinnertime - would bring Tringy out from his little hut, shouting. Between there and his hut, was the Ist.X1 football pitch, right outside the wooden changing rooms. Even this pitch had a bad enough slope to it. Then, way over on the left and dropping away out of sight at a sickening angle, was the so-called Under 14 pitch. If ever a home ground had an advantage attached to it then this surely had.

A haul up to the top of the Field would reveal a pitch that straddled the watershed - tolerably good and somewhat better than the one below it, which often became waterlogged and unplayable. But now we are into the boundary and through the gate to Longley Park. Here was an excellent flat pitch that, in fact, was the Home ground for Crowder Sports, a boy's team that I captained in the late 'forties. This was often the pitch to which the also-rans in the Form games were banished and I have to admit that included me on one occasion. (What on earth happened that day?) There was one terrible drawback to this pitch. If the ball was booted too hard and cleared the trees, which bordered the touchline on one side, then it would disappear down the steepest and longest grassy hill in the area. Despite dire warnings this always happened, and it could take many minutes of valuable playing time for the miscreant to retrieve the ball from the precincts of the outdoor bathing pool far below. I remember a certain pupil as being a fitting culprit. A large, happy-go-lucky lad, always smiling, always in trouble, but brighter perhaps than we all thought him, and that included the masters, who perhaps regarded him as an ignorant lump of a boy.

The changing rooms were attached to Tringy's warm, cosy hut and did service for visiting teams, house matches, and the ever-valuable double period of football that we were all allocated. The memory of football studs clattering on the wooden floor of the huts, and then onto the concrete apron, and the squelch of wet grass, still sends a shiver down my spine.

For me it was always football, but some of the, shall we say, odder or anorak types, ran a game that centred on an open changing hut a little farther on. This was backed by trees; their game consisted of one of their number being chased by another (who could be named, I suppose, the stalker) around this woody labyrinth, wielding a stick. The chosen victim always seemed to end up in the hut, standing on the wooden bench seat (perhaps this was a rule), whilst trying to protect himself from the oncoming missile. What was disturbing for the onlooker was that the victim and the stalker would scream hysterically or make animal noises! It was a sort of sado-masochistic 'stick-piggy-tiggy' with sound effects. Shades of Lord of the Flies!

My mate, Reg Parsisson and I concluded that the participants' sexual proclivities had not yet gelled. It wasn't too difficult to pick out the aggressors and the all too-willing victims. Predictably enough, the same group ran the 'finger-thumb-rusty bum' game in the side yard of the school, often as a preliminary to morning assembly.

It was quite obvious that this little gang were completely uninterested and inept at sport and transpired to be either swots or complete failures academically. There's a lesson to be learnt somewhere!

For the uninitiated; this game consisted of a 'cushion' man leaning against a convenient wall, and then a human chain forming, as it were, from his belly and all bent over with heads into the next man's butt. Hands were clasped around the next man's thighs for strength, as in rugby - perhaps this was a sport! One team went down and the other team would line up and jump in turn as far along their backs as they could manage. If the bent team were able to withstand the weight of the upper team, then they had the privilege of witnessing the 'call'. If the 'bottom' team, (and I use the word circumspectly), collapsed in the meantime, they would have to start again.

The silent call was given by the last jumper who, when mounted, either showed his finger, his thumb, or the 'rusty bum' - his fist, to the cushion man- provided that he also had not succumbed to the combined pressure of the human caterpillar rammed into his belly. He then would ask the leader of the bent team, whose head was still pressed into his groin, the time-honoured question (this wasn't a modern game) 'finger, thumb or a rusty bum?' Now here's where I got a bit lost, because after that there was the added question – "Is it a fine thing or a very fine thing?" What was that all about? Anyway, if the answer was wrong then - sorry - down again. If correct, then - your turn to jump. By this time, the cushion man could well be crippled.

Again, the more sophisticated lads amongst us thought it all very 'camp' especially as there was all that screaming still going on. In truth though, it could be very funny to watch, especially as one of the teams always contained 'Biffa' Smith, a huge fat lad whose sole existence at the school seemed to be to play this game. His weight suddenly deposited with a frightening crunch in the middle of the 'caterpillar' often had the desired instant collapse effect. Here he was the master in his own time.

This was a game that had a great pedigree, certainly in the North, but in the more advanced and perhaps more cynical world in which we now live, lays shelved along with even more dubious pursuits. I'm sure Freud would have been very interested.

Apart from being my best mate for seven years, Ron was my link with the school as he had already been there for two years. Exasperatingly, and like my brother, he wasn't a particularly communicative person, so I had gleaned little information from him. I knew tradition had it that the first day could involve some ragging - I wouldn't call it bullying - and I suppose it certainly could have been deemed to be somewhat humiliating. I certainly wasn't looking forward to being ducked in the toilets but then I think this was reserved for people like Peter Swain who had, incidentally, also escaped from Grimesthorpe Intermediate School with me, and who could be arrogant and cheeky. Later on, he claimed that he had been 'flushed'. Anything for a bit of fame, you might say. Love him or hate him, he couldn't be ignored. There certainly was some activity going on around the toilet area so I kept well away. Curiosity killed the cat didn't it?

Being called a 'Fag' was a certainty - fag not being intended as a reference to any sexual tendencies that you might have, you understand. Certainly a term handed down from public schools where 'fagging' (i.e. fetching and carrying for older boys), was a constant.

I tried to make myself as unnoticeable as possible on that first morning: my only mistake being to declare myself a Sheffield United supporter, when, as I quickly learnt, Sheffield Wednesday was far more popular - the ground at Hillsboro' being only about three miles away over the hill and far more approachable than Bramall Lane, which was more familiar to me. My failure to conform cost me a forfeit of having to sing a song but as I liked singing this didn't particularly bother me. Fags were running for dear life and a few tears were shed, but it wasn't nasty - just a tradition.

Having got rid of any sadistic tendencies that I might have had, on my older brother, I was never interested in indulging myself in later years at the school, although one of my friends, Reg, loved to have a flick at fags' ears in the crowded corridors- painful! - or 'flip' their trouser buttons open as they nervously hurried by. Reg was a fun-loving guy but he could be very naughty.

I felt that as a third former, my street mate Ron was just vain enough not to acknowledge our relationship, especially when he was in the presence of some special friend such as Pete Perrott, already heading for the dizzy heights of the First X1 football team. Back at home, however, he rarely ventured out without me and I was certainly his best friend, even if he didn't always care to acknowledge it. I also still had the ever-solid Tony Reynolds (also a Grimesthorpe escapee), Brian Clarke and even, on occasion, Max Watson to fall back on. Ron and Tony shared my fast-increasing interest in football and I was soon ambitiously working on the idea of a local team. I called this Vale Rovers and it survived for a number of seasons, albeit with a makeshift group of lads drafted in to make up the numbers. Some of these were the best players around the area, mainly because we were in a position to press whosoever we fancied into service rather than having to play some weaker souls whose dads and friends happened to own the team. Tony, in fact, made the Sheffield Boys team in goal. Quite a few FPGS lads such as Alan Lee, Reg Parsisson and Denis Marsden were regular players for the Vale. Brian Clarke always played for Firvale Boys Brigade, who were no pushovers, and also had one or two formidable players. But we'll leave football for now.

It wasn't unusual for fags to get lost in the school and be found wandering around the corridors not knowing quite where they should be at any one time. The curriculum for the whole school was always pinned up in the entrance hall - if you could find that. We always had our own form copy but the problem was knowing just where a particular classroom or lab was located and how to get to it! Even I as a budding 'ace' at map reading (later in life finding my way around the wild Pyrenees, for instance) occasionally succumbed to the heart-stopping revelation that you were the only one left in silent corridors.

We were all designated a House - the choice being quite random - except that I noticed that one or two particular boys of shall we say, a more 'aware' disposition, managed to gain the house of their desire in order to be with their mates. Brian Clarke was the only person who I might possibly have deemed to be a mate at the time but I wasn't even sure what being segregated into Houses meant, so any attempts at conniving seemed pointless.

There was definitely a difference existing. Some boys were all too obviously from better-class backgrounds and seemed to have more say in what was going on. Not of their ilk, it was only my diligence in passing the Eleven Plus exam that had put me there and, to my credit and Ron's, we had done it without outside help and lifted ourselves from the mentality of the back streets. I felt that some of the boys had an advantage and to some extent were already known to each other and therefore were more in line for any opportunities that might come along. Call it Class if you like. The awareness of this wasn't altogether immediate but it had the effect of self-segregation - we knew our place without even mentioning it. This was an early indication to me that I was now, for the first time, rubbing shoulders with boys who had wealthier and/or more influential parents than mine. One boy in particular, Tony Sedgewick, had already seemed to have acquired position and be known to some of the masters. Later on I learnt that his father had been a teacher at the school but tragically had succumbed to a serious illness. Tony always had an easy relationship with the elite of the brotherhood and his clean, bright self-presentation, together with his superb athleticism, grasp of academic subjects and personal charm made him one of the most popular boys in the school. My form photograph shows how clearly he stands out. His charisma soon attracted a small sycophantic group around him - something I chose not to join. Instead I preferred to associate with boys whose attributes were nearer to my own and whose lower disposition I could more readily associate with. There seemed to be no jealousy or grudges held - in fact Tony Sedgewick and a few other superior mortals were there to be lauded and admired. An active and no doubt valuable member of the Scout Group, his easy association with Spike, the Scout Master, soon became apparent.

The Houses were named after War heroes. Mine was Beatty - even I knew him to have been an admiral. I also knew of Foch and Haig but I never knew, or bothered to find out, who Kings was. Perhaps it referred to - well - Kings. The trophies that we competed for were displayed in cabinets in the Assembly Hall, which doubled as the gym. They were enthusiastically competed for in all the available disciplines. I was happy to be with Beatty, although the premier sport football (thank the Lord we didn't play rugby!) was dropped from being Top Team when I arrived, to being not so successful later, as excellent older players like Barry Blenkinsop and 'Pongo' Rooth left the school.

After trials I was thrilled to be picked for Beatty and, after the first match, even more thrilled to receive a "Well done" from our Captain, whose father, Ernest Blenkinsop, incidentally, had played over four hundred times for Sheffield Wednesday and had also captained England. I had just touched glory.

mel

Form 1A   Firth Park Grammar School   1946
V.Oliver Brian Clarke Tony Sedgewick B.Revill P. Webster G.Teanby Brian Sumner Dowswell P.Elliot
Kirbyshaw M.Lee Greaves Reg Parssison Wilson B.Gillot W.Buck J.Flint D.Hardy
K.Tupholme J.Smith K.Cockayne D.Creasey Mr.Montgomery P.Hurst K.Addy Brian Kelk Terry Millard
M.Simmons Bryan Woodriff T.Hindle J.Brailsford E.Buchanan B.Barker

16   A happy form led by 'Monty'

I found myself in Form 1A - again quite arbitrary, as no fag, up to that point, had had his academic potential assessed apart from the Eleven Plus, which I assumed was common to all. As time progressed, credibility was stretched as certain pupils appeared to show little or no aptitude for learning and seemed unable to make the bridge into this higher education. They suffered, as did the masters who tried in vain to educate them further. I had never actually possessed much in a material sense before and now I was the proud owner of a satchel with a shiny set of compasses, protractors, set squares and a fountain pen with a bottle of ink and goodness knows what! It all had a certain exciting smell and uses for which I couldn't even begin to imagine but which I was very soon to find out.

The form room was located at the very top of the old part of the school, under the roof, in fact, and overlooked the quad from a pretty vertiginous height. We were quickly informed by our form master Mr. Montgomery (Monty- a very special name at the time- 1944) that we were not allowed to fall out of the windows! It beggars belief that pupils would be allowed to be exposed to such danger in modern times. Monty, a benign, somewhat old-fashioned gentleman was one of the maths teachers and also ran the stockroom next door where we could trade in filled exercise books for new ones. The full ones were signed by the appropriate teacher as being ready for exchange. In later, more confident years, there was quite a trade in forged signatures in order to gain an illicit exercise book to draw in. Some of my friends were guilty as they were drawn from the less scrupulous side of society. I admit to enjoying observing such skulduggery without being implicated, which is why I numbered the likes of Parsisson and Swain as my close acquaintances.

80

I suspect that with Swain's expertise with a pen, no teacher's signature would have been inviolate!

All connected by a narrow, somewhat dingy corridor, this floor also housed another attic maths room and the Prefects Room. I suspect that Peter Swain was called in more than once for punishment - probably a brief strap on the bottom - and this would probably be for cheeking the prefects. I had a theory that he did things like this on purpose in order to draw attention to himself and make sure everybody knew who he was. He was a total show-off and generally 'up-front' to anyone he encountered. Given the chance, he would stammer away constantly. Although small in stature, with his dark hair Brylcreemed into an over- large wave, Peter could not be overlooked.

From being at Infants School at Owler Lane, I had always admired his artistic skills and I saw him as a natural artist. Even then, he would talk as he painted; his tongue wagging or hanging out of the side of his mouth like a lurcher after the quarry. He never stopped for inspiration; his paints and crayons flowed non-stop, creating pictures full of animated life. Peter, whatever became of you and your talent?

We had a potential bully in the form, but he quickly learnt that the bad habits that he had brought with him from an earlier, more primitive school really didn't fit at all in this rather more sophisticated environment with lads who were, in most cases, much brighter than he was. He was quickly rendered down to a level of his own, which he soon realised he didn't like. He turned out to be useless as a sportsman (except swimming) and academically, which inadequacy probably prompted his bullying tactics in the first place. There just wasn't any space for negativity in this school.

We did have a few fragile lads who tended to keep themselves solitary or team up with souls of a similar disposition. Likewise, the better sportsmen amongst us tended to drift together even though there was a huge competitiveness in operation.

I suppose I fitted in somewhere in the middle. Quiet and shy by nature, I was more of an observer than a do-er. As I have intimated, I was drawn to lads who had a similar, poorer background and who had perhaps lived on the streets rather more than the better-spoken, better-off students had.

I didn't get to be taught by all the masters but one came to know most of them in brief encounters. Many of them were friendly characters but others were not so. When the curriculum was called at the beginning of the term, it was fingers crossed and an intense wish that the best masters, as you saw it, would end up on your agenda.

My poorest subjects were chemistry, closely followed by mathematics. Unfortunately, these subjects were taught by two of the strictest and most feared teachers. However, it was noted by me that familiarity and the confidence brought on in the following years could lead to a softening of the liaison between master and pupil; some of the Sixth Formers could even be seen to be having a joke and a bit of banter with masters as the master/pupil ratio was reduced to what seemed to be a cosy get together, probably emulating the situation they would likely find themselves in at university. I could look on and wish - this wasn't to happen for me.

Perhaps the most feared master, apart from the highly respected Head, Walter Padfield (Big Walt) the crossing of whose path couldn't even be considered, was Willie Gagan. His name alone made boys quiver a little and in all honesty, he wasn't the handsomest of men. His face always seemed to have half a grimace to it, as if he was constantly working on some obscure problem of high mathematics. I never even saw a glimmer of a smile cross his countenance. He always seemed to be a little late for his lesson and when all the other classes had wandered in at leisure, his class would be left lining up in an otherwise empty corridor, hardly daring to breathe. He would appear looking just a little unkempt, loping from Moke's Alley and usually finishing off his last cigarette. I was very happy that I didn't encounter Willie until my final year when I was not so easily fazed by authority figures. By this time, I was quite intrigued as to know what he was really like. His classes were held in an atmosphere of absolute discipline and every boy did his best to avoid any confrontation. It wasn't difficult to see that he could possibly lose his temper but I never saw it actually happen and I began to think that perhaps it was all a myth about Willy; there were though stories of him using the cane. One unusual moment came with this somewhat mysterious master at, of all places, Castleton in nearby Derbyshire. I was waiting with my parents to go into Treak Cliff Mine to view the semi-precious and rare Blue John mineral. There was Willie smoking and standing with, I suppose, his wife. Willie's got a wife? Jesus! As I had on my uniform, as usual, I doffed my cap as he caught my eye. He briefly acknowledged the gesture without letting his face slip from the stony grip that held it in place. Just for a moment though, he seemed a little more human. I found algebra difficult and although I tried really hard with the introduction of trigonometry, at a later date, I eventually got lost in a wilderness of angles and cosines. In the early years, my father would try to help me with my homework, but as he had never even heard of algebra, (an old-fashioned butcher really didn't need it), he had to start by reading the textbooks from the beginning, and this proved to be a slow process. However, he always enjoyed a challenge and would never admit defeat. If it was logical, he could handle it.. Being almost reared in a butcher's shop and serving customers from an early age, his mental arithmetic was without parallel but his algebra, I'm afraid, became a great source of amusement with all his butcher brothers -and there were eight of them!

Chemistry and physics seemed very impressive to me, with the sinks, Bunsens and all the glass paraphernalia laid out by the young, sympathetic lab assistant, ready for the next experiment. The lecture hall next door, with its deeply raked wooden benches and huge blackboards appeared particularly redolent of very advanced learning but this, together with the library seemed, largely, to be the preserve of the Sixth Form.

Unfortunately, my school career was interrupted several times by illness and much of my time was spent in vain attempts to catch up on subjects that to me had whole chunks missing. I use this as a possible reason, or excuse, for not entering the realms of the academic elite. I remained an average student getting average results and sometimes feeling very average.

As I said, chemistry was my weakest subject, although in one particular term I managed to scrape together a magnificent 52%! How on earth did that happen?

I visited two chemistry teachers over the five years: 'Prods', one of the senior teachers, was a very large man - portly would be an adequate word to describe him. He carried his watch on a chain that decorated his ample pin-stripe frontage. When confronted by some uninformed comment from one of our weaker intellects his fat cheeks would judder and enlarge. "Hrr-ubble - Hrr-ubble" It sounded like some half-submerged bullfrog. Catching the tram to school in the mornings at Firvale I would usually find 'Prods' occupying the first seat (for convenience) and reading his daily newspaper. I was obliged to say 'Good morning, Sir' but I wasn't guaranteed a response.

'Prods' became my nemesis as the only master, apart from 'Briggsy' at Grimesthorpe, who actually physically assaulted me. My own fault, of course. As usual, his lesson was going way over my head and I was crass enough to fool around with the lad next to me. What followed was only heralded by a sudden tension falling over the colleagues in my immediate vicinity and an awareness growing in my consciousness that I was the centre of attention.

The sudden explosion in my head almost threw me off my stool. His podgy hand was delivered in the same flat trajectory as his voice as he dealt out Boyle's Law with one and 'Prods' law with the other. You know what? I can't even remember his real name. There again - it was Rhodes. Truly a Colossus!

The other notable occasion of embarrassing reprimand was in the other chemistry lab with Mr.Hilton. For me, just for me mind you, he managed to make the subject even more boring than 'Prods'. He was noted for innocently coining the catch phrase "and the net result is......" On this occasion, the net result was that he noticed my attention had strayed far enough away as to be consumed in some innocent connivance, again with my neighbour. He stopped the lesson to proclaim that I was becoming "a sly cheeky individual". I didn't consider myself as sly or cheeky - but then, he didn't know me that well. Some of the lads loved it of course, and my mate Reg would frequently remind me of what I was.
I felt on safer ground with the very senior physics master 'Daddy' Machin, and my marks reflected this, even once attaining top exam mark for the form! - unbelievable! -mainly (artistic talent employed here) because I managed to draw a perfect Leclanche cell! Reg liked to do his impersonation of 'Daddy' by pulling his cheeks sideways and uttering the typical "a shinee bakeelite surfayce", delivered rather in the manner of Wallace asking Gromit for cheese.

Another 'dreadnought' was Draycott (Drags) - he was a smoker. He looked mean enough with his thin moustache and set features and by all accounts - he was. He taught German and, to be frank, I felt that he wouldn't have been out of place in Hitler's Gestapo! My choice of second language was Italian, so apart from a few French lessons where he explored the realms of Guy de Maupassant with us, our paths didn't cross academically. Some masters however did 'dinner duty', and, after leading us in the prayer …. 'For what we are about to receive'..…in which Reg always replaced…. 'may the Lord make us truly thankful' with ….'may the Lord give us iron stomachs'…, they would be obliged to sit with us and consume the same food. There were no chips or anything else that a young lad might desire - except occasionally roly-poly or jam pudding in which case there would be a mad dash for any seconds that were offered. Having a master sitting at the end of the table wasn't our idea of an easy meal, especially as the fare often included the likes of boiled potatoes and cabbage - but in all fairness, considering the wartime rationing, it was much better than at my former school of Grimesthorpe.
On this occasion, I didn't do well with the meal and Draycott spotted that I had committed what was tantamount to being a criminal act in those days - namely - wasting food. He demanded an essay on the subject by the next day. I thought it a safe bet that he wouldn't remember and on discussing it with my father, we both concluded that I shouldn't be punished for not eating something that my father had, in fact, paid for. Unfortunately, the next day, Draycott chose to disagree and was spitting with temper when I explained the decision. Not wishing to pay a visit to Paddy the Head, I had to climb down from my lofty position. That night my father and I concocted a cynical piece of writing on gastronomy and the ethics of force feeding. I don't think 'Drags' even read it but at least 'face' had been saved.

In the Fifth Form I found myself with 'Drags' as my form master but this didn't affect us all that much as he rarely appeared in our break time; choosing to spend it smoking in the Staff Room. Smoking, of course, didn't carry the stigma that it would in later years. It wasn't unusual to be aware of masters smelling of tobacco and one master often smelt of alcohol - detected on his breath as he bent over to address some problem.
Bill Hinchcliffe was one of the more popular boys - again because he was a good tricky footballer, as I often found out at first hand when I played left back and faced him on the wing.

On this particular occasion, for bravado, he had taken the pole used for opening the top windows and dislodged a trapdoor in the ceiling. Unfortunately, he was having a lot of trouble replacing it.

"Don't panic - don't panic," he was shouting. No one was panicking - only Bill. We were all watching and beginning to wonder if he could get it back in place before Drags appeared.

The bell rang to summon the end of break and the reappearance of the master. It slipped into place just in time and as Drags appeared in the doorway, we were all heads down in our desks gathering the next set of books and trying to hide our giggles.

It was Bill who gave me the nickname "O-O". This was derived from a song in the musical 'Oliver!' that had recently become popular. "O Oliver - O -O -Oliver - he knew a thing or two". I was sometimes pointed out as knowing one or two things. This didn't last long and was eventually replaced, due to my presence in the Italian class, with "Vicchio – Vecchio"- Old Vic!

Firth Park was a great school for languages and was the only school in Sheffield to teach Russian. Language fairly dominated our existence and many of us found it fascinating. Reg in particular loved playing around with words and loved to posit 'ag' throughout his name and those of his friends. He became Regegaginagald Pagarsagissagon - you have to admit it had a nice ring to it, although the idea probably wasn't original and could at times appear just a tad juvenile. I became Vagictagor Ogalagivager and our colluding friend, Leonard Staniforth, became Lagenagoagard Staganagifagorth, or even Nasty Froth. Alternatively, spelt backwards, I became Rotciv Revilo, Reg became Dlaniger Nossisrap (nice one that) and Lennie became Dranoel Htrofinats. Fun with words. We became a bit of a secret society, drawn together by our similar circumstances and interests. Reg lived nearby on the Oval. He was certainly a one-off and certainly not to everyone's taste. We had a passion for drawing in common, albeit Reg's efforts were often limited to drawing men with spotty faces and stubbly beards. All three of us were freethinking, a little anarchic and didn't mix too well with anyone else. I think Len must have had a communist father as he occasionally propounded the theories of Marxism; on one memorable occasion in Spike's history lesson, much to that legendary master's astonishment. Maybe his dad called him Len after Lenin - I should have asked. Football brought us together and both of them played for my Vale Rovers - Len specialising in a very accomplished sliding tackle - not an art easily acquired without crippling the opponent! Reg and I, both fullbacks (although I often played centre-half), had a good understanding between us- something rather rare, as most defending players were only concerned with belting the ball out of their area as hard as they could. We developed a nice offside trap, which at that level was quite a sophisticated concept. The trouble was that it often went unnoticed and left us in the lurch. We had to wait for the rare times that 'Tringie' - allegedly once a professional referee - would agree to run a game for us. Then it would be appreciated.

Partnerships were not that common in our experience of youth football - but Reg and I had one. I elaborate further in 'That Football Thing'.

Neither Reg nor I were deemed good enough for the School Teams although we both made the House teams. I played for Beatty and Reg played for the all-conquering Foch. Reg did however play for the school at cricket and was a very convincing spin bowler. His secretive side kept this from me for a long time - it wasn't done to brag anyway - and it came as a bit of a shock when I first saw him decked out in his cricket whites. Reg in white – come on!

The teacher who had the most profound effect on my future life was undoubtedly Joe Over - 'Joke Over', as some boys christened him- and it certainly was when you entered his sanctuary.

He taught me the basics of French and Italian, which certainly gave me some grounding and confidence to travel abroad later on in life. He was a tall man with a commanding presence. Whether it be striding along the corridor with his black gown billowing out, or leaning threateningly over some poor wretch who couldn't get his verbs quite right. "Clay! You are well-named, lad!" "Swain - are you a swain?" If you were not good at the subject he could be a terrible tyrant and the bane of your life. The dunces of the class would tremble and stammer their way through the lessons. Fortunately for me, I had a lot of feeling - even passion - for the French and Italian that was loaded onto us and they were two of my best subjects. Had it not been for the presence of Wilf Durham, I would have been consistently first in the class. Wilf was either a genius or a complete swot! He appeared to get around 90% in every subject that he sat exams for. Sport was not his thing but I couldn't help noticing that he was often picked as right full back for Beatty when I was playing left full back and he even played for the First X1 whilst I was humbled into running the touchline! He didn't seem to have any true feeling for the game; I think it was some collusion on a master's part to give Wilf a respite from his books.

Nevertheless, I liked the guy. His academic brilliance was worn without conceit. In fact, at times he appeared almost apologetic for his success.

Joe Over was very methodical and frequent tests would put us in class order - the dullards being in front, wilting under his withering gaze and being the recipients of his wrath. Wilf and I were usually only called on to help out when all else had failed. His system seemed old-fashioned, more in the line of Victorian teaching I would have thought, but I suppose it had the required effect. Joe was moody and had an awful temper. The tension would sometimes lift in his good moments and he would reveal a less brooding self and even offer a smile and an attempt at a joke occasionally. His right hand was missing and had been replaced with a heavy black leather glove, which wouldn't have been out of place on some later James Bond villain. Perhaps this glove and the events promoting it were the real reasons for the black cloud that often hung over him - we were never to know. With the glove, he would often beat out the metre of the verbs - they being his speciality. The rhythmic pounding on the desk could be heard down the corridor of the Gym Wing and put the fear of God into most of us. But I certainly learnt French and Italian! I was genuinely interested in languages and I carried a hidden desire that I might, one day, travel to France and Italy. Joe had framed photographs of the great places in Italy - Florence, Rome, Venice etc. hanging in a framed frieze around his classroom. Nobody seemed to look at them but I was interested enough to hang back one day and examine them. As he had not left the room, he seemed delighted at my interest, pointed out one or two of his favourites, and urged me to go if I ever got the chance. Joe - I went - and thanks.

Mr. Hayward was the Russian teacher and must have been worth his weight in gold. Spanish was taught by Mr. Thornton - 'Toffee' for obvious reasons. Denis Marsden, another contemporary and brother footballer said Spanish was easy - but then - an upside-down question mark at the beginning of a sentence? Easy but crazy? 'Toffee' could be a bit crazy as when he caught the intrepid Sherwood surreptitiously goofing over a girlie magazine in a free period. Come on Shirt! Not that free! Anyway, 'Toffee', who wasn't one to mince words, gave him a right cross to the jaw. Unfortunately, this had a knock-on effect between Shirt's head and the wall and we were not sure which was the hardest as Shirt didn't even flinch. Toffee apologised profusely but we all thought it was fair doo's. You had to try and get it knocked in somehow. 'Toffee' played manfully in goal for the Staff v School Annual Match and to see the likes of 'Blenks', 'Pongo', Wildsmith and Perrott all bearing down on him at once was a scene never to be forgotten.

'Jock' McKay ran the gym class. A chance for the talented to show off semi-naked, and- in the showers -completely naked. Probably regarded as not PC now, it was anybody's game then. The discreet and demure amongst us would studiously forget to bring our towels every week, whereas the more free-thinking types - you know who you are - (Sumner, Royston, Kirby et al - oh! yes) made the most of it, although I did sometimes manage a quick run through (water was definitely not my medium- in fact, I think I was the only one in the form who never learnt to swim). 'Jock' would put a stop to the jolly proceedings by having a swift whack at a few bare arses. We had respect for Jock. He could do things on the beam that, to us, seemed impossible. I did learn to climb a rope, not by strength which I never had a lot of, but more by technique; this gave me an entrée into being suspended needlessly above ground, which certainly helped when I later took up caving and rock climbing in Derbyshire. There were strange talents on view in the gym as well as in the showers. A certain Wilson, for instance, could not only hold a handstand but actually walk about upside down. I saw this as some sort of miracle and as his name echoed that of Wilson in the Wizard -he of the nine-foot stride- I expected to see more, but apart from a whipped forehand on the Firth Park tennis courts, it crumbled into disappointment.

My other favourite teachers were both benign gentlemen and any threats were always delivered with a sense of humour.
'Percy' Pascoe was a Cornishman, had hairy ears and even had hairs growing on the top of his nose. He taught geography, one of my best subjects. His particular deterrent was a strap which he insisted came from a tree in the Gran Chaco in South America and in its native country was called 'quebracho'. There it was used for tanning hides; the joke wasn't lost on us. He also engendered the myth that the greatest source of streaky bacon came from the pigs of Fundy Bay on the Canadian seaboard. Due to the fact that the long, narrow inlet from the sea engendered massive tidal waves- the biggest in the world- the local pigs had to run the length of it twice a day - hence the streaky bacon! Well, it was certainly a graphic way of teaching.
I always got good marks, mainly because I loved to lavish my artistic talent on drawing the required maps - mine being always in full splendid colour, but not necessarily befitting the Ordinance Survey brief.
'Percy' was also the Beatty House Master and was therefore expected to attend any House matches. As I usually occupied the left back or left half position, I invariably found him running the touchline alongside and bellowing in my ear, especially as gravity insisted that the ball continually veered to the low side of the somewhat sloping First XI pitch. "Come on Beatty! That's the way!" His deep sonorous voice was always an encouragement, especially when I would be feeling exhausted with taking so many throw-ins!
I was also very good at English Language and Lit., invariably attaining high marks and thereby currying favour with Mr. Hartley, Dr. F.T. (Hefty) Wood, and Kate Moxon, all excellent teachers of the subject. 'Hefty' was particularly highly qualified and bent over backwards trying to treat us as intellectual equals. His intentions were often misplaced, I'm afraid, as his gentle manner was sometimes taken advantage of, especially when he pointed out grammatical discrepancies which he would pore over, see the funny side of and, giving his characteristic laugh, expect us to join in. We didn't always get the joke, but we laughed anyway. Dear old

'Hefty'. Many years later I was thrilled to come across one of his books in a second hand bookshop and I cherish it still.

Another gentle soul was Creasy, the Religious Instruction master -or Scripture as I preferred to call it. There were pupils who took advantage of certain teachers who tried to display the finer points of humanity, shall we say, by refusing to raise their voice or their temper.

A joke was a joke but when behaviour became destructive to the class, I felt that certain individuals were, in effect, cheating me. I had no sympathy with their disrespect and attempts at disruption.

No such state of affairs ever existed with the most popular master, 'Spike' Johnson. I didn't do History as an advanced subject and I wasn't a Boy Scout so I never became one of his brood. You could say that he outlived the school and the legend lives on in better annals than mine.

Strictly a Boys' school, the female presence was very limited, and anything approaching femininity or even a subtle sexuality was never overlooked. Chances of a flight of fancy were very few but the young secretary who brought around the dinner tickets every Monday was a girl, wasn't she? Well, the only person resembling a girl in this cloistered arena. Lining up with your two shilling piece to hand under the eagle eye of Joe was tricky, if at the same time you were discreetly trying to see if her top blouse button was undone or not. "Pay attention .boy!"

"I was, Sir!"

"Don't answer back!"

Kate Moxon, a teacher of English, was not without charm and a sense of fun. On one memorable occasion she revealed to the class just what a desirable figure she had! This was a staggering event by our standards, to say the least. Some important exam answers had been left on the board; in order to cover them up- whilst a selected boy was designated to obliterate them with the rubber- she spread wide her black gown and thereby couldn't help adopting what seemed to us sex-starved individuals, a most alluring pose. She revealed that, underneath a gathering cloud of chalk dust, she was indeed - a woman! Jaws dropped. Thanks Kate! She was also responsible in staging the end-of-term school event in the Hall. Certainly not a play, it was more a joke, song and dance act aimed at lampooning the staff. This was highly successful, especially when stalwarts such as the Deputy Head, 'Duke' Wetherill, and the ginger haired History mistress, 'Flossie' Zeiher (a great take-off by Hallas) were highlighted.

The other special occasion was Speech Day, which usually took place at the splendid Victoria Hall in the City Centre. This was mainly a prize giving event for pupils who had done particularly well. It's significant that the only pupil that I can remember who received a prize -for most improved pupil- was none other than Peter Swain, whose schooldays had shadowed mine from the age of five at Owler Lane Infants School. A showman to the end. A flashy goalkeeper, a flashy cricket stumper, and now a flashy academic - ye Gods!

We all sang, and the Special Choir - how did they get picked? - sang magnificently. Mr. Benoy expressed himself so energetically that he had to constantly shove his spectacles back onto his nose. The Masters were also magnificent in their gowns - some specially fringed around the neck- and all the parents and friends filled the Hall - magnificently. I couldn't help noticing that the immaculate Sedgewick had what appeared to be - a - a girlfriend? - sitting next to him. Some guys had all the luck -or perhaps it was just application.

Big Walt retired and Little Walt took over. Dr.W.R.C. Chapman had to be called 'Arsy' didn't he? What was he thinking about? Although half the size of Big Walt, we didn't mess with him either.

A thrill went around the school when a young French teacher was introduced for a short period. She was very friendly and sympathetic and we tried our best to encourage the bonding process, especially when we had to squeeze past her on the narrow upper flight of stairs! "Excusez-moi mam'selle." Try out all the French you could think of, fool! We'd never seen a mam'selle before - what a thrill!

You would have to say that Polly Charters was female but you could be excused if you were to think otherwise. She was the Art mistress. I was amazed when I first entered the large Art room high up on the Library Wing. It was bright and airy and had huge windows at each end - one set giving a lovely view of the quad and the Tower. A circle of easels dominated one side of the room. This was impressive. I already fancied myself as an artist and instead of restricting my drawing to an exercise book from 'Woolies', resting on the top of a mangle (the only kitchen table we had), I could now draw on a large sheet of paper resting on a real easel! Powder paints could be mixed with water and laid out in a tin tray. Was this for real? The only down side was Polly. Her strident aggressiveness brought forth my shyness and culpability and I was unable to do anything worth while. Fortunately, she retired soon after and I was set free. We had a succession of Art masters after that and I admired them all. One young student master had shown us some abstract prints and suggested that we try something similar for homework. This was for me. I gave it my best shot.

"This painting is as good, if not better, than the ones I showed you". "Whose is it?" My blushes were not spared but I was thrilled to acknowledge that it was mine. This was something new. I'd never seen anyone's work picked out in this way. Heads turned.

"You seem to understand tone. Do you?"

"Yes, sir." I had to admit it. Sarcastic groans emanated from certain members of the class. Fortunately, he didn't ask me to propound the meaning.

"Well done!" I had
arrived.

17

An early drawing of the Hospital at Firvale .We called it the City General then, and I was incarcerated therin in my late teens, thereby missing chances to shine brighter at Firth Park Grammar School. I would have drawn it from the watershed at Osgathorpe. There was an old house there, standing in a field. We used to play there but we always regarded it as haunted. One day, the gent who owned it came out and told us we could play there as long as we didn't make so much noise! There were other drawings but my father saw fit to throw them out, along with my schoolbooks, when I left home.

That Football Thing

If you have no interest in football - the beautiful game - then the following pages will be fairly meaningless. Only if you have felt the excitement and the glory will you fully understand.

For those of us who were tolerably fit and able to run and kick, football presented a world of release from lessons or work and a chance of glory, albeit on a very minor and local scale. If you were good at football then you were a star, no matter if you were an academic flop or a social disaster.

Firth Park Grammar School was a force to be reckoned with in the days that I was privileged to be there. The Under Fourteen XI dominated their league and the senior teams were always a power in the City of Sheffield.

In a way, this prevented me from having the honour of playing for the school - something I would have been so proud to do. If the school had not been so full of star players, then I might have had my chance. I was a competent stylist but not exactly brilliant and, in fairness to myself, I did suffer periods of illness that depleted my strength and energies.

Firth Park was 'tops'. I'm sure that having our own school field had something to do with this and helped us enormously. We only had to cross the road in order to enter a different realm.

When I arrived there from the 'dark satanic mills' of Grimesthorpe, I had never played in a formal game and, outside of the school yard, no one that I knew owned a tennis ball, let alone a real football. This wasn't so with some of the Grammar School boys. As youngsters they had already played in junior teams and learnt all about the game. Many of them had regularly attended professional matches at Hillsborough where Sheffield Wednesday held sway. Here they learnt all about the dynamics and the heroes of the game and some of them went straight into the Under Fourteen XI. Mixing them at my new school gave me different perspectives.

To me this was all new, but the moment that I stepped onto the school field at the tender age of eleven, the touch paper was lit. I wandered on to that hallowed ground with a few more 'fags' (First years) in a mixed state bordering on excitement, trepidation and actual fear. Immediately by the gates, an elegant Senior boy by the name of Jack White- who I noticed had different coloured eyes, something else I'd never seen before - was in the nets and cracking a very hard cricket ball with a power that I had not previously witnessed. The hardness of that ball put me off team cricket forever and I decided there and then that it was football for me! Not that football didn't have its dangers of course, but like choosing between flying and rail travel, I felt that the chance of survival lay in one direction.

My most intense football memory was on the day of the First XI v Masters Match. I hadn't been at the school long enough to know who some of the masters were, let alone the Senior boys, but standing behind the bottom goal and seeing fit young men bearing down on 'Toffee' Thornton, the Spanish master who had elected to keep goal, was a sight not to be forgotten. The First XI at that time included top flight players such as Wildsmith, 'Pongo' Rooth and Barry Blenkinsop, the son of the Sheffield Wednesday and England player. The masters were game and wilfully cheered on by the crowd but, not being as fit, always lost. I was thrilled, bewitched and desperately wanted to play.

The curriculum designated a double period every week for 'footie'. I was delighted to be handed by my parents a pair of studded football boots, shorts, and beautiful red-ringed football stockings a la Sheffield United, complete with the requisite shin pads - most important! An ordinary white shirt had to suffice to complete the ensemble.

Over the next few years, my mother had the onerous task of washing all the muddy gear. I particularly liked my laces to be as white as possible. I thought they looked smart tied around and under the boot and they sort of became my trade mark. I did bring a certain style to the game eventually as I was always neat and slim (nay- thin!) and my hair was always immaculate, at least to begin with.. Strength, however, wasn't my forte, having been ill so often and not a great eater -there wasn't much to eat during the war period anyway. Had this not been so I might well have promoted myself even better.

As the older boys matured and left, some for University at seventeen years plus, I eventually at fifteen became eligible for the trials for Beatty House Seniors. I chose full-back as I assumed there would be less demand for this unglamorous position. I didn't mind - a chance would be a fine thing.

I remember all the Beatty boys who were interested showed up after school down on the Longley Park pitch, which was the flattest playing area of all. We were chaperoned by the two admirable senior prefects, Blenkinsop and Dilger - both well-loved.

Peter Swain- another survivor of my Grimesthorpe days - was much in evidence and was already well known to the prefects - mainly for being cheeky. He was no footballer but, in later years, he earned himself the position of goalie- but not on this occasion, as Beatty had arguably the best goalkeeper in the school - namely Senior, nicknamed affectionately as 'Sos'. The position ultimately gave Peter the chance to do his usual showing off with somewhat exaggerated ducking and diving - not always successfully. He carried his dramatics into the form games of cricket where, of course, he always elected to be the stumper. The bails used to go flying for no obvious reason. Yes - dear old Pete certainly put some life into the proceedings.

I did what I thought I was supposed to do and put everything that I had into that game even though all my experience was conditioned by local and form games. My main attributes, I suppose, were ball control, reliability, and accuracy- with perhaps a bit of style thrown in.

Shortly after the trial I met Brian Clarke in the break period, at the bottom of the stairs in the main hall. We had both been in Form 1A (the First year) under Mr. Montgomery (Monty) and had been close friends at Grimesthorpe.

"You're in then" said Brian in a flat voice.

"In what?" I enquired.

"In the team".

"What team?" I hadn't any idea what he was talking about.

"Come here" he said, grabbing my arm. He pulled me over to the notice board by the master's canteen. "There!" Pointing.

I couldn't believe my eyes. I was down as left back for the next House match! I hadn't particularly looked at the notice board before and didn't even realise that matches were posted there. It was difficult to contain my joy as I began to glow inwardly. I had entered the 'prestige zone' and been identified - but I was very nervous!

The match went well. We still had some of the older boys (in all the House teams) including, in ours, the dour and indestructible Salvin, who, as I was playing directly behind him had, I suspect, been told to keep an eye on me in case I began to flounder. Thankfully I didn't. 'Sos' was in goal. Blenkinsop- the quintessential Captain- would fly down the right wing, arms flailing, and put in tempting crosses for 'Pongo' and Pete Perrett.

'Pongo' was rumoured to have had trials for Sheffield United. They were all highly respected, as I also was about to be.

In the changing room after the game, there was a "Well done, Vic!" "Thanks Blenks!" I blurted.

I glowed again- I had made it.

We had been narrowly beaten by Foch who already had strong young players in their ranks, notably Kenny, the best left-footed player in the school; the powerful Royston who was soon to play for Sheffield Boys and then Yorkshire Boys and also Kirby, a bundle of muscle who also had the honour of playing for Sheffield.

But the great days of Beatty were quickly drawing to a close as 'Blenks', 'Pongo' and other Senior Beatty boys left the school. I continued to be chosen but we never had such great players again whilst I was there and the coveted shield never came our way. The best of my contemporaries didn't play for Beatty!

Foch quickly became the champions. One of my mates, Reg Parsisson, was eventually picked for Foch at full back and had the privilege of playing with Kenny Kirby, Gord Royston and Brian Kenny. I was on the receiving end.

Gord was all power and impossible to shake off the ball as he was so heavily built. He was good natured and had a sleepy drawl and demeanour in class, but on the field he was unstoppable at inside forward and had an awesome shot. Kirby was all energy and then the stylish Kenny was on the left wing. They were all strong, vital and impossible to beat.

Haig were next in line, mainly through the services of the admirable Sedgwick. Tony was small in stature but big in heart. He was everywhere, neat and dapper - another bundle of non-stop energy. They also had the dominating Fearnehough at centre half. He was tall and a fearless header of the ball, which in those days of heavy leather wasn't easy to come to terms with. Contact with the ball on any part of the anatomy had to be seriously considered before taking it on; whether you turned your back at the last second or not, especially when the likes of Royston booted it straight at you. When the ball was wet, heavy, and covered in mud it was a lethal weapon, the prominent lace being a real cutting factor. On a heavy pitch it required a lot of effort to move it forward. A lasting image was of Fearnehough, parallel to the ground, heading the ball through a ruck of players. They also had the admirable Bashforth. If ever a guy was well named, it was he. Again, tall and strong, his tight wavy hair would bob up all over the place. He had big feet and was one of the few players who could tackle Royston and come away with the ball. Having just been robbed by 'Bash', Gord once turned to me on the field-

"He's got feet like bloody canal barges". An apt enough observation, I thought. I never remembered 'Bash' speaking. He was just an icon of strength and silence and was selected to play for the First XI, with the elite, long before the usual age lapse.

Many years later we had an encounter, both backpacking and miles away on Ogwen Bridge in North Wales.

He didn't speak then either!

Sedgewick, Fearnehough and Bashforth certainly formed a formidable half-back line for Haigh.

Despite our depleted force, we usually had a fair chance to beat Kings. My long-standing friend Brian Clarke finally got his place, having put on a spurt of growth and strength. Joe Corbett was probably their best, and certainly their most popular player. He had come from being Captain of the Under Fourteen XI, and with Sedgewick was probably a dominant factor in that team's undiluted success. Unfortunately he didn't develop in size or power and survived by dint of close control and tricks he had learnt.

He was a benign sleepy sort of lad and spoke in a slow drawl. His reputation and popularity kept him afloat when I thought he had become a little lazy and certainly not the power that he had been. Their other favourite player and also tricky with it was Bill Hinchcliffe- again very popular and full of fun. He played on the wing and so we often confronted each other. We had several battles of will and I was happy if, at the end of a match, I had managed to contain his abundant enthusiasm.

Occasionally I played wing -half for the House and it was in this position that I almost had my moment of glory. As the First XI pitch -where all the House matches were played- had a sideways slope to it, it was sometimes difficult to dig the ball out from the touchline. It would keep coming back I remember; I was getting increasingly more irritated and exhausted with taking uphill throw-ins, especially as it rained all through the match and I was wet through. However, on this particular occasion and well within my own half, I met a ball on the half volley. As any intelligent sportsman will tell you, timing is everything and "if you ain't got that - you ain't got nowt!" My timing was always good and helped to make up for my lack of strength.

I hit it as sweet as a nut and it soared high and away in the best tradition of Roy of the Rovers. Percy Pascoe the benign Cornishman, my geography teacher and our House Master (he never missed a match), was standing right by me on the touchline -

"That's the way- that's the way!" he bellowed. I felt that everybody on the field was gawping and watching as the ball headed for the top corner of the Kings goal. I'd never seen that happen before - time stood still.

Now you understand that to score a goal in such a fashion, (Beckham did it later on!), could alter my whole football career and shoot me into the School team. Certainly it would be a talking point for a long time and I would certainly be feted in Beatty House. I watched the ball curve and drop like a bomb. It surely must go in.

What a shame! I forgot to tell you. Another player of note in the Kings team was Ted Taylor who now happened to be the School First XI goalkeeper ('Sos' having left.). Ted made one of his spectacular leaps and scooped the ball away. Ted - why did it have to be you! Damn it! And he was such a nice kid I couldn't even hate him. Ho hum!

Attempting the impossible and hoping for a repeat, I took the next ball on the half volley again, except that it bobbled and I missed it completely - an air shot! Fortunately, I was quick on the recovery skills and brought the ball under control, hoping that no one had noticed - some chance!

The other excellent player that Kings had access to was Vernon Haw. Another bundle of athletic energy who with his dark, curly hair and good looks was also something of a lover boy! He would appear again as we both played for Hartley Brook Youth Club. Alan Lee, also of Beatty, became a great friend. Although not deemed quite good enough for Beatty Seniors he turned out regularly for the Brook as did my school mate from earlier years - Tony Reynolds. We all played for other teams too.

Some of the pitches that we had were pretty awful. Most of them sloped- the worst of all being our own Under Fourteen pitch, which dropped at an alarming angle making it almost impossible to score at the top end. I suspect that our Under Fourteens milked this to their own advantage in Home games. I only played on it one or two times. Conditions could also be diabolical generally. We played in pouring rain, in bitter winter winds; on pitches thick with glutinous mud (especially in the goal mouth), which, if it was freezing weather would turn into hard knobbly ruts, the ball bouncing around with a life all its own.

Cameradie was the name of the game and I built up a rare understanding with Reg Parsisson (when we were not opposed - he playing for Foch); often both playing full back we would employ the off-side trap, especially if 'Tringy', the groundsman was refereeing, which he sometimes did. The legend was that he had been a professional referee so we could rely on him not to miss out on our finessing.

He also gave Royston and Kirby an occasional workout in tactics etc. heading as they were for the dizzy heights of Sheffield and Yorkshire Boys. We lesser mortals usually only got to hear of these coveted honours by way of the School Magazine as bragging wasn't an option - except for Swain that is; you may be labelled a 'Big 'ed' - and he was. I would have loved to see the boys play at this top level but I never did.

The nearest that I got to that was being offered a place as reserve for the First XI and being thrown the coveted shirt by Jock, the ultra fit PE master. As it was, everybody turned up (at some school pitch on the outskirts of Sheffield), and I found myself running the touchline - but at least I saw the lads in action.

Ill health interfered with my football (and my education). I found, one sad day, on looking on the notice board, that I had been dropped from Beatty and replaced with an admittedly better player - a young giant of a lad who had risen from the ranks of the glorious Under 14 and was sweeping all before him - including me.

It was 1949 and I was still only fifteen. Running previous to that heady year, concurrent with it and succeeding it, I played for other teams, and I am privileged, sixty and more years later to still be able to write about them.

18. Me in 1949, aged 15 years. Posing outside 52 Skinnerthorpe Road

Working: The Steelworks

I left Firth Park Grammar School in August 1950. I was almost seventeen.

The fact that I had to leave the cloistered life of the school brought mixed feelings of some profundity to my sensitive nature and somewhat delicate constitution. Up to this point in my life I had been guided and told, more or less, what was expected of me. Now it seemed I would have to make my own decisions. The school had been my great turn around. It had given me a wonderful grounding of knowledge and understanding but now was the time that I would have to put all of that into practice, stand up, and be counted.

I would have to get a job quickly. Although my parents were always kind and as helpful as they could be, it would have been some hardship for them to support me for too long. My father's job as a butcher with the family had only ever brought in a modest amount.

At school, we had been shown how to write a job application letter and one or two of the more confident boys had already been offered positions by companies in the city.

Perusal of the job column in the Star - the evening paper- prompted a few feeble attempts at jobs that I felt I

19. Longley Park 1950 (17years)

was wholly unsuited for and certainly not qualified to do. My first attempt was an application to an insurance firm directly by Sheffield Cathedral in the city centre. On attending the interview, I was quickly informed that they had already taken on Reid, an excellent pupil (and cricketer) from my year. I obviously didn't measure up to his acumen, as they didn't consider me. My next application was to an advertising company - I thought that my drawing ability just might be thought of as a plus factor - but, of course, it wasn't. They read my application letter and having questioned me about this, they thought that it was too good for me to have written - which was true. I couldn't think of one job that I might like to do or indeed would be able to do. Languages and Art - my fortes - where would they fit in?

I had already announced to Dr. Chapman, the School Head, in a gathering of school leavers in the hall, that I would really like to have a job that would involve my artistic talent.

"Well, Oliver - not very likely in a place like Sheffield. How's your physics and chemistry?"

My physics was passing fair but my chemistry was definitely sick. Together with mathematics, I had absolutely no passion whatsoever for the subjects and had only managed to stagger along with them as mental burdens during my years at the school.

I approached my father with the problem. Having never done anything but butchering, I didn't expect a result from him. I think my time at the school had always been a bit of a mystery to him and he had already suggested that a career as a meat inspector might well be in order. The thought of having anything to do with animals, especially dead ones, did nothing for my frustrated ambition or sensibility. My brother, five years my senior had been managing a butcher's shop from being eighteen years of age - having left school at fourteen. My father, in fact, had left school at twelve and gone directly, together with a selection of his eight brothers and five sisters, to work for his father.

To his credit, he asked around and soon discovered that my uncle Harry, the shop manager, had a friend who ran a small company making cinema posters and the like. Now that sounded interesting! In those pre-computer days, the posters had to be hand painted to start off the process and then the resulting images of the film stars were printed and plastered outside the cinemas and on hoardings around the city. The quality of the work was usually excellent and many of them became collector's items.

On one of his rare days off, Father put on his best suit and hat -always essential for a town visit- and we set off on the tramcar in an effort to seek out this establishment. Behind the Town Hall in the City Centre lay an area of sheds, yards and brick buildings, many of them occupied by the 'little mesters' - small companies making the hand made cutlery for which Sheffield was famous. Amongst this rabbit warren of activity was where we located our destination. A flight of wooden steps led up to a long wooden shed where four or five men and a youth about my age were lettering and copying photos of film stars onto paper in preparation for the films about to appear at the City's cinemas. It looked fascinating and I would gladly have made a start there and then but, the boss explained, as I hadn't had any training I was already too old! Father ran out of ideas after that, except to reiterate the question of my becoming a meat inspector. I choked at the thought and asked what else I could do. "Well, tha'd better get thissen darn't t'ot job office." "Where's that?" I asked nervously.

"Well there's one darn't 'cliffe'.

By this, I knew he meant Attercliffe; with a curious mixture of excitement and dejection at having to settle for an absolutely mundane solution to my problem, I cycled, the next day, down to the Attercliffe Labour Exchange.

Oh yes! They had a job to offer me - an office boy at Charles Meadows & Co. for £2 -ten shillings a week - Saturdays off. I took the slip of paper and went to look for C.M. &Co.

I reached Broughton Lane Bridge in no time at all and there enquired of a lingering workman, smoking the ubiquitous fag, if he knew of my intended workplace. He turned and flicked the end into the canal below. A factory was tucked away almost out of sight beneath its raised banks. "Cutty Medders" he prompted.

I cycled down the side of Tinsley Canal, known locally as the Cut and entered the large wooden gates.

A small office by the gates- the Time Office- served to weigh lorries and 'clock' men in and out. Inside, an elderly dignified gentleman with only one arm greeted me in a loud almost stentorian voice. At my enquiry, he laid down his pen, and pointed through the dirty windows at the Mill Office, which stood right in the centre of things. As I walked over, I passed, on my left, a huge shed that housed furnaces, some of which were leaking flames; several pneumatic hammers of different sizes were making the most appalling noise. As I turned a corner I came face to face with another huge shed with more furnaces and ranks of metal rollers which were gradually reducing billets of intensely white hot metal into ever lengthening ribbons. These snaked menacingly across polished flagstones and were then guided by sweating men back into the rolls to be reduced even further. It was all quite new to me and a bit of a shock.

I pushed open the ill-fitting office door. A fattish individual sat behind a counter.

"Yes - can I help you?" he said in a mild abstracted voice.

"I've come to apply for this job". I showed him the paper.

"Oh. Just a minute - I'll see if Mr.Hopewell is in." He wobbled off his stool and proceeded to knock on an inner door.

There were several people sitting in this outer office - most of them bent over paperwork. One of them, tall and wearing a trilby hat, was looking out of the grimed windows but with a detached look on his face, which indicated that he wasn't really seeing anything. A youth at a switchboard turned to see who had arrived. To my surprise I immediately recognised him as Derrick Beacham - a fellow pupil at the Grammar School that I had just left- but I think two years ahead of me.

I relaxed a bit - this was better - but then he failed to show any sign of recognition. I later learnt that this was just a 'face'. I assumed that he didn't want to surrender any superiority that he might already have. He turned away as the switchboard buzzed into life.

"Send him in, Thompson", came a voice from the interior.

I made for the door, knowing that fate had intervened in my life in a big way.

A small, fat, ginger-haired man of about fifty years extended his podgy hand and introduced himself as Mr. Hopewell, the Works Manager.

"Oh! I see that you're from the same school as the other lad out there." He gave a grin; his teeth broken and nicotine-stained. "The job's yours - £2-10s. a week - Saturday off. Start on Monday 9am."

Derrick was hard work to start with. I suppose, to him, I was still a school fag. There were plenty of scary moments when I had to save face and he didn't make it any easier for me. I was still desperately shy whereas he was very personable. On the other hand, I was tolerably good looking and had, at the time, a beautiful girlfriend, whereas Derrick was no dreamboat and, I suspect, often had difficulty getting a date. His fair hair, in tight waves that you didn't really have to comb, was already receding and revealed a high rather knobbly forehead. Together with his over large front teeth, this gave him rather a somewhat pugilistic appearance - not ugly you understand -just a bit ill shaped. I soon learnt, however, that he had no fear and could charm the socks off a donkey.

To my dismay, I realised that my main job would be to answer the phones. I had only ever spoken once on a phone, and that to my father, when I was a child. This was going to be very difficult for me.

The switchboard had two outside lines, which could be connected to four internal offices. These were - the Boss's office: Ronnie's Office (a twin to the one I had already been in, with a connecting door): the Engineer's office (across the yard and opposite the Time Office where I had first put in an appearance) and the all important Top Office, which lay up stone steps at the far end of the mill and where all the accounts and finances were handled. There was also an internal phone; this connected to all our offices and those that came under the umbrella of Arthur Balfour & Co. These included the large Engineers Tool Works situated on Broughton Lane -the main road above us- and miles away, near the centre of the City at the Wicker Arches, the head offices of Arthur Balfour. Within a short time of my arriving, Balfour's were to take control over Chas. Meadows Alliance Forge and Rolling Mills but it didn't, apart from a later redesigning of our office and some redistribution of our work practice, make much difference to our working life.

The switchboard buzzed constantly - little metal flaps dropping down when people rang in from the outside, and metal 'eyelids' dropping like some one-eyed drunk whenever anyone wanted a line out. I absolutely hated answering the phone and, at first, I had no idea who was calling, whom they were asking for, or what they wanted. Derrick knew of course, and callers would quickly become exasperated and even angry when they realised that they were not talking to him but to someone who had little or no clue. Derrick was less than helpful. If I offered him the phone, suggesting that I didn't understand, he would walk away from the desk or snap - "Get on with it!"

It took a long time to get used to the phones and I never felt really comfortable. The regular callers didn't make it easier either as some of them had been making boring business calls for so long that they didn't expect to have to go to any unnecessary announcement as to even who they were. Guttural shouts, often with heavy background noise or some inaudible, timid female voice had somehow to be interpreted.

Derrick and I sat side by side and his only escape was when he had to disappear with a message down into the bowels of the works or to one of the other offices. At least my presence gave him the liberty to do so, theoretically anyway. It took a long time for him to soften and share some of his thoughts with me. Paradoxically, he was extremely friendly with most of the workmen and called them by their first names or even their nicknames - something I never did, even four years later. He would often be down the forge -if Mr Hopewell wasn't around - having a joke with the likes of Pilkington, the handsome young giant on the Top Hammer, or Joss, one of the popular older hands who led the team operating the Big Hammer that dominated the middle of the forge. Some of the men were less forthcoming, being uneducated and having seen little life outside their cloistered environment. The cinema, the pub, a football match and a walk down the Cut, was all that they knew or even required. The men who operated the hammers were very skilled. It was fascinating to see how the parameters of these steam pressure tools dictated their styles and rhythms. The small guy on the small tilt hammer, scruffy working cap pulled down to shield his eyes, (amazingly, no one wore goggles), swung back and forth on a metal seat that was suspended from a girder overhead. As he swayed, he ran small ingots back and forth through the jaws of the stammering machine that rattled like a machine gun.

The Big Hammer was quite different. This demanded a team of four or five disciplined and experienced men to operate it. Each man wore a smock and the traditional white scarf that was used to wipe away the constant sweat that was promoted by the searing heat of the furnaces where the ingots were brought up to the correct temperature for manipulation. The huge metal bars would be rotated on the anvil as the pressurised hammer would jerk down with a quick stunning force. The floor would shudder with the shock; sparks would fly, and pieces of red-hot shale would fall off as the bar was beaten to the required size. It seemed extremely dangerous and each man had to be very precise in performing his particular part if he were to avoid calamity to himself or to his fellow work mates. Burns and cuts were frequent and the men in the stockyard who handled the cold bars were particularly prone to having to suffer steel splinters in their fingers, more difficult to extract than wooden ones.

Bill Thompson, the fat-faced clerk behind the counter, had the job of collecting workbooks from the Mill; George Meadowcroft, he of the trilby hat and Forge Manager, had his own clerk to handle similar matters in the forge. The time would soon come when Derrick and I would take over these particularly onerous jobs. We were then termed 'progress clerks' as it was our job to monitor, with pen and ink, the progression of the steel through the works, from its original entry by invoicing, making out the men's worksheets for the job in hand, and then seeing that they were paid for the work done. I often wondered how Bill managed as he obviously didn't find it easy to communicate with anyone and most of the workmen had the same problem. He also had rather a nervous disposition and, despite our efforts to provoke him, seemed to prefer his role as the office loner. He was about forty five. Derrick divulged that he was a Salvation Army man and did his share of marching. We suspected that he probably played an instrument - likely the big drum - as he never walked down Broughton Lane to catch the tram home without whistling some marching tune to the rhythm of his hurried step. He would never set off without the whistle - this started up as soon as he hit the office door. Although he seemed perhaps a little simple or even stupid, I fancied that he had some inner strength and he certainly couldn't be deviated from his task, firmly refusing if one asked a favour of him, such as answering a phone call if we were under pressure. "It's not my job" he would always politely proclaim.

His counterpart, on the forge side of the office, was Ben. This wasn't his real name, but one given to him by George, his immediate boss. George either didn't like his name or, as Bill and Ben were very popular on early Children's television at the time, perhaps saw it as a way of promoting the humorous side of his own personality or maybe just a way of showing his power over him. George was like that. Either way, Ben didn't have a say in the matter. Everyone else below George's position was usually addressed as 'Son' and this included all the workmen except the top men. This had to be fine-tuned when we were eventually granted the grace of 'daughters' onto our staff!

Ben also had a curious personality, albeit quite different from Bill. Being a Christian, Bill saw it as a sin to smoke, whereas George and Ben were continually bumming cigarettes off each other. They both smoked constantly; Derrick and I didn't. I was already getting quite serious lung trouble and so this became quite an issue for me. All we could do was cough along. Ben was unconscionably shy and could never look you in the eye when he spoke, although some twenty years our senior. When he did speak, it was often quite difficult to understand him as his words were often delivered in a quick, mumbling tone accompanied by an apologetic sounding excuse of a laugh. Still, he seemed to perform his duties well enough as George's clerk - his man. It somehow seemed a typical act when, one day leaving work in the maelstrom of men rushing from the Engineers' Tool Works and adjacent factories, he ran between two cars that unfortunately for him were joined by a tow-rope. Over he went and appeared back in the office, a few days later, with some facial battering. George made a big joke about this and Ben tittered along behind his plasters.

George's trilby hat seemed to have the same power as a badge of office. Although not yet bald - he was well in his fifties - he never left the office without it and would often keep it on in the office, only removing it to scratch his head. Oddly enough, he also never looked you in the eye when speaking, although in a somewhat different way to Ben. This was more of an upward look. A man wanting not to forget the words about to be delivered and perhaps involving a little look heavenwards for some spiritual affirmation that what he was about to say would be understood by the inferiors that surrounded him. "Son - go down the forge and tell Joss I want to see him - make sure he comes back with you - don't leave without him, Son. Tell him Meadowcroft wants to see him" Then he would repeat it. George was a large, heavy person and overtly coarse, rather like his wit, but he obviously had an undercurrent of intellect. He handled the responsibility of the Forge with some aplomb - calmly and efficiently. I never saw him flustered. He was generally friendly to his men and treated the old-timers as his buddies - but still let them know that he was the boss. He never shirked his duties and when it came to a disciplinary action he would have the offenders - usually for fighting - brought into the office to give them a dressing down. They were usually young strong men - dirty, sweating and shod with steel tipped boots that could break a leg in a trice.

George also had huge feet and when confronted with a problem he was disposed to walk from one side of the office to the other, his eyes introverted and often closed. Resolution would come and he would turn to us. "Son - get me Hamer on the internal phone - Hamer Crapper, Son". This unusually named denizen of Balfour's could be found in F Department and appeared to be one of the more enlightened senior staff whose wisdom was often sought by George, along with plenty of banter delivered in a loud voice. On the other hand, a call from lesser mortals would find George making for the door and throwing over his shoulder "Tell him I'm not in, Son". Through the window, he could be seen making his escape into the darkness of the Forge.

This would immediately put us on the spot - especially me - as some of the customers wouldn't take no for an answer. This pertained particularly to a certain Mr. Hurst who called on a regular basis. At first, I couldn't even understand to whom I was supposed to be talking. "Hurst - Hurst!" he would bellow down the phone like some drunken colonel, which formerly he could well have been. "Haven't you heard of us? Who are you? Get some one who can understand me. Put the other lad on the phone - the nice chap. Come on - I haven't got all day." At first, Derrick wouldn't respond. He would just stare at me with a venomous look. But then, when I threatened to just put the phone down or leave it lying, he would snatch it up to be met by "Hello - hello - damn it! Where the hell is Meadowcroft?"

"Hello Mr. Hurst - very sorry Mr. Hurst," Derrick in his best diplomatic tone. "We just don't know where he is at the moment Mr. Hurst." "Can't ye go and find him, lad?

"'Fraid not Mr. Hurst - but as soon as he comes in I'll tell him you were asking for him".

"Alright, lad - but don't forget me." Grunt. Slam down phone.

How could you not forget him? Never a please or thank you. Sometimes we would just sit there and check orders whilst Hurst awaited our return from a mythical search of the forge, and sometimes George would just be sitting there smoking with his back to us, nudging Ben, who would lean over and chortle some sycophantic drivel. I also quickly learnt to be a devious soul.

All in a day's work - George smoking and pacing - boots clomping on the floorboards; phones buzzing and ringing; background clamour from the forge and mill; flat bed Lister trucks clattering past the windows, their small wheels catching in the rutted, potholed surface of the passageway into the mill; a couple of billets performing a cacophonous dance on the small metal body of the vehicle. Shut the windows to cut out the noise - asphyxiate. Open the windows for some air - papers covered in soot. George's opposite number was Ronnie Hollingsworth whose office was a twin next to Hopewell's. He couldn't have been more different. He was a middle-aged bespectacled, dark-haired good looking man although rather plump. Very circumspect, he would give little away. Usually appearing in his office doorway, papers in hand- quietly- "Er - put me a line through would you -er- Derrick?" Neatly suited and conscientiously playing his cards to his chest, he had apparently passed his exams but he had certainly never passed a steel billet through a roller! I never had a conversation with him in four years.

Ronnie's assistant and using the same office, on the other hand, was a load of fun and a bit of a live wire. Bernard H. Overhill, in a way, was our immediate boss. He told us who and when to ring and what and when to write. He would pop out of his office usually to see if we had written any messages in the phone book, which we were expected to keep up to date. This often involved queries about orders of steel that had been placed and not yet delivered. He usually wrote "four to six weeks" in a large fluid hand and we would have to relay this to the customer.

Apart from being a very efficient servant he was also quite skilled as a magician and had certainly mastered the art of palming coins, often making them disappear altogether. This used to completely mystify the person who had been designated as a sweeper and cleaned the whole Mill part of the works; a man very short in stature - under five feet and consequently known as Jockey, though it's probable that he had never been near a horse in his life. In the brief morning time before office work started, Bernard would entertain us by evoking expletives of incredulity from Jockey who was quite happy to be bewildered and disassociated from his sweeping up.

Bernard was very precise with an acute mental disposition. He called us by our real names; we were happy to do his bidding. He would deliver instructions with sharp, terse words which were usually very accurate. He knew that we had had an education and he wasn't afraid to acknowledge and even to avail himself of it.

"Vic, how would you spell 'expedite' and does it mean the same as 'expediate'." He bowed to our grammar school education but sometimes even baffled us.

It soon became known that I was interested in painting.

"You should visit St Ives in Cornwall. You'll see artists working away there on the harbour with their easels. You would love it."

This must have been the first time that I had heard of St Ives and a seed was sown, although it would be another three years or so before I was to embark on that voyage of discovery. Bernard was the one who tried to be really friendly towards us and not just treat us as office boys - although he did ensure that we were on the mark with our work.

He asked us if we had heard of Ken Wolstenholme and, of course being both footballers ourselves, we had. We were quite familiar with his name and voice and his occasional appearance on Pathe News at the cinema, as a commentator. "He's a personal friend of mine, Vic - a very nice gentleman."

I would say that BHO, as he adroitly signed himself, had never kicked a football in his life - his only sport probably being card manipulation whilst having a tipple in some local bar. He asked me if I had heard of Seigfried Sassoon, and of course, I had. He said that his delight was to take himself off to some hotel in - say- Torquay, lie in an expensive bed and read Memoirs of a Fox hunting Man. I was impressed. He was a confirmed bachelor but it was well known that, usually after Hopewell had gone home in the afternoon - BHO watching him cross the yard - he would slip around the back of the office and visit a portly lady of the same age who lived across Broughton Lane, the road which divided this area of the steelworks. He would talk discreetly on the phone to her before he left and we would overhear words such as - 'ham sandwich' or 'five minutes'. "He's kept her happy over the years,' said Cliffy Mills, the metallurgist. But perhaps it was the ham sandwich.

It was good to have respect from such an intelligent gentleman.

He and his colleagues had less respect for the manager, who they regarded as somewhat of a blustering bungler.

I never saw any of them lose their temper or their cool - they were all a bit too clever for that. Whereas Hopewell's freckly grin and bumbling speech seemed to lack a deal of sincerity. It was well known that when Arthur Balfour & Co. took on 'Cuddy' Meadows Alliance Forge and Rolling Mills he had been quick to ingratiate himself with the directors and particularly the young Mr. Mark Balfour, the handsome offspring who would occasionally arrive in his sports car to view the complex that seemed to have been presented to him as a family gift.

Ginger head at the door - "Er boy- two teas for me and Mr. Mark and two of those -er-cakethingys."

"Yes Mr. Hopewell - I'll go Derrick" and off I would beetle to the Works Canteen.

This early photo shows the canal ('The Cut') that ran past 'Cutty Meadows & Co. before joining up with Tinsley Rolling Mills and other steel factories. Eventually most of this area was demolished and much of it converted into the Meadowhall shopping complex.

It was a chance to buy ourselves a couple of cup cakes and wolf them down whilst he was engaged. Often he would forget to pay us and we would have to remind him- two shillings was quite a bit of money

The tea was often like -er -no- not quite as bad as that.

At Christmas he would call us into his office and give us ten shillings each from his wallet. We were happy with this but whilst giving away a few groats he would, every year, load up the works car with the generous gifts -usually alcoholic- bestowed on the firm from other customer friends.

"Boy- er -get me the driver - er -what's his name." The driver/mechanic would cross the yard and then recross it loaded down with a well stocked box or two.

"There it goes Bernard." George spying from the wide front windows. That's your share gone home early for another year."

As the car drove away, Bernard would give out a bit of doggerel to the tune of that well known hymn. 'All is safely gathered in - Low Moor's Whisky - Stern and Bell's Gin.'

Ronnie Hollingsworth, whom everyone thought should be works manager in Hoppy's place would stand at his door saying little or nothing but thinking much.

Most of the workmen had little education and some of the highest paid rollers and forgemen sometimes found it difficult to write up their 'work done' in their grimy notebooks. Some had bad eyesight and were unable to read.

Derrick and I had the never-ending task of transferring details from incoming orders onto a triplicate works order pad. We still hadn't been issued with Biros, and we certainly couldn't afford to buy one as they were quite expensive. They were an elitist tool and we were left to grind out these documents with a steel nib and ink. Dickens wasn't dead yet. George on the other hand would ask us to ring the stock department and demand the extra thick type for him. Of course, they couldn't refuse the Forge manager and Biros would appear. He had a habit, whilst talking on the phone to a client or other department, of going over the order number until it enlarged in size and power on the order form -blazoned there with Biro ink. This seemed effective because he appeared to have an uncanny recall of works order numbers.

Derrick and I were well educated in writing and the task presented little difficulty except that in attempting to make legible the instructions for the workmen or transport men, which had to, via carbon paper, render three copies, we would bend up the points of steel nibs by the score. Sometimes the orders would be returned to our desks, after being around the works, looking as if they had been savaged by dogs with very dirty paws.

The minions of the office changed from time to time and I was eventually appointed as progress clerk together with Derrick, who also became George Meadowcroft's assistant and consequently gathered even more bonhomie and recognition to himself down the forge.

It became my job to collect the grimy workbooks from the little wooden lockers where the top men kept their battered white enamel tea-cans and other personal bits and pieces. These stood right by their individual areas of operation. Later on, I also did it for the forge when Derrick eventually left. This was the most hazardous part of the job as I wasn't always sure where I could walk safely. The problem was that the men knew where all the red-hot bits, large and small were going -and I didn't! Glowing billets and strips of hot steel would swing across your path or snake around your feet. The men were certainly not going to stop the flow of work and take me by the hand; the most help I could expect would be a big shout if I happened to step into the wrong area but as there was so much noise and shouting in general, the message would sometimes get lost. I was lucky I never got injured. If you survived long enough to understand what was going on, then you stood a chance.

Walt from the Top Office (where the accounts were done) wasn't so lucky; being unused to such risky adventuring, he got burnt on the ankle. Health & Safety? - What's that? Fights would sometimes break out and George would do his strong, fatherly dressing down in the office.

All of this was eclipsed one day when George summoned Big Fred, the largest fellow in the world - a gentle innocent giant of a man. To be honest, he wasn't too bright and was mainly employed doing the menial odd jobs in the Forge.

"Get me twenty Senior Service across the road -good lad" Off he went clutching the money. The shop was situated up a side street across the main road. The houses were protected by high fences as they backed on to a scrap yard that reduced metal into shards by dropping a huge steel ball from a crane.

On returning from the shop, Big Fred was hit by a piece of metal that flew over the fence, shot between the only gap in the buildings and decapitated him. Smoking can damage your health. Having just lived through a war where life was cheap, this event was quickly absorbed and pushed into the background.

There was much filing of orders to do in the early days but later girls were taken on to do this and answer the irritating switchboard. Thus Derrick and I were promoted.

A bit of feminine interest certainly lightened the atmosphere.

One of the perks of the Balfour amalgamation was the fact that we could now use the excellent Sports ground at Whirlow, which on the western boundary of Sheffield was almost into the splendid Derbyshire hills.

Hopewell was keen for us to use this facility, genuflecting to Balfours. He asked us into his office to explain what Whirlow had to offer.

As we entered, he bounced out of his chair - his podgy hands gesticulating.

"There's lots to do up there, boys - tennis and - things -er er- and there's girls up there!" His red face beamed and his mouth broke into that now familiar grin. "OK sir - we'll be up there!"

"Good -good -good!"

21. Surrounded by Balfour Beauties at Whirlow 1951.
'Ike' is on my left-hand side.

I had already learnt to play tennis at Firth Park, after leaving school.

Derrick by now had softened to my gentle charm and we used to meet there for a game, not only of tennis, but joining the old regulars in the noble art of bowling on the excellent crown

22. Doing my Frank Sedgman impression at Whirlow.

green. I didn't have the social grace that Derrick had and in the Park he would chat away to anyone who crossed his path, in this case making friends with several of the old bowlers, and the Park Keepers, of course. We transferred our affections to Whirlow and had many happy hours on the courts there - and the tennis was free.

There were indeed girls and there Derrick met his future wife Iris (or Ike as he liked to call her). I personally wasn't attracted to any of them being already romantically attached to the beautiful Beryl.

But Whirlow was a huge gulp of fresh air.

I was a great follower of Wimbledon on early black and white TV and I particularly liked the style of the great Australian player, Frank Sedgman.

I watched him carefully and tried to emulate his style.

In fairness, you would have to admit that I developed a wonderful swinging serve and beautifully developed ground strokes. The trouble was that I didn't always get the ball into the court. However, the good news was that my clean and classy look got me into the Balfours

Tennis Team, whose players were so excellent that I only ever made the third couple! I didn't particularly like my partner, who was a particularly morose, uncommunicative type, and this did little to help our results.

Someone from C. Meadows making any Balfours team was pretty unbelievable anyway, as our office staff was extremely limited to say the least, but I wouldn't say that there was any prejudice or favouritism involved. They just knew talent when they saw it!

A similar situation cropped up with the Balfours Football Team who played in the Drake League and always did extremely well. Coming from Meadows & Co. I was rather like an alien, whereas all the other players would work with and see each other on a daily basis, hence becoming buddies. I suppose it was only due to my educated right foot, honed at the Grammar School, that I got a game at all. None of the workmen at Meadows saw fit to enter such goings-on; probably seeing them as valuable time taken off pub hours.

Derrick generally played for Unity, a very good church team. Chacun a son gout! Balfours had a prolific goal scorer at centre forward, an attractive youth called Barry Beeman. On one of my non-playing occasions, I took Beryl together with Derrick and one or two other friends to watch Balfours play in a match, against, of course, another works team.

It slowly began to dawn on people around - and myself, that our prolific goal scorer, who was about to get yet another hat-trick, looked extremely like my sweetheart! For a while this became more important than the match! They could easily have been brother and sister. I wasn't keen to let them get too close, so we didn't hang around after the match!

Coincidence? Listen. Barry Beeman and Beryl Bulloss.

I used to cycle to work on my much-loved white Viking racing cycle.

Tram lines had to be negotiated. Sheffield was a city that ran on tram lines. Most cyclists had a degree of skill but eventually the lines would win out. I once came a 'purler' on entering the infamous Upwell Street bridge. Apart from the fact that it periodically flooded, being the lowest point around for miles, it held a wicked bend after entering this gloomy place. There was little space between the outside line and the built-up walkway. Tram cars left no room for cyclists and suicide was imminent.

But still we would attempt it!

This wasn't my only cycle trauma. On one occasion whist joining the madding horde pouring out of the works and flooding over Broughton Lane Bridge I was hit from behind by a flat-capped workman on his old bone-shaker as he joined the Lowry-like mob of men rushing to get home. He just never looked where he was going and I was furious. All I could do was to shout insults after him as he pedalled away over the bridge, in the hope that he would lose his temper and come back. My back wheel was a figure 8. I was so angry I went to Attercliffe police station where, of course, they could only suggest that I tried to catch him next time. Some chance. Incidentally, the only German prisoner of war to bother escaping from an English prison camp (in the Lake District) eventually got bored with his freedom and handed himself into that very same police station. What the hell was he doing in Attercliffe?

Another incident happened after an evening with BHO and his blind chiropractor friend. We had spent an interesting interlude together where, at Bernard's request, I had recounted my adventures in France on a cycling trip with the lads, Pete, Terry and Frank. Then I had my neck vertebrae popped!

I cycled home in the dark, my lamp spreading a feeble patch of light before me. The roads were deserted at that time of night. I entered the canyons of the steelworks at Petre Street. I never saw the black cat that hit my front wheel. What a stupid cat! Again not looking where it was going, just like the man on the bridge.

I knew where I was going - recognising that agonising moment as I flew over the handlebars. Again, I had wheels that didn't match and I was walking home once more.

"Got back alright, last night, Vic?" enquired BHO.
"Nope."

One of my final jobs as a clerk was to work out the load accomplished every day by the mill rollers. They were hard, strong and usually sweaty men.

They earnt about £20 a week, which compared with my £8 (by then) was a small fortune. They would fling open the door so that it bounced against the counter where I sat, asserting their authority, you might say. They would collect their scruffy work books that I had tried to decipher and by long, sometimes complicated, mathematics had worked out the amount in cwts. qrs. lbs, of each order they had worked on. At the weekend, if their wages didn't agree with their calculations, I would be in the firing line.

"Sixpence out - see to it will you?"

The Rollers would come in straight from the heat of the Big Mill furnaces. They would lean over and glare - sweat starting from their foreheads and rolling down their jowls.

They reeked of the unique smell of steel and perspiration.

Langton - bald head and muscle -usually joking. Ginger chest hair poking from his vest.

Ketteringham - dour, tall and unsmiling, cloth cap pulled over his eyes.

Men you had to treat with infinite care.

Derrick on the other hand was never phased - "Hiya Bob! - Hiya Tom! - Hiya Pilky!"- he was everyone's friend. In a way I was a foil to his sunny personality and he saw me as a somewhat, over-sensitive troubled youth who perhaps wasn't counting his blessings. After all, I was tolerably good-looking, intelligent, educated, a good sportsman - had a beautiful girlfriend - a steady job - but I still wasn't satisfied. There was something missing.

It took a while but eventually I was embraced by the men too -particularly in the Roll Turners shed- and was showing photos of my sweetheart. They were of a more educated nature and played chess in their lunch hour.

"Asta introduced Fagin, yet?"

"Oh aye!" Enough detail there then.

Derrick had a secretive side to his nature. He didn't necessarily confide in me over certain things, whereas I was very open.

For one, I mentioned Unity, the church football team he played for, which reached the League final. I assume this involved going to church -he never mentioned it. He also ran a local junior team from his home at Shiregreen. He never spoke of it. Unbeknown to me, he was attending City & Guild lectures on steel production at the University. This could lead to management. When I accidentally discovered this, I asked why I couldn't go with him.

"What's stopping you - see you next Tuesday 8pm."

I duly turned up and joined a host of suited, ardent, young, prospective managers. I quickly realised that I wasn't one, especially after listening to an hour on Bessemer Converters. I wasn't convinced that Derrick had his heart in it either, but I didn't mention it further. Despite this he was a great friend and we would meet many times for tennis at Firth Park or Whirlow and we even met occasionally after he had left 'Cuddy' Meadows for Hatfields - another steelworks and eventually marrying his 'Ike'. He also did his National Service in the RAF and I wrote to him from time to time with the 'Home' news. A great guy and I loved him.

The 'Top' office housed a different set of animals. Mainly typists and accountants, they had to be somewhat better turned out; they certainly didn't have to contend with all the dirt and noise that blew in through the Mill Office windows as their office was divorced from the mill floor by a flight of steps, into a yard with an escape door out onto the relative peace of the canal bank. No - the Top office crew were smart and unsullied by our somewhat drear existence down in the mill. Our one consolation was that instead of looking out onto brick buildings, we had quite a grand vista down the stockyard and over the slag heaps, which on a good day could almost be mistaken for Derbyshire outliers. In fact, on one sunny summer day - yes, even Sheffield had them - I persuaded young Don, the new office boy, to have a go at climbing them with me in the lunch hour. Not to be countenanced on a wet day! Aberfan was an example of what could happen - but our heaps were smaller.

The star of the Top office was undoubtedly Betty - a tall, soft mannered blonde with a breathy voice and a curvaceous figure. She was in her early twenties and engaged. This didn't stop me being enamoured of her.

At five p.m. our office theoretically shut down and we would all make our escape from the top gate. This had to be kept locked and therefore we had to call on the staff to release us. Hopefully this would be Betty. If so, I'm afraid that I never missed this opportunity to ask her for a kiss - and always got one! Crushed up against a brick wall in a dream of perfume and feminine charm. It wasn't all bad. It was a bit of fun - something to relieve the monotony of the work. The Top office had an upper floor where the records were kept and tea was made. This also occasionally was a place for fun and certainly not lost on Walt, a small, sociable, popular, curly-haired guy who liked to chat with we lesser mortals.

The other two office girls, one being Norma and the other a rather flighty married one, also liked to lighten the atmosphere somewhat, and not surprisingly. Their office was run by the Levitt brothers and I must say they were unique.

At the least sign of shenanigans Fred Levitt, appointed overseer by his brother Stan, would put in an appearance at the top of the stairs, which was supposed to subdue everybody into a quiet conformity, but as no one had any respect for him, especially Walt, his presence would be deemed to be merely as a spoil sport.

Fred was fat, pompous and in charge of the safe. My frequent sorties for petty cash, mainly for Hopewell's tea parties, would take an interminable time as he would have to count and re-count a row of sixpences laid out on his desk before allowing me to leave with it.

Brother Stan in his partitioned-off twin desk was his alter ego. Small and quite badly truncated with a spinal fault, he dominated Fred and the office.

There was some attempt by Derrick and Walt to pair me off with Norma, but she had just a little bit too much attitude for me despite her large brown eyes and good figure. I was easily frightened. My relationship with Beryl was decidedly blowing on and off, so having a date wasn't exactly out of bounds.

On the switchboard, it wasn't unusual for us to get crossed lines and on one occasion, Derrick, as positive as ever, chatted up a girl who just happened to have butted in on our conversation. He was cheeky enough to set up a date with her and her twin sister in the City.

As I was slicking my hair and polishing the chains on my shoes, Beryl unexpectedly turned up at the house. "Where are you going?" "Me and Derrick have got a date with twins - up town." "No you haven't"

"Well, you had a date with John Connealy last week- why shouldn't I have one?"

"Because I don't want you to!"

We discussed the situation as we walked along the Front to the tram stop.

"You know there's nothing between John Connealy and me!"

"Well, I haven't even met these two!"

She grabbed me as a tram approached.

"And you're not going to!"

She had that stubborn look on her face, only slightly redeemed by her dreamy green eyes.

"You are not getting on that tram!"

How could I? I loved the girl and she was gorgeous.

The trouble was that our love never ran smooth.

She loved dancing. I actually met her, one dark evening, about to enter the Welfare building opposite the Paragon cinema at the bottom of Sicey Avenue at Firth Park. I had noticed her twice before and had been attracted. She was always with her friend Betty Bramall (another BB!) and her small white terrier. Painfully shy as I was, I bit the bullet and crossed the road.

"What happens in there?"

"Who's asking?"

"I'm Victor - I live at Firvale."

"Old Time Dancing."

"Can I watch?"

"From the door-you're not a member. Do you like dancing?

"Not much."

She was a tall fifteen and I was a shy sixteen.

We both became members of Hartley Brook Youth Club, near where she lived. She danced, I joined the wallflowers.

From there she graduated to more sophisticated friends than Betty and to the dance hall at the City Hall, extremely popular with the young generation, of which I was supposed to be a member. It wasn't my scene and I knew that very well. I didn't need to go there. On Saturday evenings I usually went to the Paragon with Tony and Alan - Ron by now had fallen out of my favour- as Beryl insisted on going dancing at the City Hall. I trusted that her promise of faithfulness would be maintained.

Peter Coates, a recent new friend had a job (amongst others) of managing the entrance tickets to the hall and he enlightened me as to what went on there apart from the dancing. After that, I was completely disenchanted.

Beryl also went on holiday with a girl friend to Blackpool of all places. Was she faithful? -er- well - no.

When I was ill and hospitalised, my school friend, Reg casually mentioned that she had been seeing Frank Limb, another footballing friend who, as it happened, looked very much like me! Perhaps she got a bit mixed up - but then again later, she had a date with Reg, who certainly looked nothing like me. He said she was 'hot stuff'. As I had just staggered out of the hospital, this cheered me up no end. I hadn't had a girl friend before and it wasn't easy for me to divine how 'hot' stuff could be.

"That's the trouble with good-looking girls" declared wise George whilst we were chopping down trees for the Forestry Commission- "everybody chases them. Get yourself an ugly girl, Vic boy."

The delicate aesthetic side of my nature wouldn't allow this of course. I thought it would be better to do without, and for five years, that's what I did.

Things were changing at the works. This was the time of the first advent of immigrant workers into the industry and suddenly we had a quota of Pakistanis injected into this arena of full-blooded Yorkshire men. I knew nothing of race relations but it soon became obvious that the men disliked them. The mill office had also had a facelift and a screen now separated us from any workmen that might choose to enter - usually with some complaint or other. The bonus for me was that I didn't have to answer the phone any more; the only thing that I missed was Betty's sexy voice. The other benefit was the influx of office girls. The first one to take up residence was Jean. Derrick called her 'sex-on-legs'. She was only just approaching sixteen. Men stopped what they were doing as she sashayed across the stockyard to the Time office.

An Attercliffe girl, she was quite cheeky - in both senses of the word, as it happened. She could easily deflate any response from lesser-witted, uneducated workmen and her tight-clad bottom was a joy to behold.

We virtually sat back-to-back in the office and it was impossible for me not to be in close contact with her. We very soon became interested in each other. A stolen kiss in the stockroom led to cinema dates and trysts on Wincobank Hill, and at Concord Park and Whirlow. She didn't play tennis but she would often come to see Balfours play- or was it just me. I was never sure. She also spent time with Timmins, the Balfours six foot three inches centre-half. She always referred to him as Timmins, which I thought somewhat humorous - and curious. Fortunately for me, he was only aggressive on the football field.

She would drop off the tram at Page Hall and we would do the long walk to Concord Park and Wincobank Hill - then laying together looking at the stars and trying to make sense of our lives. Often we would drift into romantic mode but we only ever got serious on a singular occasion. We liked each other but I never felt that it would get further than mutual fondling.

I invited her home on one occasion. She charmed Dad out of his socks as she sat in her preferred position on the floor. The wriggle of her sexy bottom was not lost on Father. Mum thought she was a bit 'fast' and preferred Beryl whom she liked very much and would gladly have had as a daughter-in-law.

Jean and I were good mates while it lasted. One funny eventuality was when I periodically picked her up at lunchtime by Attercliffe Baths near where she lived. I had recently acquired my DOT trials bike which to be frank wasn't really built for passengers. The back foot rests were very high, consequently she had to hoik up her already very short skirt and wrap her naked legs under my armpits! This phased her not one little bit.

Legs and one arm wrapped tightly around me and the free hand brandishing a half-peeled banana - the residue of her recently consumed dinner- we would arouse all the workmen that we passed as they lounged against the gates of the factories. A DOT with its two-stroke engine and noisy exhaust always attracted attention anyway and I was often jeered on. With Jean and her banana on board, the symbolism was not lost and the response quite different, especially as we sputtered our way into our own stockyard! Down tools-up tools! We would certainly have remained great friends had she not left Meadows for pastures new. I later bumped into her in the City and she revealed that she now had a job selling office technology.

I'm sure her charm and strapless flowered dress would have served her well. Dear Jean. My next office encounter was Doreen who liked to have the 'o' in her name expressed as a 'u'. I was happy to comply. Again I found myself sitting back to back - our chairs almost touching. Although not as exciting as Jean, we gelled more on an intellectual level. She was very efficient in the office and rarely called on me for help once she had learnt the job. She was already engaged, but from time to time, seemed disenchanted with her fiancé, so much so that we would occasionally sound each other out. Having recently finished with Beryl altogether, I was fancy-free to indulge my whims. In a way the element of forbidden fruit added the necessary spice to the arrangement and I think that she felt the same. I certainly wouldn't have pursued it otherwise. There was no question of intercourse - that would have been crossing the line, but the usual intimacies began to happen. We were very young.

Alec, her fiancé, rode a motor bike and on hearing of our now flourishing caving adventures, he elected to join us on the occasional weekend meet. His idea, not mine! Doreen made an attractive pillion passenger. Having pitched their tent, she proved to be a great improvement on our attempts at campfire cooking! Sausages her speciality!

On one such occasion, the lads took Alec off to explore the nearby Gautries Hole (near Castleton). I had recently been quite ill and at this time it was deemed better that I didn't get cold and wet through, which was par for the course in our caving activities. Doreen opted not to go as well, it not being her scene. Consequently, we were left to explore each other in one of the tents. I concluded that Alec must have been far too trusting or a bit simple. In fairness, he didn't seem to be that bothered and I certainly saw more of her than he did, during the day. I had no intention of attempting to take her away and when I asked her why she stayed with him, she simply said " He needs me."

The boys found it a great source of amusement when I suggested that Alec should have a turn at the bottom of our favourite dig - a near vertical, silted-up stream passage of, then, about forty feet. Whilst he was enthusiastically digging away at the bottom of the shaft, Doreen and I took the opportunity to roll around on the grass together.

"What's Vic doing with Doreen, Pete?" asked Frank, loud enough for anyone to hear.

"I don't know - what's he doing?"

"I think he's lying on top of her, isn't he?"

"It looks something like that."

"Does Alec know?"

"Ask him."

"Do you know what Vic's doing, Alec?"

Grunts from below - Alec seemed to have been bitten by the caving bug!

He certainly seemed to be more interested in what was going on underground than what his fiancée might be getting interested in. He certainly wouldn't be the first guy to have broken off relations in order to pursue a troglodytic life at the weekends and I was no exception when Beryl decided to diversify. Sometimes one has to accept the obvious.

It was very odd. Doreen was so passive and mild - something new to me, whereas Beryl could at times be quite fiery. Anyway, did they split up? Probably not, but shortly after, I left Charles Meadows & Co. for fresh fields and pastures new - literally - and so lost touch.

These weekend pursuits – underground, mountaineering, camping, cycling and later motor bikes, would often find me falling asleep in the office! BHO was by now very sympathetic and would suggest that if I had finished my work then I should put my head down and doze off at my desk. He always kept an eye on Hopewell's movements and often a well-aimed paper clip would warn me of his imminent arrival! I was tempted on my last day to leave a sign over my desk proclaiming that 'Vic Oliver slept here' but then thought better of it!

Caving Days

This is the story of three Sheffield lads who became so inseparable that we were christened 'The Three Musketeers'. For Athos, Porthos and Aramis read Pete, Frank and Vic. As you will see, as the story progresses, there were many D'Artagnans but they all fell away. Some couldn't stand the pace - some realised our way wasn't theirs and some just couldn't understand what it was all about. I dedicate these writings to the members of the DSG.

Someone once said that if you hit the Peak District in Derbyshire with a giant hammer, it would ring like a bell. This would only refer to the so-called White Peak, which is largely composed of limestone and is fairly riddled with caves and potholes and therefore certainly has a fair percentage of airspace beneath its apparently solid covering. If you hit the High Peak however, particularly Kinder Scout, with a large hammer, you would get very wet and covered in bog.

As I write this in 2011, we now know for sure that Castleton, that limestone wonderland, can claim, in Titan, to have the deepest pothole in England - at least.

Mine is a simple enough story but had our efforts in the middle fifties come to fruition and our intuition shown to be justified then the story would have been very different. We could only guess at the largesse that might exist beneath our feet as we wandered over the landscape but there were indications enough, especially in the Castleton area, which boasted the famous Peak Cavern and the other extraordinary show caves. The fabulous Peak Cavern, with its enormous resurgent exit, nestles at the back of Castleton village and in days gone by was quaintly known as the Devil's Arse of Peak!

Some two and a half miles heading west along the Castleton to Buxton road one reaches Eldon Hill with its well known hole punched eighty feet deeply into its summit. The hole is almost as wide as it is deep and one could assume that this might be the entrance to the Underworld that every caver dreams of finding. But no. There are a few ramifications where hopefuls have dug, and a few indications of mining, but certainly no sign of the enormous lake of local legend and fantasy.

Impressive enough to attract the attentions of one Edouard-Alfred Martel (1859-1938), a French geographer and great early pioneer of international speleology (the scientific exploration of caves), even he could make no impression on it. Turning his attention to Gaping Gill in Yorkshire, he made the first descent in 1895. Lots of old rope needed there M'sieur! (The trail down the magnificent Gorge du Verdon in the Southern France bears his name, by the way - I would loved to have known him.).

Eldon Hole remains a tempting enigma.

Too tempting for one local farmer who, according to local legend sent a goose down one of the rifts at the bottom of Eldon Hole believing that it was bound to come out at the resurgence of Peak Cavern. Well it did - but it was naked, having lost all its feathers on the way. I did say it was a legend.

We are at Perryfoot and you could be excused if you passed along the road without a glance, it being merely a small lane junction where a stream runs past a farm called Whitelee and disappears under the road. But this was the site of one of the special caving systems in the area. Being a member of the Derbyshire Speleological Group (DSG), as we were, didn't necessarily give you any access to some particular systems; in fact, some were covered and locked. This was essentially to prevent ignorant people wandering in and doing damage to the cave flora - the sometimes wonderful displays of stalactites etc. The British Speleological

Association (BSA) were very good at this and permission would have had to be obtained to explore these special sites. We were expected to respect other cavers sites, particularly digs, and this we did. My friends and I operated under the umbrella of the DSG and in the middle fifties, to which all this refers, there was plenty of leeway. In 1960 however, when we had long gone, the different clubs in Derbyshire were brought to task in order that they wouldn't be treading on each other's toes (and the stalactites etc.) and duplicating work and so forth.

We knew that the systems at Whitelee were BSA, so that we respected. We also knew that their explorer there was Les Salmon who lived in Sheffield but who occasionally caught the same bus into Derbyshire as we did. As far as we were aware he would spend every weekend at Whitelee, presumably digging away, but there was also a rumour that he was courting the farmer's daughter! Anyway he deserved our respect and Frank would point him out at Pond Street bus station in a very quiet, somewhat mock reverential tone, as was his wont.

"That's Les Salmon, Vic"

"Yes, I know that, Frank."

"Les Salmon, Pete".

"That's definitely Les Salmon, Frank".

Perryfoot for me marked the end of a geological unconformity that ran from here back to Castleton, but on the opposite side of the Buxton road to Eldon. At the Castleton end, this important area for a caver started at Windy Knoll. From here one could within a short distance be on Mam Tor (The Shivering Mountain - and it did) with views into the beautiful Hope Valley or North into Edale and the beginning of the Pennine Way. But the geologically important event that had happened here was that the gritstone massif of Kinder Scout (2088feet) with its outlier of Rushup Edge was butted up against the northern edge of the limestone mass that stretches across to Buxton and down to Matlock and beyond, forming the White peak.

Kinder is notable and very impressive as a high acidic boggy area with its deep gullies (groughs) and its river running dramatically over the Downfall and into the reservoir at Hayfield on the Manchester side of the Pennines.

All the acidic run-off on the South side flows down Edale Valley, except that from Rushup Edge which attacks the Windy Knoll-Perryfoot depression and bores into the limestone, creating hundreds of feet of passage, much of it impenetrable. Yet there are many places here that have been explored by cavers, notably Giant's Hole, which was extended by the BSA in the fifties and joined up with Oxlow Caverns and Maskhill Mines in the sixties to produce a trip, albeit dangerous, extending over 13,000 feet. Further possible opportunities were explored all the way down to Perry foot - some of them productive and others not. Gautries Hole at the far western end, just before we hit the road again, was another system explored and surveyed by Les Salmon.

The places of water entry into the limestone corridor were originally, for convenience, called P1 to P8 and this to me became quite confusing. P8 was probably the only one recognised by us as we knew this to be a going opportunity for the BSA. In fact with the help of the Cave Diving Group it was later opened up for a considerable distance and is now known, appropriately enough as Jackpot. As far as we were concerned our particular dig didn't have a number. We just called it '1Bull Pit dig' as that particular shakehole was very nearby and above us. No doubt it had at one time had something to do with the same system.

Having visited the area many years later, I couldn't even recognise it - the whole area had been turned over and there was even a small pond that certainly had never been there before.

Systems had been opened up and many man hours had obviously been spent digging, struggling, crawling, squeezing and blowing things up!

When we were active in the area, we were happy to conscript anyone who fancied spending part of the day down a thirty foot (eventually) steep incline scraping away at a wall of compacted silt that had been sluiced down over a few thousand years by the action of the water running off Rushup Edge. When we first arrived at the site doing our usual thing of looking for Jules Vernian opportunities, the water still ran into the fissure onto a bed of silt but as we realised that the aperture was just about big enough to accommodate a man we began scraping.

As we progressed and gained a little depth, we thought a bucket might be a good idea, so on the next trip we hopped off the bus at Castleton as usual, but then headed for the local rubbish dump. We found a very serviceable old bucket! - and some rope.

As we gained depth, it became harder to drag up the filled bucket -wet grit is heavy!

Another call at the rubbish dump provided us with a wooden top from an upright piano that fitted our excavation perfectly and facilitated the bucket's journey to the surface. Of course, we couldn't do anything about the surrounding rock so we could only employ a solitary workman at the face at any one time, and thus progress was slow.

The great discovery of Titan at Hurd Low in 1999 put a whole new perspective on British Caving, as up to that point the deepest pothole in England had been Gaping Gill in Yorkshire at 450feet. The Yorkshire potholers never failed to remind us -we tended to go in sideways - not down!

A further 65feet had to be opened up from the surface to allow a top entry to Titan, making a grand total of 529feet.

Well, who knows. We might have been the lucky ones that suddenly dropped into an apparently bottomless pit, but as it happened we were on the wrong side of Eldon Hill!

1954 - The Genesis

On the 1st October I borrowed a book from Firth Park Library.

It was called 'Ten Years under the Earth' and was written by a famous French speleologist named Norbert Casteret. He became so adept at discovering and exploring cave systems that he was eventually employed by the French hydroelectric services to plot underground streams and lakes. He went on to write 'More Years under the Earth', 'My Caves' and 'Cave Men Old and New'. Later, I acquired these books for my collection and fiftyseven years later I have them still on my shelves. I also acquired Tazzief's 'Caves of Adventure'.

Later on, as caving became more and more popular, many other books were written. To say that I was fascinated would have been a great understatement.

My father, to his great credit, had always been attracted to Derbyshire, on the outskirts of Sheffield. He loved to get away from the pollution of Attercliffe, the area in which he worked, and take my mother and me on a bus ride into the Peak and spend the rest of the day walking - or rambling, as it was known. The show caves at Castleton were on his itinerary, although he hardly had the money to do but two, as I remember- Speedwell and Treak Cliff. My brother, five years older than me, usually preferred to chase the girls with his cousins. The steelworks area of Attercliffe was a playground to him - not a problem. So I knew of the caves, but I yearned to know more - especially after reading Casteret.

I had known Peter Coates and Frank Wicken for just a year now but I knew that they would be up for anything that I might suggest, provided that it be legal and adventurous. They were already my brothers.

I asked them around for a meeting at 52 Skinnerthorpe Road, the diminutive house where I was brought up. It had to be when my parents had their weekly outing for an evening drink at the Working Men's Club at Page Hall, a short tram ride away - otherwise there wouldn't have been any room to move. Perhaps that's why I didn't suffer from claustrophobia.

"Have a look at that lads!" slapping the book on the table.

"Hmm! Interesting!" said Pete perusing the photos. "Must be a good swimmer".

"Can't get to France", murmured Frank, screwing up his bad eye to get a better look.

"We don't have to go to France, Frank - we've got caves in Derbyshire. Admittedly they aren't on that scale - I mean he's goin' down a thousand feet - we can't do that -but- well what do you say?" Pete grunted.

"Aye- let's 'ave a go. We've got no'wt on this weekend. What do wi' need?"

I was just about to suggest a bicycle lamp and washing line when Frank blurted – "Ey - somebody said that there were a cave in Dove Dale. That you could stay in!"

I never liked to discourage Frank as his forte wasn't swooning over books and maps; in fact neither of them had been educated much beyond an elementary level. They had pulled themselves up with their own bootstraps and had not resigned themselves to their relatively poor backgrounds. I was always ready to accept their opinions and points of view.

"Well, two points Frank. I'm not sure that the Dove Dale caves - like - do anything - and- how do we get there?"

I had Saturdays off work but I was very much aware that they didn't - consequently, apart from holidays, our escapades had usually to start around midday on the Saturday or even Sunday morning.

"The only bus would be to Bakewell and that's bloody miles away from Dove Dale - and anyway - where do you suppose we sleep - even if we get there? There is Hartington Youth Hostel but I'm not sure we could get there by ten p.m. lock up - and then, that's not exactly Dove Dale is it". I always had to supply the rationale and let them knock it down.

"Sleep in the cave, Vic,vic,vic", Frank, quietly.

"Ay - then it wouldn't matter if we walked all night - an' we might gerra' lift!" Pete always optimistic.

"OK! Let's do it! Saturday Pond Street. We'll need the usual cook-up stuff and as many clothes as we can carry. It is October!"

It wasn't what I had in mind, but then - what the hell. I had been ill - sometimes seriously- and in and out of hospital for the last six years but I wasn't prepared to take an invalid route. After all, what better place to freeze to death than Dove Dale!

Saturday 9th. October 1954

We get the bus for Bakewell and then set off on the long walk to Dove Dale!

Well - fortune smiles sometimes. We thumb and get a lift somewhere along the way. This takes us to Parsley Hay, which is in the middle of nowhere - but - half-way there!

It's getting dark.

"We need some light to get down the Dale, chaps, or we'll be up to our knees in watter. That manky old torch of yours, wain't be much good Pete - its dark in't countrie' lads - no gas lamps".

Why worry - this is Frank's night out.

An old van pulls up and drops us at Alsop-en-le-Dale. The clue is in the name. We are at the head of Dove Dale and as we pick our way down into this beautiful, wooded limestone gorge night starts to enshroud us. We were lucky to get the lifts!

The cave isn't difficult to find as it is directly opposite Ilam Rock, sitting sentinel-like across the river. The cave was called Pickering Tor Cave.

Comfort? Well -no. The rock is deadly hard and paralysing to the hip bone - the modern light-weight bed roll hasn't yet been invented.

My one blessing was my huge lined jacket, which made me look like I had just discovered the Yukon. Of all the things that my brother Ernest handed me down, this was perhaps the only thing that I wanted and needed. Mind you- I did have to pay him £1 for it! The lads called it my 'Jimcaneyt' coat as it reminded them of a character we had met at Ewden Youth Hostel whose prowess as a prolific eater was being extolled by his ageing friend. "Aye! Jim can 'eyt all'reyt. I've seen 'im 'eyt a whole bluddy chicken to his'en. Aye! Jimcaneyt!".

I had a reasonable night considering, and was delighted to hear Frank complaining that water from the roof had been dripping on him.

The next day we had a look at the other caves in Dove Dale and then carried on down by the lovely River Dove, (which incidentally marks the Derybyshire-Staffordshire boundary), all the way to Ilam, with its stately Hall (another Youth Hostel). Sharply tuning back north we follow the River Manifold back to Wetton and then on to Hartington where we were lucky enough to catch a bus to Buxton. Bus back to Sheffield. Job done - now we could start some real caving!

The following weekend we were ready. Equipped with bicycle lamps, washing lines and boiler suits, we caught the train (again from Pond Street) and chuffed our way into Derbyshire.

We were staying at Rowland Cote Youth Hostel for the night. This was where Pete showed his bit of expertise. I didn't really like communicating with people all that much whereas Pete didn't have a problem - so he was the one designated to make any bookings etc. that were required - we soon got to know which venues were popular enough to have to do this, whereas we knew other Youth Hostels where we could just turn up on spec. Pete also had the convenience of working in the very centre of Sheffield. He was a piano tuner at Wilson Peck, the large music store dominating a corner of the City Centre, and there was only a short walk down to the YHA shop that delivered the goods that we required - that and the Army & Navy Stores - also nearby.

The train stopped at Edale before plunging into Cowburn Tunnel and going on its way to Manchester. Overlooked by the brooding presence of Kinder Scout- the site of the first mass trespass- Edale was popular with ramblers, and was eventually designated as the start of the Pennine Way. It had a sense of romance about it - it was on the edge. Kinder to the less hardy was a barrier and not to be taken lightly. The men's dorm at Rowland Cote wasn't a doddle either. Situated high up on the side of Edale Moor -Kinder's outlier- it was reached by a long wooden staircase, named Jacob's Ladder after the notorious scramble that presaged any advance on Kinder from Edale Head. Having arrived at the long hut, the issue was one blanket and no heating. It often made for a very cold night!

I have to introduce you to two of our D'Artagnans here as they had decided to join us on this trip. I don't think that we ever refused any gesture in our direction but we did see ourselves as somewhat exclusive. The first, Brian Gutteridge - not a pretty name but fairly descriptive of his origins in the back streets of Brightside, was more of a stickler than any of the other satellites that drifted into our orbit. This was probably because Pete, Frank and he all lived within the proverbial stone's throw from each other and contact was almost daily. I don't think that Pete had the heart to refuse him.

Brightside was an area of back-to-back houses on the edge of the highly polluted industrial area of Sheffield. Its saving grace was probably that parts of it were elevated on the slopes of Wincobank Hill and so didn't necessarily have the oppressive congestion of the Attercliffe area, which lay in the flat overcrowded valley bottom of the River Don. Here it was difficult to avoid the poisonous multi-coloured smoke from the forest of chimneys, domestic and commercial, that would often form a shroud of smog, which covered and penetrated the whole scene. In fact, if you had to be there at all, then Wincobank was the place to be. It has to be said that it had a great view over the steelworks! It also had the charisma of having been a Roman camp and in WWII sported a gunsite - and it was also popular with courting couples! Pete would often ring me at work to report on any bookings that he had made for the next weekend so that we could adjust plans if necessary. It was usually then that he would report that "Brian's coming". It wasn't for me to complain or even conceive of a suppressed groan as, after all, they had almost been brought up together- but there were times when we would have just been a bit slicker without Brian! I think that it was mainly that he couldn't contribute anything, except a big grin and a happy-go-lucky demeanour even when we were in trouble! Neither did he seem to have any propensity to learn or even show interest, which, after all, was largely the object of the exercise. His major asset seemed to be that, having a weak bladder, he could be relied upon to find a toilet quicker than anyone else!

Our next D'Artagnan couldn't have been more different than Brian. Terry Phoenix, apart from having a romantic name, cut quite a romantic figure. Tall, good-looking, dark wavy hair- he could have been any girl's dreamboat. He joined us on the Sunday morning having caught the train to Edale.

For our first cave, we had to climb out of Edale valley and broach Mam Nick - a natural crossing place into Hope valley. Windy Knoll was easy enough to find - just across the road, and sitting on this high point between valleys, it really was windy! Quite an impressive, broad entrance cave with small chambers doesn't engage one for long. Its claim to fame is that it has yielded hundreds of animal bones in the past, many of which are in museums. Okay. We didn't need the washing lines!

We followed the obvious line of subsidence that I have discussed and eventually arrived at Giant's Hole, by now well known to cavers and the more adventurous rambler. A meet of the Orpheus Caving Club was happening and, quickly hiding our washing lines, we fell into conversation with the members. They were based in Salford near Manchester and so had about the same distance to travel as we had in order to reach the caving area -though they did have their own transport. We waited for their departure and went in as far as we dare. It was extended in the late fifties by the BSA to over three kilometres and therefore was one of the most advanced caves in Derbyshire. On this and further visits we were able to explore dry passages in the roof and then get thoroughly wet following the stream passage as far as the 'Curtain', where the stream dipped under the surrounding rock. From here it became a serious system, and one which we were not equipped to do.

Hiking back to Castleton for the bus, we had plenty to discuss.

"We have to get helmets lads - and them 'eadlamps that go 'bang' and shoots out flame! Pete - get darn the YHA shop and see what they've got will ya?"

"Bloody right!"

At the time, I was working as an office boy, graduating to a progress clerk, at Charles Meadows - Alliance Forge and Rolling Mills, which was situated by the canal at Broughton Lane, just off Attercliffe Common, which was part of the main road that ran virtually from Sheffield to Doncaster and encapsulated most of the steelworks area of South Yorkshire. The only relevance regarding my caving adventures was that I now badly needed a miner's helmet and on enquiring, Sid the works dispatcher, a good friend, soon came up with the goods. There were plenty of coal mines in Yorkshire! The lads had made similar enquiries amongst relatives and been fitted out.

An outlay of fourteen shillings and sixpence each gained us an Acetylene (Carbide) Lamp from the YHA shop and as I seemed to have a bit more cash than the lads - I was after all earning about £5 a week by now! - I invested in a hundred feet of 5\8 hemp rope.

That same afternoon we were on our way to Castleton to book in at the Youth Hostel.

Terry joined us. Having made our beds and dumped our stuff, we were off to Winnats Pass and the Suicide Cave! Not of any great consequence, Suicide was easy to get to and fun, and therefore probably had more visits by young people than any other cave, other than the series at Stoney Middleton. It has to be said that Stoney, easily reached by Baslow Bus, and Castleton by train to Hope, (Castleton was often referred to as 'beyond Hope'), could, in summer, be overrun by youths seeking romantic or even sexual encounters - the caves and mines only being an excuse - and ideal, it has to be said -to chase someone of the opposite sex into long, dark galleries with plenty of discreet corners. The screams weren't always genuine cavers falling down shafts! The complex maze of mines at Alderley Edge, near Macclesfield in Cheshire, also had a reputation for this, though we never went there. We christened the ten a.m. Sunday train from Sheffield - 'the Sex Express'! Pete and Frank were not really that interested in such goings-on and had had little experience. I was two years older than them and, on the other hand, at twenty, had only recently terminated a four year relationship with a very beautiful girl, which could have concluded in marriage. However, she seemed to want to expand in one direction and I in another. Meeting and getting to know different people was quite common at weekends, bumping into them at the same frequented Hostels. Often they were from the Manchester side of the Pennines, and I wasn't averse to greeting a particular girl from Stockport with a warm embrace and a friendly kiss. She was called Beryl like my former girlfriend, but that's where the similarity ended.

Daphne and Valerie, having noted our caving gear, expressed a wish to go down a cave, and in the early evening we were happy to show them the delights of Suicide! We had pointed out that they were not properly dressed but that didn't seem to worry them. Very nice girls and well brought up, I would say - unlike some on the 'sex express'! The next day we walked them up Bradwell Dale and said goodbye as we had an appointment at Bagshaw Cavern.

Meanwhile, on this occasion with Terry, we had a look at Hal Tor Lead Mine at Winnats. Much of Derbyshire has shafts and adits relating to the lead mining that had gone on for centuries, even back to Roman times.

Although warranting extra caution, largely owing to rotting timbers, we spent many a happy hour exploring them. Some of them, including the intriguing but commercial Speedwell Mine nearby, broke into natural cave systems and if not for that particular one, the mighty Titan might never have been discovered.

Memory fails and details of the different caves that we explored merge into muddy crawls, difficult drops, ladder pitches, very wet streams - sometimes running down your neck-beautiful calcite formations, but above all, interest, humour and companionship.

Winnats Pass is a fairly rough road going between towering limestone bastions and in early times must have held a few terrors for travellers. It gave access to a direct route from Shefffield to Cheshire before the road under Mam Tor was built. Although less severe, this new road wound its way right beneath the open face of the 'shivering' mountain. Always prone to landslip and fissuring, in recent times the mountain demolished the road altogether, leaving travellers to cope with the gradient of Winnats Pass once more. At least the horse had been succeeded by more powerful horse power. For the moment, our caving activities had to be undertaken on foot or by public transport, which meant that a trip up Winnats and the subsequent drop down the Perryfoot depression could be up to two miles, depending on which cave was to be visited - and two miles back to get the bus at Castleton! A change of clothes, food and any equipment had to be carried over the top. Having garbed ourselves with helmets, headlamps, rope and boiler suits -fitted incidentally with car inner tubes around the lower legs and boot tops in an effort to stop water penetrating too easily- we felt ready to have another go at Giant's Hole! It was late November 1954. A month had slipped by since we had made our initial trip down Giant's. This time we were able to explore the West Passage, the East Chamber and the Stream Passage as far as feasible. Brian Gutteridge had by now made his mind up that caving wasn't for him, although he did often put in an appearance on our rambling and cycling trips.

The Youth Hostels were a real godsend, particularly Rowland Cote at Edale and Castleton Hall as they gave us a quick and early entrée into the caving area.

A week later, the Three Musketeers were at Castleton YH again and meeting friends - including Beryl. We had time to cook up a bit of grub in the Kitchen (always called the Self-Cookers) before hiking up Winnats and having another scramble down Suicide. On the Sunday we investigated any prospects in Bradwell Dale, then had a chat with an old watchman looking after a building site, warming ourselves around his coke brazier. It was November and very cold! Down the dale, it wasn't difficult to find Bradwell Dale Cave, the large entrance being easily reached from the road. We had a nice surprise, as, with it being winter and pretty wet, the muddy area at the back of the cave had been transformed into a beautifully atmospheric lake. This was the first troglodytic lake that we had seen - we were impressed. There was also a collection of stalactite formations but over the years these were vandalised - the price often paid with caves that were in easy reach of the general, and sometimes ignorant, public. We were all too aware how these calcitic formations had taken aeons to produce and in many cases were still growing. It was regarded as a terrible sin to break them.

On the way over from Castleton, we had stumbled on a small group of lads who were busily exploring a cave or mine adit near Hartle Moor. We attempted to engage them in conversation and perhaps swap a few caving notes but it soon became obvious that they really didn't want us there. On enquiring, they claimed to be the Sheffield Potholing Club, although we had never heard of such a group then and since. They were in contravention of unwritten caving code that suggested sharing of information in order to gain knowledge. We never had any problem with this concept when, on occasion, we bumped into groups from Derby, Nottingham or Manchester, examples being BSA, Pegasus and Orpheus. They were always friendly and helpful. It was a matter of mutual respect. This wasn't the case with these guys. Maybe they had a big secret to hide! They certainly weren't going to share it. Oddly enough they weren't very far from the as yet undiscovered Titan - but it certainly wasn't them that did find it! It wasn't done to interfere with other people's digs until they had finished with them and we would certainly have respected that too.

With all that attitude - and aggression - we had to label them as Yips, which was the name given to the type of young person that came to the Peak and brought their ignorance with them. An early form of Hippie, I suppose - but without any of the better attributes that some of that cult carried with them.

The following weekend found us at Ravenstor YH which although not as easy to get to on a Saturday afternoon as were Castleton and Edale-it not being on a bus or rail route- was still one of our favourite hostels. A beautiful mansion with a fine wooden staircase, it had vast views over Millers Dale and the surrounding pastures and woodland. These splendid buildings- Ilam Hall being another one- gave us an insight into how better appointed people than ourselves had lived. We were from very underprivileged backgrounds and I personally was brought up in relatively poor conditions during World War II.

I had met Pete and Frank in September 1953 and over the past year we had stretched our legs walking and cycling together. By now we knew our strengths and limitations. We would usually spend every weekend pushing our boundaries and I would often finish up on the following Monday hobbling through the steelworks and nursing my blisters. Later on we all saved up enough money to buy a decent pair of hiking boots!

This weekend wasn't untypical in that we had to walk four or five miles to the hostel and then the same back, with the deviation of exploring some valley or other in between. We also had to make sure that we caught the last bus back to Sheffield! We always managed this even though some Sunday evenings found us breaking into a crippling jog along an obscure Derbyshire lane in the pitch black.

Staying at Youth Hostels incurred having to do a 'duty', which in a way was a privilege. After all, the hostels gave us a chance to savour a new way of life and we also regarded them as 'ours'. We were not averse to sweeping up or washing down the members' kitchen but we were very happy when we were asked to cut wood or chop down a small tree! Ravenstor and Castleton were good for this as they both had associated land, Ravenstor's being a veritable woodland in our suburban experience.

So, on a cold misty morning in early December, we stood in front of the great house and plotted a cross-country route to Lathkill Dale, a Derbyshire jewel and one of our favourite haunts. Pete enjoyed map reading and I usually left it to him to fill in the details. Brian Gutteridge was with us but maintained his aversion to caving.

Walking down Millers Dale following the course of the River Wye to Bakewell was always a joy. The mills and workers' cottages of Litton and Cressbrook were now quiet and quaint, having finished their business long ago, and the noise of steam trains and machinery no longer impinged on the bucolic murmurings of the river, and wind rustling the leaves. Then the picturesque meanderings of the deliciously named Water-cum-Jolie with its turrets of white limestone and on to the beauties of Monsal Dale with its impressive rail viaduct, now silent.

But we were short-cutting - down to Taddington Dale where we were seduced into a quick game of kick-can - something that the increase in traffic would not now allow and then over the hill to Sheldon village and into the upper reaches of Lathkill.

We wanted to look at Ricklow Cave. This we found in Ricklow Quarry where in the past marble was quarried. The passages are short and blocked and the mine workings not to be interfered with! Further down the valley is Critchlow Cave, which in later years was pushed to three hundred feet, but was always tight and muddy. It has some formations but whether these have survived is pure conjecture on my part as I have never returned.

This top end of Lathkill is a dry valley but here that story ends. Across from Critchlow is Lathkill Head Cave which, especially at this time of year, becomes the resurgence of the River Lathkill. An enormous amount of water can at times burst from the wide mouth of the cave, having gathered its force from deep underground, and this day was no exception. This starts the river off in great style on its way to join our stately River Wye after it has passed through Bakewell. Soon after, the Wye joins the much broader River Derwent at Rowsley in Darley Dale and continues flowing South.

Anyone not suffering a physical disability or extreme claustrophobia can explore the first section of the cave in dry weather. After the six feet high entrance this quickly reduces to a stooping crawl over slabby rocks, not gentle on the knees or the head! 'The Wringer' is soon reached. This is where the entrance passage ends and drops to a lower level. The sight of water trying to bubble up the short rift in the floor is enough to encourage you to return quickly to the entrance! Given a period of dry weather, it's possible to drop down the Wringer and crawl along a surprisingly beautiful bedding plane. You are crawling as if on a beach, albeit a very narrow one! The roof, a few inches above your head, has been artistically wrought by the action of the water and the whole passage has a sense of purity about it. Unless you are lucky enough to have a person willing to sit out the time at the entrance watching out for a possible cloudburst, it's not a relaxing place to be, and even then it wouldn't be that easy to extricate oneself quickly. The system was explored to a length of 3,000 feet. After our days were finished there it attracted quite a few responsible caving groups. Parts of it were only viable after an extremely dry summer. We hobbled our way back to Bakewell to catch the bus home.

1955 had almost arrived. New Year's Day and the following Sunday found us doing one of our longer rambles, this time traversing the main body of the Peak District and back again. This was triangulated between three of our favourite places - Castleton, Buxton and Bakewell. A matter of eighteen miles as the crow flies, only our feet complained - we were happy wanderers. Holidays and festivals with family had been left well behind. Brian was again with us.

Christmas dinner, for instance, might well be dry biscuits on the top of a mountain in the Lake District or celebrated down some God forsaken hole in the bowels of the earth in Derbyshire. Having finally reached twentyone, I thought it time that I doffed my mother's good looks and started to look more like a man - so I started to grow a beard; I never shaved it off. Ten years earlier, nearing the end of the WWII I had rubbed shoulders with American airman in Nottingham - one of my cousins was a GI Bride. I decided that I would emulate them by giving myself a crew cut. There were times when I had more hair on my face than on my head. Romantic life having come to a halt with the straying of my beautiful sweetheart, I felt that I had to recreate myself and explore life and my potential rather more fully. Two and a half children wasn't really what I wanted. Beryl eventually had three but apparently did little else except carry on smoking, having a drink and watching TV. Chacun a son gout!

I had always had a talent for drawing and I began to be more interested in the possibilities of developing in this direction; I bought some art materials.

But back to our long walk.

We missed the 6.15p.m.bus to Castleton on New Year's Eve so this meant that we had to pay the single fare of two shillings and three pence and catch the 6.55 train to Hope, (which lies at the end of Edale valley), and then walk the mile and a half to the Youth Hostel. My diary reminds me that Castleton and its hostel are very dead. A cold hard bed and a walk to match obviously not being everyone's idea of bringing in the New Year. I tried to cheer things up a little by giving the boys my rendering of Home Sweet Home on my harmonica - but it didn't help.

Castleton is famous for its show caves, the largest being Peak Cavern. The entrance is a huge hundred feet wide by sixty feet high and is set in a perpendicular limestone cliff. Inside it stretches for two and a half miles. Sitting on the cliff nearby is the ruined Peveril Castle.

The back of the castle overlooks Cave Dale; this is only a hundred yards or so from the hostel and was the beginning of our route. This discreet narrow valley (it is so discreet, in fact, that it is not named on the one inch Ordnance Survey map), provides an easy access to this part of the White Peak -although we never called it that. We made for Eldon Hill, crossing Hurd Low, and in so doing it is now obvious that we probably walked right over Titan itself! If only we had known!

We dropped down into Peak Forest, which barely has a tree let alone a forest. Although a village with a church, and sitting on the Stoney Middleton/Sparrowpit road, it always, to me, seemed to be in the middle of nowhere. But it did have a pub - and we celebrated the New Year with a rum and peppermint. Each, that is; we weren't that hard up.

The Romans crossed over these parts but not the way we were going. Dam Dale, Hay Dale, and Peter Dale are conjoined valleys heading due South for almost three miles and have a wild romantic aspect. Although dry valleys, they can still occasionally be slippy underfoot and they are probably best avoided in wet weather. Eventually the problematic path drops into Monks Dale, and carrying on the romantic aspect into the wooded river valley of Millers Dale, leads on to our beloved Ravenstor.

But we are heading for Buxton so we turn west and find ourselves in a completely different landscape. This one has been blasted apart. Great Rocks Dale is virtually a limestone quarry two miles in length. Everything is white, including the trees, and the area has been massively quarried and transformed in the gaining of this useful and valuable commodity.

We are soon in Buxton and happily ensconced in Sherbrook Lodge, the Youth Hostel, where Pete gives us a tune on the piano. Yes! Pete plays the piano! He tunes them for a living in fact and is to follow an assiduous course for the next few years until he himself becomes a teacher - albeit in New Zealand! For the moment he is happy to teach me how to play 'Chopsticks' so that I can accompany him! Yes - many a quiet Derbyshire pub has been livened up with our musical extravaganzas.

At 1000 feet above sea level, Buxton is the highest market town in England. Chatting to two local old timers they were keen to reveal that snow once fell during a cricket match in July! It also has a grand pavilion for hosting festivals and the like, and a crescent in the Doric style that puts one in mind of Bath, that other great spa town.

I told you that the Romans were around here somewhere! They certainly came to Buxton. Attracted as so often by thermal springs, they built their baths which, after neglect, were rebuilt in the 16th. century. They named the town Aquae Arnemetiae. You can drink the therapeutic waters in the Pump Room - rather you than me.

The next day was Sunday, 2nd. January 1955 and we wanted to investigate Deep Dale, which although only two miles away, left us with another eight miles to do to reach Bakewell and the bus home.

It had been snowing but not too heavily - just enough to give a bit of contrast to the beautiful landscape we were walking through. Duke's Drive was probably built by one of the Dukes of Devonshire; why Devonshire and not Derbyshire? Consult the history books! This gave us a direct route out from the Youth Hostel, having said our goodbyes to friends heading off in other directions. The boys quickly made a new friend in a large pig that wanted them to warm up its ears.

Deep Dale is yet another of those exquisite dry limestone valleys that abound in the White Peak. You don't have to be a caver to enter the large, very obvious entrance that sits halfway up the valley wall. Archeologically researched as long ago at least as the nineteenth century by the early pioneers, it, like many of the other rock shelters has given up its trove of animal bones - some exotic - and particularly in the case of Cresswell Crags - human bones. Sitting there, it's not too difficult to transport yourself back a few millennia.

Climbing out, we are quickly into the village of Chelmorton, which has row after row of white stonewalls outlining the ancient mediaeval field system, probably after deforestation had taken place. Certainly this relatively upland area between the villages of Monyash, Flagg and Sheldon can seem fairly bleak, especially as it is snowing again and the light is fading fast. Sheldon is on our route, that is after crossing yet another Deep Dale - this time with no caves but plenty of mining for lead that had gone on in the distant past.. We reach Bakewell and shiver in the cold until the bus arrives. The snow continues for weeks and is the worst for thirty years. It still lies thick on the ground in Derbyshire until the middle of March.

The next week was spent between walking the two miles to work, the deepening snow having brought all transport to a halt, and then spending a couple of days in bed with one of my special chest colds.

I had by now woken up to the fact that I really needed a better camera than the one that my father had been given by some relative or other. My acquisition was strictly governed by the fact that I had little money and was loathe to spend what I had.

A Kodak 127, which had a plastic body, a separate yellow filter and a screw-on close-up lens was about the cheapest camera on the market - but it worked!

I am essentially isolating here the interest that we had generated in exploring caves and the surrounding limestone areas, but it's necessary to point out that we were concurrently rambling into other areas of more mountainous aspect, which included sorties into the English Lake District and Wales. Also we were keen cyclists and spent many weekends and holidays eating up miles of road. Watch this space!

The snow continued and this for the time being put an end to our caving activities. Undeterred however, we continued to trudge and flounder through the Derbyshire snowdrifts of the first three months of 1955.

The photographs that I took on the 13th of March that year show why we couldn't get to do any caving at that time - the entrances were well and truly snowed up and high levels of water in the systems due to melting snow would have increased the danger factor.

This didn't stop us catching the 'Sex Express' to Hope yet again and walking on to Castleton via the field path. Up the secretive Cave Dale again and on to the tops above Castleton.

Nettle Pot is on our way but isn't easy to locate unless you know. Quite an extensive system, it was first explored in 1934 by the Derbyshire Pennine Club and is far from being straight forward, the first sixty feet being very tight and probably impossible to effect a rescue should this become necessary. It contains a 170 feet natural pitch - previously the longest in Derbyshire, but not now! Moving on we pass Frog Hole near one of the many old abandoned quarries. Nothing to write home about and, as is the fate of many holes in the ground, a depository for rubbish. Over Eldon Hill and we drop into Perry Dale and the Castleton to

Buxton road at Perryfoot. Here we are on familiar ground with Gautries Hole, Bull Pit, Giant's Hole and the neighbouring swallets looking attractive in their snowy mantles. Over Windy Knoll, past the famous Blue John Cavern (Treak Cliff) with its rare deposits and fabulous view down Hope Valley and finally, at the impressive fissure that is Odin Mine. An ancient mine, it has long been unsafe and probably best left alone, although it has been explored. There are also two caves nearby that have chambers and are relatively safe.

And so to Castleton and the bus home.

The DSG Story
(Derbyshire Speleological Group)

The extreme weather had, for the time being, been responsible for the abandonment of our caving forays. By the 2nd. of April, it had at last improved enough to make our first cycle run of 1955. We were as happy cycling as we were caving and rambling, which is probably why we were not obsessively devoted to any of them.

23. The Three Musketeers - "They're off!!"

As often, a Youth Hostel was our venue, this time York.
Brian Gutteridge had decided to come along and I must say that we often had to stop and wait for him as he didn't seem to have the energy that we had, and his bicycle wasn't the cutest thing on the road.
At the Hostel, we were astonished to see the walls of the dining room decorated with the most amazing photographs of caves. We were even more astonished when we realised that we looking into the bowels of none other than Peak Cavern itself! Cycling obviously wasn't going to keep us away from the mysterious underworld!
The Vale of York is as flat as the proverbial pancake and as far as I knew had no connection with caving whatsoever, so it was all the more surprising to see the Wonder of the Peak just where we weren't expecting it.

A bespectacled, rather plump fellow had noted our interest.
"Hi, lads. I'm Tony. What you're looking at are photos taken by Ron Frost of the DSG."
"DSG?" I queried.
"Derbyshire Speleological Group - Speleology - stuff about caving?"
"Yeah - I've read a couple of books. We've been doing a bit ourselves - we're from Sheffield."

"Well, you're laughing then, lads - Ron Frost lives at Darnall." He wrote down the address. "I don't get down there much these days but if you're interested like that, why don't you look him up - he'd be delighted to see you. Tell Ron I sent you! Join the DSG!"

On our return, we did just that.

A year earlier, almost to the day, we had joined the FYR - the Fellowship of Young Ramblers. We were not keen on the name as by now we didn't regard ourselves as being that young, but after consideration, we thought that the FYR might be a bit more adventurous - and fun- than the Rambler's Association (RA), whom we suspected might be rather too staid for our taste - although we did have the occasional meet with them. The three men who ran the FYR were intelligent, humorous, knowledgeable and approachable and we had many happy outings with the club. They also ran a clubhouse - a Nissan hut (how useful did they prove to be after the war!).

On the outskirts of the town, it was just a quick bike ride away and we made many friends there - but we were always the Three Musketeers! Just a bit separate and a bit different.

We found Ron Frost to be a great personality, a talented photographer, a great pioneer caver and he had to be regarded as an honourable man. We perceived, however, that his former, more adventurous life had by now escaped him. He worked for the English Steel Corporation, as many did in Sheffield, but as a machine worker, perhaps on a lathe, he had had the misfortune to lose an eye. He was always accompanied on our jaunts by Terri Rains, his constant female companion and, incidentally, club secretary. She was soon to disclose how the loss had effected his self confidence, not only in caving but also in rock climbing. The boys and I were quick to see that the great days of opening up places like Peak Cavern had gone and Ron, now in his early forties, was not the dynamo that he had once been. But he was still highly respected and I suspect that what he had lost in activity, he had gained in intellect. I always assumed that what he didn't know about British caves and especially Derbyshire caves wasn't worth knowing. I also assumed that he must have read every available book on Derbyshire geology, and possibly that of Yorkshire too. How the references that led to the discovery of Titan escaped him, I shall never know.

We learnt things from him. Essentially where caves and swallets might be located, often in places that we would never have discovered for ourselves. We also learnt words like 'vadose' - common in caving parlance but not in the Oxford Dictionary, and 'phreatic', which was.

Whilst wading through some underground passage up to our hips in water, Frank would relish in his new found knowledge.

"It's phreatic, Vic,vic, - phreatic".

"You're dead right, Frank,frank"; me trying to stay on two feet as I couldn't swim and didn't like water. Pete would chuckle –"It's bloody freezing".

Vadose was a lot easier - dry passages, often in the roof of a system, with the stream passage far below and stalactite formations above.

Around at Bray Street in Darnall, Ron, because there was no other way, lived with his parents and a huge old Alsatian dog. There we joined the DSG. Ron was delighted to hear that we had met Tony. Ron loved to tell caving stories and we were immediately regaled with how they had feared for Tony in the bowels of Peak Cavern one particular trip, as he had failed to show up as expected. Later, to their relief, he was seen hanging on the end of a rope, high up in an aven, spinning gently, and explaining in his high-pitched voice, that he had gone back to the village for one of his beloved meat pies - that he was now consuming whilst hanging on with the other hand!

We were treated to other stories - such as 'Wobblegob' Simpson, who never stopped talking - even in a constricted tube, and then, more brilliant photos of Peak Cavern.

Realising that there were further passages beyond the Show Cave area and expressing our amazement, Ron was quick to point out, with his characteristic throw away laugh that they were – "big enough to drive a bus down". We were intrigued to see how areas of large passageways or chambers could be lit up by judicious placement of magnesium powder and ribbon, which when ignited gave off a brilliant white light and revealed far perspectives that the camera lens would otherwise have been unable to probe. Unfortunately we didn't even have a camera worthy enough to take underground but we did play around with magnesium ribbon just for the hell of it. Our main toy was the acetylene lamp. Early road users, cyclists, motorists etc. would have been well acquainted with such a device that would light up the road ahead. The cavers' version was a two-part metal container with a dish reflector, fitted on to the front of the helmet. The bottom part of the container was filled with acetylene powder and the top part with water. A lever on the top regulated the water, which dripped onto the powder creating acetylene gas. This fed through a small nozzle on the face of the reflector. This had the same flint gadget that an ordinary cigarette lighter had. Flicking it with the thumb often had no effect - the fun and very effective thing was to cover the dish with the hand until a quantity of gas had built up - then strike down! The resulting bang and shooting flame was part of the thrill and charisma of caving. In contrast, we would sometimes extinguish all lights - first making sure that at least one of us had water and powder in the can! - then sit in the complete darkness and silence - an experience that is probably not possible in any other circumstances where there is usually some light, the eye having a miraculous ability to detect it. Not here! The 'drip' had then to be turned down if the flame was to last for the whole trip - sometimes a matter of hours.

Ron suggested that we make our way to Buxton at the weekend in order to meet one or two other members and maybe look at some swallets in the area.

On the Saturday, Sherbrook Lodge the YH at Buxton, once more proved invaluable.

The next day we met up with Ron and he introduced us to Terri his long-term lady friend, and John Larsen and his family; his wife Joan, and two pretty blond children. They arrived on motor bikes. Ron and Terri with BSA bantams, popular two-strokes of the time, and John and family on an ageing sidecar combo.

We arranged to meet at Ladmanlow, a road junction about a mile away on the South side of town, near Poole's Cavern, another famous show cave. From there a short track led us on to Stanley Moor and its reservoir. This lies between Axe Edge, the gritstone heights that carry the Macclesfield Road, and to the East, Grin Low and Anthony Hill. Again, water runs off the more impermeable ground of these hills and collects in the declivities of the limestone below the reservoir. The streams formed burrow their way into the unconformity of the rock creating passageways into it, called, hereabouts anyway, - swallets. Not too different then from Castleton and its swallets at Perryfoot.

Ron pointed out the main one, aptly named Stanley Moor Swallet, closely followed by Plunge Hole, and then 'shakeholes' in the area- declivities in the ground, rather like old shell holes, where possible caves, or mines, had collapsed. Nearby was 'Jimmy Putrell's Hole'. Jimmy, apparently, was an early explorer and with a name like that we agreed that one day soon, we would do him the honour.

Penetrating Stanley Moor Swallet wasn't easy as the entrance was quite restricted and the small stream of water, one of the many issues from the dam close by, could not be avoided, usually trickling down your neck. Not extensive, but the sloping chamber gave a good close-up view of some fine straw stalactites, many discoloured by the rust deposits at the dam. The area was of interest to other caving clubs -we bumped into Orpheus more than once- the thought being that it might be possible to forge a link with Poole's Cavern in Buxton. Water certainly ran underground into it from Stanley Moor. Plunge Hole nearby looked good, despite the front bumper of a lorry wedged into the entrance pitch! In 1992, I re-visited it with Bernadette, my long-term partner.

The bumper had been replaced with a concrete platform and the system had been extended - but not to Buxton!

I suppose it being the mid fifties, we could be regarded as the early middle generation of cave explorers- there certainly had been plenty of activity with the early pioneers, but I suspect that the heavy loss of young men in the two war periods delayed interest.

24. Camping on Stanley Moor – Buxton.
22nd May 1955

Certainly after us there was a big expansion in the science and sport - cave diving for instance opening up many systems where water sumps had denied entry. This was serious stuff and we weren't about to take too many chances ourselves.

We were pleased to meet John Larsen and his family. As his name suggests, he was of Scandinavian extraction; meeting his ageing, but characterful father later, this was confirmed, as we struggled to understand him. We liked his father enormously, but to be honest, John was a bit of a show-off. On this occasion Ron had to admonish him for climbing above Frank whilst our beloved brother was attempting to delve into the bowels of Plunge Hole. A dislodged boulder could have proved extremely dangerous.

So, whilst it wasn't hard, at the moment, to believe that Ron was the Chairman of any meetings of the Derbyshire Cave Rescue Organisation, credibility was a bit stretched to discover that John was the Treasurer!

The following weekend, The Three Merry Lads from Sheffield were once more ensconced early in Castleton YH. A meeting of the DCRO had been convened at the Bull's Head in the village, and thirty cavers had gathered, overviewed by the Committee, headed by Ron, John, and a secretary that we didn't know. Actually, we didn't know anybody else either, as this was the first meeting that we had attended. It was of great interest to us, as we listened to accounts of new discoveries, abortive digs, pitches with psychological belays, unexpected dunkings in underground lakes and then someone being heavily chastised for frightening tourists by unravelling ropes in the show cave part of Poole's Cavern!

Ron introduced us to Brian Edey. Then seventeen, and keen on caving, Brian was very happy to make our acquaintance.

The next morning, the DCRO had arranged a practice cave rescue. This was at Bagshaw Cavern in Bradwell Dale. Bagshaw was privately owned and therefore couldn't just be walked into, although the family were generous enough in opening to school parties etc. It had a history dating back to the early lead mining era at the very beginning of the 19th century and extended to a length of three kilometres. Not to be out of the limelight, John volunteered to be the 'rescued', which in this case was more like being 'the victim'! Being tied in a stretcher and carried along by four people underground isn't easy but, in this case, Bagshaw's passages are so wide at this level that it wasn't too demanding. On the way back passing the' Dungeon', a huge eighteen foot hole in the passage floor, John was quick to urge caution! God help us if a rescue had to be effected in narrow constricted conditions.

This was the first time that we had been underground with Ron and we were quite astonished that he eschewed a helmet, preferring his usual flat cap! Hardly a good example to set but then - he was a legend. He didn't wear a helmet whilst riding his Bantam either (although Terri did). It wasn't compulsory at that time but when we three acquired motorcycles our heads were not found wanting. Whilst he wasn't looking, we mentioned the oversight to Terri.

"Oh. Never has done - can't get on with helmets."

We had quickly learnt the hard way that banging your head on the cave roof could become a painful second nature, but then perhaps legends didn't do that.

Into the daylight and eventually the group dispersed. For the rest of the day, Brian Edey tagged along with us and we walked the four miles to Eyam, the village that contracted the plague and bravely cut itself off from the world and now attracts tourists. Dropping down the valley, we arrived at Stoney Middleton, where Carlswark Caverns attract the passengers of the 'Sex Express'! Despite this, it is a serious system that spreads itself extensively under the wooded cliffs of Middleton Dale. Again, it is associated with early mining activity. The small village of Calver is one of the many places where 'soughs' (pronounced 'suffs') were excavated. These were long, deep ditches that were intended to lower the water levels in the lead mines. They didn't always work as the mines often went deeper, some becoming inoperable because of the flooding. We catch our bus home at Calver.

The next Saturday and we are on the 3.15pm bus to Buxton, Frank as a butcher's mate having to scrub up early in order to catch it. Not for the first (or the last) time, we were accompanied by a selection of likely lads who had no interest in caving but still caught the same buses as we did and headed for the same hostels. Barry, Buddy, John etc. were just some of the

Sheffield lads who teamed up to tramp the Derbyshire hills rather than jive at the City Hall and we always got on well with them.

Pete was the one who made friends easiest. I had always suffered from a chronic shyness with people and it wasn't until my mid-twenties, after I had moved to St Ives in Cornwall, that I started to recover from this social stigma. In fact, Pete was really good at finding things out, so to speak. He would often stop and talk to men working, or anglers on the riverbank, for instance.

"Ah they a bytin' er terdai, mate? Ah yer cawt ani eh?"

Frank and I would look at each other.

"Why is he talking like that, Frank?"

"Don't know, Vic. He thinks that they'll understand him better".

"Better than what, Frank? Speaking plain English?"

"Well, it's like - er - talking their language, like".

"They don't talk like that do they? Most of them are from Sheffield".

"Well, 'spose not- but he always seems to get on alreyt wi' people".

"Where did he learn that funny accent, Frank?"

"Well, he does sometimes talk about having holidays when he was young -at Dog Dyke - in Lincolnshire. He said he was allowed to drive a tractor across the fields".

"Is that a Lincolnshire accent then, Frank?"

"Don't know, Vic,Vic- probably not but it seems to work."

"They've caught nowt" said Pete.

The next, morning, we were expecting some of the DSG to turn up, well, at least two - but no. In the modern world of today- it's just a text or a quick word on the mobile, but in those days, it was guesswork.

Once more, on Stanley Moor. Orpheus Caving Club were laying out some gear on the grass and Pete was communicating in what he thought was a Manchester accent. "He's doing it again, Frank, frank." "What did they say, Pete?" "Don't know - they talk a bit funny". It wouldn't have done to clutter up the area, especially as there was also another group camping there - namely 'The Idle Bergers'. "Are you sure you got the name right, Pete?"

We had Brian Edey with us and we decided to explore the 'shakeholes' around Anthony Hill. Not having any success, we climbed up to the folly known as Solomon's Temple, on Grin Low, in order to have a bird's eye view of the surrounding landscape. The hills of Upper Dove

25 Frank, Brian Edey, Pete. Stanley Moor 22 May 1955

Dale looked inviting and we were soon to have a closer look.

Still having plenty of time before having to catch the 8.30p.m. bus home, we sported a shilling each and descended the show cave of Poole's Cavern. My diary says that it was 'very good' but I have to admit that I can't now remember anything about it. In fact, if you told me that I had never been down Poole's Cavern - I would believe you.

Brian Edey was a reasonable companion, mainly because he was committed and also brought ideas along with him. One of his ideas was that we should meet, just we four, at the Blue Boar, which was situated at West Bar in the town. Here, for a period that lasted just a few weeks, we would have a pint and listen to a small band playing live trad jazz on Friday nights. My musical appreciation had been grossly neglected and had been reduced to listening to Jack Jackson, an early DJ, and Radio Luxembourg, on late Saturday night radio - I wasn't a drinker either. It was a lively venue and proceedings became even livelier when the local 'bobby' dropped in (as he always did), looking for underage drinkers and any other trouble. Edey, being seventeen was, to be accurate, an underage drinker. It was fun watching him trying to shrink from view in the crowded smoky pub - not easy, as he had sprung a surprise on us by bringing along his girl friend, Janet. She was underage too. It wouldn't have been too bad if she had been a looker, or interesting in some way but, I'm afraid, she was quite the opposite. The pub wasn't too far from the University and the noisy students provided most of the clientele. We were never quite sure about Edey as we knew nothing of his background (apart from his boring girlfriend). We thought he might have had university connections as he certainly wasn't dim; he would waffle on about being an existentialist, but as far as I could ascertain, his interpretation of this seemed to be not bothering with too many rules, such as trespass, and drinking in pubs, and then wherever possible, putting his feet up on the table and having a smoke.

This didn't go down too well in Youth Hostels where it wasn't allowed, but he had his points. These sessions didn't last for many weeks as 'we three' were not drinkers or smokers and as it happened, we weren't too fond of university students either. We would often have to share space with them at the Hostels and we usually found them rather fatuous and their behaviour generally irritating.
We were the serious students of the Nature that surrounded us and we were completely engrossed and dedicated.

Midweek we called in on Ron Frost and he showed us more of his amazing collection of cave photos.

Pete had revealed that they both had to work on the Saturday morning. This wasn't unusual and I arranged to meet them at Matlock, late Saturday afternoon, where I thought to surprise them with yet another of my progressive ideas.

As it was Easter and I had extra days off -the steelworks shut down to give the guys a rest- I was getting itchy feet and felt like wandering off, albeit on my own. Sometime later, Pete talked of how different it was, just being alone in the landscape and having to make singular decisions with no one to confer with. I did have a loner streak in me, so this wasn't exactly a new experience for me.
Friday and I caught the 6.25pm bus to Bakewell - cost: one shilling and nine pence. From there I got the bus to Matlock - cost: one shilling and one penny. As the sun began to dip, I walked on to Matlock Bath and then up into the woods of the Heights of Abraham. It was getting late and I was looking around for a barn, perhaps, where unwritten law stated that travellers could lay down their heads for the night. Not all farmers had, unfortunately, heard of this law, so one had to be a bit careful. There was no barn to be had but walking along a back lane, I came across piles of hay in an open shed in an allotment- so there I made my bed. Cocks crowed early and woke me up. Not wanting to be compromised by some early gardener out picking rhubarb with the dew on it, I fell out of the shed and stumbled along the lane. 5.00 a.m. was far too early to start rambling and I figured the Lord came to help as the spire of Bonsall church came into view. The benches were hard but I thought that I could hardly be thrown out or arrested!
The sun broke through the early mist and I was off on my adventure. I made my way to Cromford and then up onto the dizzy heights of Black Rocks, above the oddly named Via Gellia, with its strange house looking a bit like something out of Hansel and Gretel. I researched this later. Apparently, a local lead mine owner called Philip Gell had built the road in order to facilitate access to the smelting works and canal at Cromford. The name he gave to it referred not only to himself, but to possible connections that he thought he might have with the Romans - well, of course!
The house was made of tufa! A mite unusual I feel, and it looked it. Tufa is a spongy form of limestone that can popularly be seen at so called 'dropping wells' where sedimentary deposits

coat placed objects and – "turns them to stone - ee' by gum!" There is a famous one at Knaresboro' in Yorkshire viz 'Mother Shipton's Well'.

Ron had mentioned Ball Eye Mine and I could locate this from my elevated viewpoint on Black Rocks, but I thought perhaps I had pushed enough luck as regards trespass. I'd better wait for the master.

I dropped down through lonely woods on the way back to Matlock Bath, where I had arranged to meet Brian Edey at 12.30 p.m. I had seen hardly anybody all morning.

Being alone in woods never bothered me. I liked to commune with nature- so to speak. I was soon shaken out of my reverie, however. I had been surprised to see a rail line running through the trees - I crossed over it and then was even more surprised to hear a great clattering from above my position - and then - a huge open metal wagon burst from the undergrowth and thundered past me at great speed. Well, no level crossing there then, or even any warning signs - but then I wasn't on a road or a path even. I suppose the noise would have warned me in time, but I thought it decidedly scary. Wandering loose can have its risks!

More research. My stretch of line was part of the ramifications of the Cromford and High Peak Railway, which was built to carry limestone from the quarries as far away as Parsley Hay and the Buxton area. It was built as an alternative to extending the Cromford Canal. This was thought to be far too expensive and difficult.

In 1967, the railway was abandoned and converted into what is now the High Peak Trail. They could have found a squashed Bramley in the woods and I'm not talking about an apple.

Edey turned up like a bad penny and after having a 'drink and a bite' in the fleshpots of Matlock Bath we spent the rest of the afternoon searching out Romantic Rocks cave and mine, though now, as I write this, fiftysix years later, I remember nothing of it. Oh! Fickle memory! Pete and Frank arrived on the 5.00 p.m. bus.

I had summarily explored the abandoned buildings on the Heights of Abraham. I concluded that the large edifice which I assumed was once the dance hall that would have been connected to the gay high life of say thirty or forty years ago- when the spa was at its height- would make a good place to sleep out. The fact that we would have a roof over our heads would make it even more appealing should it rain.

We walked steeply up into the woods and the lads were not a little surprised to see this once rather grand building apparently standing desolate and decaying. Some of the windows were gone and the door was open, but at least the walls were standing and, apart from a few leaks, the roof was still where it should be. Exploring the floor above wasn't really recommended.

One could easily imagine finely dressed folk alighting, maybe, from horse drawn carriages, in the forecourt. At the moment it was a free car park.

Sleeping out was our only alternative should there not be a Youth Hostel in the area. It did give us a sense of independence and not a little sense of adventure and, not to be taken lightly, a sense of being oneself and not being cradled in the bosom of the family. Why not camping? Well, for the moment, I didn't even have enough cash to buy a decent pair of hiking boots and neither did the lads. This state of affairs was, by a stroke of fortune to change very soon.

The next morning, Sunday, as arranged, we met the Bantam-borne Ron and Terri at Ball Eye Mine at Via Gellia. Some of the easier levels of the mine could be walked into and as we had no caving equipment with us (except a flashlight) we had to settle for that. The system is extensive and involves natural caverns as so many lead mines did. Owing to its proximity to the quarry, much of it is unsafe. Ron seemed to be more interested in whether the quarry hut had been left open as apparently, this was the easiest way of acquiring a bit of 'Nobel's

Hammer' should a bit of persuasion be required on a stubborn cave passage. Stealing justified, of course, in the name of scientific research! Nobel would have been proud of us.

References suggest that the skeleton of an elephant (not from a circus) was discovered in one of the natural cave parts of the mine and also that silver was extracted from the galena deposits.

Ron and Terri liked tea and buns in little cafes, so whilst they rode back to Matlock Bath, we walked.
Bakewell was our destination for the Sheffield bus and this was seven miles away, but we may have picked up a bus from Matlock. My feet always told the tale.

Over the last four years I had graduated in my job at the steelworks from being an office boy at £2.50 shillings a week to a Progress Clerk at £8 a week. Pete had splashed out £5 and bought a pair of Beva Boots - an early edition of a boot made specifically for rambling - with Vibram soles! He was keen to show us how waterproof they were by standing in a stream! We were suitably impressed and got fitted. I was glad to reduce my blisters by at least a half! But, of course, they weren't for caving. Caving Boots had to have holes in order for the water to run out! My diary also reports that I had put a £1 deposit on a tent: earlier in the year, the FYR had entrusted me with the job of buying a tent out of the club subs and looking after it. It was to be rented out to members for a small fee. This only happened once as we were the only members who were interested in camping anyway - that's why I got the job. I nipped down to the YHA shop and spent £5.7 shillings and sixpence on a tent called 'Viking'.

The combination of Buxton YH and Stanley Moor proved to be somewhat irresistible however and the following weekend we were there again, Edey tagging along. We had another good look down the main swallet - getting pretty wet in the process. Ron and Terri and two mates of Brian's put in an appearance later. We weren't expecting, by now, to see Ron or Terri get wet. They were very much in their comfort zone. Ron could rest on his ample laurels.

The same venue on the next weekend but this time we camped. The Wednesday previous had been recorded as the worst day in May for many years - snow having fallen heavily in the Peak District. Happily, most of it had cleared and the weather brightened by the time we arrived at Stanley Moor. Stripping down into caving gear and then getting wet through wasn't too exciting in the best weather, let alone in freezing conditions. Ah! Dedication! I had scraped up the money to pay for my tent. Pete took the loan of the FYR'S' in his stride and Frank had always had a tent. Well, I say tent. It was made of some heavy dense fabric that managed to keep out all of the existing light. It would have served well in the Crimean War.
"Frankie - are you in there?" Pulling back the heavy flap.
"Of course, I'm bloody in here - where else would I be?"
"Oh -sorry Frank - I couldn't see you". Dodge the flying boot.

Orpheus were down the swallet on the Sunday. Ron arrived with Terri and the Larsens - John's ageing father, Jimmy, handling the old sidecar combo with great aplomb in the ruts of the ancient track.
Ron showed us where another Jimmy, Jimmy Puttrell had laid claim to a hole he had discovered just across the moor. Puttrell was an early pioneer of the Derbyshire Peak, when it was a lot wilder than it is now. In those days, places like Kinder Scout were best avoided. It wasn't difficult to get lost and there were wanderers who had died from exposure or from the

results of injuring themselves. It wasn't unknown to also get shot at by a gamekeeper! The mass trespass of 1933 put an end to that but people still got lost!

27. *My beard but not my hat!*

26. Terry Phoenix, Me, Pete and Frank outside the Barrel Inn at Bretton 1954.

The Forestry Commission

It was August 1956. Roger, a young friend, had mentioned that he had worked for a short period for the Forestry Commission at Wharncliffe Side, on the outskirts of the City. The pay was not good and he was now bricklaying.

I needed some fresh air into my damaged lungs and it sounded good enough for me. I rolled out my trusty DOT motorcycle and soon found my way there. It was hardly a forest, more a well-wooded escarpment, an outlier of the great Derbyshire gritstone edges of the Peak District.

The main Langsett road, passing through Oughtibridge, heading for Barnsley and the North ran along the valley bottom, as did the great River Don. The railway from Wadsley Bridge actually ran along the bottom of the wood and although not a main line it could prove a fire hazard due to flying sparks.

I took the track into the woods and found the centre of operations. It was a farm that had been taken over by the FC. The forester's small manufactured office had been deposited in the yard. Mr. Bowns, the Forester, was generally serious but friendly enough. He enquired whether I had any experience. Roger anticipating the question, had told me to mention that I had done a bit of gardening! This obviously didn't impress him so I admitted that I had come straight from the steelworks but added that I had an outdoor background of mountaineering, potholing and rock climbing. He didn't think any of that would be of any particular use but he took me on anyway, at the very minimal wage of £4 a week - Saturdays off.

I liked the guy, smart in his uniform and brass insignia; he presented a figure of authority - someone that you could respect.

My caving and travelling friend, Frank Wicken, had by now also received the news and had given up his butchering career to join me.

The following Monday we duly arrived at the farm and met the rest of the lads. All young and ardent except for a more mature man, who I soon found out didn't much like work and spent most of the time grumbling about the basic pay and conditions. We suggested that he ought to go back to Sheffield.

George, the most experienced of the bunch, was benign and we were soon learning how to fell a tree the correct way, how to clear a patch of ground, dig a ditch, and erect a pyramid of unwanted trees, branches and undergrowth and then burn it.

We liked George. He was never lost for an entertaining insight into human nature. He also liked to probe into our immature sexuality, he having lived with a woman! "Have you not yet had a soapy wrestle with a naked girl, Vic?"

"Er - no."

"Oh, dear!"

I explained that getting the tin bath out might be a problem.

Essentially, we were there to do Mr. Bowns's bidding, although George sometimes questioned it. Our main purpose was to clear the ground of old unwanted trees, also acres of fern and undergrowth, in preparation for the planting of fresh young trees that were only a foot or so high and were delivered to the farm in boxes. Many were Corsican Pine, a fast-growing, hardy tree that gave off a wonderful scent when the boxes were opened.

Sickles, billhooks and sometimes scythes were used for ground clearance.

We enjoyed many a huge bonfire, especially on a freezing cold morning.

We were usually dropped off in the Land Rover at our particular station and there more or less left to our own devices, as Mr.Bowns rarely worked with us. He would usually be snowed under with paperwork in his little office. Sometimes we would be snowed under in reality and in case of rain, we had the use of a large canvas that we would throw over convenient branches to form a shelter. From there we would spend the time sharpening our tools, telling stories, eating, and identifying the bird life that gathered looking for crumbs.

If the weather worsened we would be called down to the farm, sometimes having to walk. We would then usually be employed making fire beaters. These consisted of long poles that we had to fashion from the raw product. A square wire frame was fashioned at the top and this was then enclosed in sacking. The results of this labour were placed in strategic positions around the forest tracks, which, of course, we had to maintain. On two occasions I was to witness their efficiency. The public were allowed to walk the tracks and so technically were a fire risk. In our case, there was also the even greater risk from the railway, mainly, as I said, from flying sparks.

One bright morning, a fire had been reported at the far end of the forest and Mr. Bowns lost no time at all in rounding us up. Breaking the rules of the road and pushed on by the sight of smoke rising in the distance, we sped off down the highway. Finally swerving into the forest precincts, we piled out.

"One day he'll break our bloody necks with his driving" muttered George.

The fire had taken hold but, thanks to clearance along the railway line, it was being somewhat starved of ready fuel, and thanks to our indulgence at the farm, nearby fire beaters were standing ready in their stocks.

We surrounded the fire and moved in a circle, as recommended in the text books. It seemed reminiscent of some Red Indian warring party surrounding the settlers encampment. Bashing the flames furiously, we soon brought the fire under control, much to the Forester's delight. Burning down Oughtibridge, Wharncliffe and the nearby Sheffield Wednesday football ground would not have looked good in his weekly report. It was exciting and, dare I say - a lot of fun.

The second occasion wasn't so funny and was personal!

The layout of the ground at Wharncliffe started with the main road, the railway and the river, which ran along the bottom edge of the forest. Beyond that was an area of soft, low-lying ground. This gradually rose steeply into the forested area until it reached the escarpment edge, culminating in an eighty foot gritstone ridge at the NW end. Needless to say we climbed this in our spare time! Beyond the escarpment was an area of planted, mature trees and then a very large plateau of scrub, fern and native trees that ultimately had to be cleared for further planting.

The rising ground was notorious for harbouring submerged rocks which had, over the years, fallen from the escarpment. Banging a planting spade into this area would often meet with a sudden, jarring resistance. Being rather delicately made, it wasn't long before this particular duty had the effect of giving me a strong dose of synovitis, whereby the wrist swells up in a painful manner, due, of course, to the sudden reoccurring impacts.

I was relegated from the available piece work rate of steep planting to the softer and sometimes boggy work in the valley bottom. This came under the standard wage of £4 a week.

My synovitis didn't diminish and I was eventually summoned to the farm. Here I was given the job of soaking the bottom ends of fire-beaters in creosote. This was intended to stop the poles rotting when placed in their wooden stands by the forest tracks. I had to place the beaters in a metal drum that contained a foot or so of creosote. A fire was lit under the drum in order to raise the temperature of the creosote to a point where it would be absorbed by the beaters. The tops of the beaters were secured to the loft overhead, where straw bales and boxes and the like were stored. All this took place just inside the large doorway of the barn attached to the farmhouse.

In my defence, I will say that I knew nothing about creosote and the only personal contact that I had with other flammables, such as petrol, was that it made my motorbike go. After the first day, I soon realised that the fire under the drum had a propensity to go out and all my efforts at fanning and feeding, mainly with any paper that I could find, were to no avail.

The following morning I managed to collar one of the workers, who happened to be a friend, incidentally, and quietly, not wanting to attract attention to my inadequacy, explained the problem.

"We've all had trouble with that," he laughed. "There's only one answer, but make sure Bowns doesn't get to know. Filch a bit of petrol from the mower and encourage the fire with that." And he was gone.

As I said, my ignorance on such matters was infinite, but as I was approaching desperation, I followed instructions.

I obviously, in my enthusiasm to get the job at least on the way, overdid it somewhat. A jet of flame spurted out over the drum and the creosote caught fire. It was obviously not going to waste time in working its way up the beaters, aided by the fumes, and I realised, to my horror, that in the loft above was stored enough flammable material to burn down the farm, if not, ultimately - the forest! Health and safety? What's that?

There was only one thing to do. I ran across the yard to the office and, trying not to panic, threw back the door and shouted "Fire in the Barn!"

Mr.Bowns was buried in paperwork and as I hadn't bothered to knock, I later felt myself lucky that he hadn't been doing anything subversive!

He fell out of the office and immediately seeing the situation, ran over to his Land Rover, reached inside and took out the fire extinguisher. Oh! Great! I thought - the perfect solution. Ooops! He turned the handle and nothing happened.

We ran over to the barn, managed to untie the smouldering beaters from the loft, lifted them from the burning creosote and threw them into the yard. Straw on the floor had caught fire, but of course, we had the perfect answer - already finished fire beaters were stacked by the barn door and, each grabbing one, we soon smothered the flames.

Disaster had been averted and, needless to say, I was very relieved.

"Well done", he said "but I've never known creosote to catch fire like that." Ah well, Mr Bowns, sir, we live and learn.

I had been sworn to secrecy about the petrol - and so it remained a mystery. No doubt I could have handled it all anyway, but I gave myself a pat on the back for not having wasted any time thinking about it.

Mr. Bowns was a quiet, introverted gentleman, who gave out orders and spoke little else and as far as I know, nothing more was said about the incident. He could well have been embarrassed by the fact that his extinguisher was a non-starter and I assume he immediately went and had it serviced! I was quite relieved that I hadn't burnt down the farmhouse.

It wasn't all bad news. On one occasion, I was given the job of producing a square-sided gatepost from a tree that had been cut down and laid in the yard for some time. This had to be achieved by standing across it and attacking it with a mattock which was swung between the legs, being careful not to cut oneself off at the ankles in the process, of course. I soon realised that I had a talent for this job and, left alone in the yard, I happily swung away.

When Mr. Bowns and the boys returned in the Land Rover at the end of the working day, they were indeed impressed that this rough old tree had been turned into a beautiful, smooth, shiny-sided gatepost. Mr.Bowns remarked that it wasn't particularly necessary to achieve such perfection - but I could see that he too was quite impressed!

George liked to tell stories and probably his best one was about Mr. Bowns - no less. Apparently it was in torrential rain and the boys had been called out to divert a flood of water that was running down the hillside and threatening to wash away a few acres of newly planted trees. There was a large culvert which was designed to carry away the effluent underground, eventually to join the river, and had been made for this very eventuality, Unfortunately the protective grating had become blocked and this had to be removed. Mr. Bowns who was never one to delegate duty when he was himself available, bent to struggle with the grating. According to George who was standing by, Mr.B slipped and the water surge disappeared into his wellington tops. The boots disappeared into the drain. I'm glad I wasn't there!

We dug drainage ditches and knocked in wooden fence posts with a hammer that we estimated to be about sixteen pounds and which some of us could hardly lift. We learnt how to fell a tree with an axe - the main lesson in self-preservation or more probably manslaughter, being not to hit the tree with the leading part of the handle instead of the blade - a flying axe head could be deadly and apparently was not unknown! The ultimate cuts were as near to ground level as possible so that little of the tree would remain. As with a two-handed saw, the technique was in the rhythm and timing - not the strength. In the case where a large felled tree had to be disbranched, there was a choice - the man standing on the trunk had the harder job of pulling the saw upwards through the cut, whilst the man standing on the ground beneath could get a quantity of sawdust over him. With all tools, the watchword was to keep them sharpened and let the tool do the job. It wasn't so good when you had a partner who liked to show his strength, which, in the case of the two-handed saw usually meant that the teeth bit too deep and therefore meant more effort on the return stroke. Keep the saw singing! Motor-driven saws were not commonly used like they are today and I never saw one used in the forest.

Beyond the escarpment at the highest point of the forest was quite an extensive plateau - a flat area of scrub and native trees that had to be cleared for planting. I thought that pieces of Africa must surely look like this. The largest animal that one could see, however, was the deer, which made its presence felt by taking the opportunity to chew any young trees that it could get to. Hence all the fencing that we had to do. The other animal that made its presence felt - or should I say - smelt, was the maggot. In the distance, a small hut could be seen. This belonged to an enterprising soul who bred maggots on rotting meat - I assume to sell to fishermen plying their craft in the beautiful Derbyshire river valleys. Working in that part of the forest, it was possible to be made aware of the 'maggot hut' if the wind was in the wrong direction!

It was in this part of the forest, that we perhaps enjoyed ourselves. Remote from Mr. Bowns and the Farm, we were left to get on with job. It was here that we had the biggest 'burn-ups' - the land being relatively open. Having prepared the pyre the day before with the material we had cleared, we would fire it on arrival the next day and enjoy its heat, and roasted potatoes for dinner! Especially welcome on winter days, when it was often severely cold. Some frosty morning would find Frank challenging himself to light this huge pile with one match!
Yes! - there were plenty of icy days and on one occasion my Dot shot from underneath me; both machine and I went skidding along the main road down to Oughtibridge - me sliding on my PVC covered behind and my lovely machine in front of me sending a shower of sparks over my head. It must have presented quite an intriguing sight. Fortunately neither of us was

seriously injured - just a bent mirror. I always got to work and back, otherwise safely but black ice could be a problem as you didn't see it until you hit it - by then your back wheel was doing the fox trot. Sometimes, deep snow would make it impossible to even get to work.

We had a young 'ganger' who, as it happened was religious and carried his feelings of honesty and integrity with him. I admit that Frank and I were not of that ilk. We were just lads from the back streets and taking a bit of advantage here and there to make the day a happier thing wasn't unknown. Our young ganger, on the other hand, did Mr. Bowns bidding by the book and to the clock. At the least sign of rain we would dive under the canvas; George would shout "Send it down David!" (according to him, the Patron Saint of rain, and directly opposed to young religious gangers.)

But - as soon as the rain eased, we would be whittled out from the canvas and be expected to work in the wet undergrowth. Good were the days when he wasn't there!

Competing with the smell from the maggot hut, an equally disgusting odour came from a certain fungus that flourished in the forest. Under the name of phallus impudicus, its foul smell could be detected at a good distance in the heart of the woods. It was a given- ganger or no ganger- that whoever found it first and pierced it with a sickle had a God-given right to hoist it on high and chase everyone in sight. Needless to say - it was shaped like a huge penis and gave off the foulest smell.

We had fun but we did take a pride in our work - the one exception being when Frank, my old caving mate, who was desperately saving up to emigrate to Canada, had volunteered to plant the hardest terrain at the top rate of pay. I, on the other hand suffering with my synovitis, was plodding away on basic pay planting young trees in the soggy bottom by the railway line. I had a good view of Frank, powering his way up the hillside with a huge bag of young conifers on his back, making the prescribed H cut in the ground and stamping in the tree before moving on.

What Frank didn't know was that on this occasion our highly trusted young ganger was following him and quietly pulling up much of Frank's efforts. Theoretically the trees, having been stamped down, should not have been able to have been pulled out with two fingers!

Poor Frank. He wasn't very pleased, but a few months later he was on his way to Canada and I was discussing with Brian Robinson the possibilities of fleeing the nest and seeing what opportunities we could find in the Art world.

Brian Robinson – The Gypsy Life

It was August 1956. I was twenty-two.

I had already bought my first oil paints long before and these had stood me in good stead, especially when I was eighteen and recovering from a lung problem. Small bottles of poster paint had been some of my treasured possessions since taking my Eleven Plus exam. My relationship with Pete, Frank and the DSG was gradually waning; we had been bosum buddies for three years.

I had given up my job as a progress clerk in the steelworks and Frank had decided that butchering was no longer for him.

He was now working with me on the Forestry Commission at Wharncliffe Side, on the outskirts of Sheffield. He was keen on the idea of emigrating and making a new life in Canada. I admit that I had put the idea into his mind and we both had medicals at the Emigration Centre in Liverpool. My brother had emigrated to Toronto years earlier and brought up his family there.

Frank had his papers duly returned to say that he had passed muster.

Both of us, together with Pete, had, a few years earlier, failed our army medicals. This seemed ironic as we were so active in our outdoor pursuits, often driving ourselves to the edge. Frank had failed mainly on his eyesight and Peter on his acne! There wasn't a war on at the time!

I had failed due to breakdown of lung tissue (bronchiactesis) in my mid-teens, and short sightedness, so I now assumed that I had failed my projected life in Canada for these same reasons. I had to accept that, and it was only many years later after my father and brother had long gone, I learnt from my niece in Canada that my father had torn up the papers, which in fact said that I had passed. He didn't want to lose another son to the New World! He had sworn my brother to withholding yet another family secret. Such things fate is built on.

Frank worked his socks off trying to earn as much money as he could before his departure. He was furiously planting young trees on piecework, whereas I was content to plod along just picking up the regular wage, which at that time was about £4 a week! Dear Frank went on to Canada working in the deep forests as a lumberjack; later out of South Africa on a whaling ship; to Australia selling hamburgers to miners -well, he had been a butcher's boy back in Sheffield! - and finally to New Zealand. He said that this was the most beautiful country in the world.

Meanwhile, Pete, still working in the City, was keen to carry on with his piano lessons, but he eventually joined Frank in New Zealand and became a teacher of the pianoforte.

Our adventures together were manifold and quite, quite wonderful.

Peter married Maureen and reared a small family in New Zealand. She was a Sheffield girl who had been brought up on the same street as me. He died from cancer in New Zealand aged seventy. I spoke to Frank at that time. He too had a family.

I always hoped that somehow I had helped them to rise from a poor background and see the possibilities that life might offer.

As to our initial meeting in 1953 - even that seemed very fortuitous.

I was trying to take my painting and interest in Art more seriously and I had plucked up courage and decided to join night school classes at Sheffield Art School in the City. I thought it would be somewhat ambitious of me to sign up for the painting section and I could only do evenings anyway, as I had to earn a living, and also I didn't particularly want to have to engage with any flashy, know-all art students. My inferiority complex was awesome.

Instead, I joined the pottery section and the clay/plaster modelling classes. There, Peter Coates, Frank Wicken and Brian Gutteridge were already busily engaged. We formed the full complement of the modelling class, in fact, and were generally left to our own devices, receiving instruction when we asked for it. The pottery was a lot busier and more fun but we didn't always get back the results of our careful work as the fatalities in the kiln were rather high. "Sorry, yours has stuck to the shelf" was often the watchword.

All this seemed to be just an introduction to our friendship, which flourished in relatively happy times - only my illness intruding.

And so, Frank had gone, and Pete had already teamed up with younger friends that we had encountered on our many outings and was still treading the hills - for the time being.

My father, meanwhile, managed to borrow some money from one of his friends in order to buy a house in a nice area at Handsworth on the outskirts of town. I gave him £100 towards it, which represented a half of my savings. A relatively modern house from the one we had left at Firvale, it had a garden and a bathroom, and the sitting room wasn't in the kitchen! The garden was relatively enormous, with a small shed and a greenhouse. As gardening had become his passion, I think that he felt that all the work that he had put in at his father's butchers shop had finally borne fruition.

To begin with, the garden was quite bare and I asked him whether there was a chance of erecting a larger wooden hut behind the greenhouse in order that I might indulge my growing passions which were painting and listening to classical music. He was happy to accede to my wishes as he realised that my small bedroom would hardly be adequate enough to contain a budding studio and Brahms.

In no time at all, I had a place of my own, wired with electricity and graced with windows down one side. I had started my artistic career big-time!

I was still working physically hard at the Forestry Commission and I admit that some evenings I found it difficult to keep awake and concentrate on my latest masterpiece. Now that the boys had moved on, I also found that exposing myself to Art at the two City Galleries was quite a lonely pursuit.

I needed some sort of contact in order to expand and understand my interest.

I came across an advert in the Star evening paper. The Royalist Art Group was seeking new members. I rolled out my beautiful Dot trials motorbike from the little garden shed. This machine of character had served me well travelling over the Derbyshire and Yorkshire hills in search of potholing adventures. I rode across the city in the evening light, eventually found the building, and entered.

Half a dozen people were sitting at their easels, painting and chatting. I was warmly welcomed by the leader. They were of all ages, although no young women to distract me. There was only one person close to me in years and we quickly became friends. It was rather like the meeting of lost souls as I quickly realised that I had found someone who reflected my growing passion for Art, although he had, despite being two years younger, already absorbed much more than I had. But then he didn't know anything about Derbyshire caves!

He was already lost in a world of Art, classical music and poetry.

Our friendship quickly grew and I soon realised what a sensitive nature he had and how vulnerable he appeared to be.

He lived with his parents as did I, and only a couple of miles apart, on the same side of the city.

He revealed that he had been in the RAF, but in desperation, he had tried to commit suicide. This, of course had led to him being taken into an institution for a short while. Unbalanced - well yes - but then someone like that being forced into service seemed bizarre and the result almost predictable. He was extremely intelligent and as I soon found out, talented in an original almost visionary fashion. There was a sense of strangeness about him; this showed in his attitude to life and also in his paintings. He was, by now twenty one, and I was already reflecting that we shouldn't be living with our parents, although he obviously needed the security of that more than I did. He invited me to his family home. He painted in his bedroom, which, in contrast to the rest of the very nice suburban house, certainly had an artistic feeling to it. He had painted the walls a soft yellow in homage to Van Gogh with whom he empathised greatly.

I found his painting exciting and original, with a very personal colour sense.

But the most exciting aspect for me was that a door had opened, and I could now spend time talking to someone about what was now becoming a greater part of my life. Often retiring and diffident, he could be quite disparaging about his so-called mental condition. I tried to point out that although he had a job working for a firm that included correspondence courses in Art and Literature, Sheffield certainly wasn't Montmartre, and the chances of meeting a real painter were pretty rare. Encouragement and enthusiasm over painting could be pretty slim.

I think we had been very lucky - or destined.

His surroundings and the hurdles that had already been thrown across his path were difficult for his fragile nature to cope with. I had had a far harsher upbringing but had managed to face up to it.

His parents and his sister were kindly caring people but they were a million miles away from understanding what he was going through. His father was a butcher but he didn't wear it on his sleeve like my father -rather more genteel in fact.

Brian had steeped himself in the French Impressionists, and contemporary painters such as Ivon Hitchens, Graham Sutherland, John Bratby, Lucien Freud, Stanley Spencer and also the likes of William Blake and John Minton who at that time was taking a close look at the bucolic and wonderful Sam Palmer. Brian was also very aware of the great Renaissance masters and our own Pre-Raphaelites; he had lots of respect for Turner and Constable. I had gained some knowledge of all this but Brian filled in the gaps for me. He also, to his lasting credit, attracted me to the music of Brahms, Beethoven, Tchaikovsky, Delius, Elgar, and his personal favourite Rachmaninov. We even explored a few living composers, such as Michael Tippet whom many years later I met, albeit briefly. The older gentleman that Brian worked with had actually seen Rachmaninov play on his visit to Sheffield. He pointed out that he looked exactly like his music! Tall, aloof and sombre, his hands could apparently stretch over notes that others couldn't span. On the evidence of this dark eminence, Brian's colleague had coined the phrase usually delivered on his daily departure from the office, "Let's all go home and destroy ourselves". I could see the point but felt that it might not be a good thing for Brian as he might just go home and do it, as he thought the comment very apt. Brian needed no invitation to get lost in Rachmaninov.

Later I realised that I had also missed Picasso's visit to Sheffield in the fifties!

Although my enthusiasm occasionally verged on being irritable to him, I felt that he shouldn't be allowed to drift into a 'slough of despond' lest he shouldn't come out of it. He had a girl acquaintance that he occasionally met up with in the city. Somewhat of a 'blue stocking', I couldn't see her bringing much joy into his life. He said that he wasn't much interested in girls and I have to say, he didn't show much interest in men either - at least, not live ones! Now Gauguin and Monet - that was different.

I was seemingly his only and almost constant companion.

We had an affinity for sure and we didn't have to wander far before we would meet up, usually at the Graves Art Gallery in town or the nearby Art shop.

I had never seen a ballet, except on very early black and white TV, or been to an opera - or a classical concert. Brian altered all this.

Almost every week would see us at the City Hall for a classical music concert - often the Halle Orchestra conducted by the effusive and popular Sir John Barbirolli - or a ballet or opera at the nearby Lyceum Theatre. 'La Boheme', of course, proved to be my favourite and I immediately identified with it.

We had little money, so we queued up for the 'Gods', which threw us together with the same people, week after week. Brian was good-looking and girls in the queue were attracted to him, but he was only mildly interested.

I would meet him in the evening, in the city, on the corner of Barkers Pool. Unlike me, he always dressed smartly and impeccably - handsome with his soft, fair hair, sometimes hidden under a fedora type hat that surely appears in one of Van Gogh's self-portraits. He had a habit of standing with one hip slightly forward - very gay - and smoking a gold-tipped black Balkan Sobranie cigarette, no less.

He did present a gay image and I couldn't help but suspect that this was his issue, bearing in mind that to be so wasn't as acceptable as it is now.

Certainly, years later, mutual female friends and my eventual wife, swore that he was gay, but still 'in the closet', so to speak. God knows what he had to put up with in the RAF. I didn't have a gay bone in my body and I certainly came from a rougher background than he did. It never worried me. If he was so, I couldn't resolve that for him.

He was never loud, never made jokes (although he had a sense of humour), never swore and never disparaged people - I did all that. It wasn't an aspect of my nature that he particularly liked: in fact, he probably hated it, but I think that he knew that I was relevant to his life at that time - he was certainly relevant to mine.

I duly asked him over to meet my parents and view my work. He liked what I had done and intimated that I might make a good abstract painter. What particularly impressed him was my hut, together with its raffia blinds that I had made! A touch of the Gauguin, we thought.

He noticed a cutting of St Ives that I had pinned to the wall. I explained that one of my bosses in the steelworks had thought that was where I should be. He didn't argue with this but thought it highly unlikely.

He was very keen on my hut idea and although he had much more limited space, he eventually convinced his parents that it was a 'must have'.

His hut was duly built in the corner of the little garden, behind a very nice but ordinary house on a nice but very ordinary estate.

There wasn't anything ordinary about the hut by the time he had finished with it. I would walk over and call on him and as I drew nearer I would catch the strains of Rachmaninov drifting down the road.

He painted the hut red and had a skylight put in. I would often find him lying back in his chair watching the clouds drift by and elegantly smoking his Sobranie.

I quickly learnt that he was a dreamer and nature seemed to absorb him in this way. He had planted some sunflowers around the hut and these grew to massive proportions, so much so that one had almost to fight one's way in! Nature absorbed the hut.

I learnt that John Minton had a show of work on in Nottingham, which was about forty miles away. It was too good to miss and I suggested that he could ride pillion on my DOT.

We set off early and duly arrived in the main square where the exhibition was being held in one of the municipal buildings. We were intrigued and inspired.

Open forums were held in the square and we enjoyed some of the controversial and often humorous proposals and answers that were put forward. Brian particularly enjoyed the old gentlemen who kept intoning in a deep reverberating voice "Deuteronomy states that …." etc. etc.

My DOT didn't suffer passengers lightly, the foot pedals being high up, and by the time we had arrived back at Brian's home at Frecheville, he found it a little difficult to walk. This condition was exacerbated by the fact that he had no protective clothing - only a raincoat. He was frozen! Poor Brian! The things we did for a bit of culture!

Our conversations were never-ending and far-ranging. Our lives had indeed become a 'vie boheme', albeit somewhat an estranged one.

We did make a brief friendship with an art student from the College and by doing so brought a bit of 'other-world' atmosphere to one or two cafes in the town mainly by dint of doing drawings of each other over cups of tea, and the odd sandwich.

"I was thinking about going to St Ives", I offered.

"There are no artists of any worth in Cornwall", he declared with some authority. There was no answer to that but the idea still stayed with me.

Our Royalist Art Group, which I quickly learnt was not founded by some long-lost member of the Royal Family, but by Stanley Royle, a Sheffield painter of some excellence and not a little fame, afforded us some entertainment but could hardly be called progressive. The only deviation from sitting painting together was a joint show with a similar Society in Rotherham; where to my surprise my somewhat unusual portrait of Brian caused comment. In fact, I soon realised that the members thought that I had a natural talent, when they saw me draw. This pleased me.

By now we were beginning to think that it might be time to move on.

Brian and I both had a serious desire to go to London and contemplate the paintings in the Tate and the National Gallery, but we had little money.

Although I had seen much of England and Wales and had even been to France, I had no hands-on knowledge of London.

Brian had been a few times with his parents and felt that, at least, he could find his way around. A day trip was out of the question.

I volunteered the idea that we had to 'take the bull by the horns' and just go, in the hope that we could find some way of staying.

On our return from France, Pete, Frank and I had spent a night in what could only be called a drop-in-centre for down and outs at Tooley Road by the Tower Bridge. It was a desperate possibility for an emergency only, and one that we quickly dismissed.

"Well we would have to get some sort of a job" offered Brian positively.

We had both by now handed in our notices.

"A job in London wasn't really what I had in mind" I replied. "We would be too busy working and paying the rent to see much painting. Anyway, its freedom I'm talking about, not getting tied up with another job". I pondered.

"I don't suppose we could camp in one of the parks, could we? I've got a tent that we could carry".

"Not in one of the parks! But come to think of it there's a place called Richmond that you can get to on the Underground and that's by the river - Thames, that is - but it's not that big there and I think it would be possible to camp on the banks somewhere. At least it wouldn't cost us anything. Just food and short trips into London". "That's good enough for me", I said.

Richmond Bridge

28

So the day came. We packed our rucksacks, said our goodbyes, took a deep breath and caught the train to the 'Big Smoke'.

Richmond turned out to be a wonderful idea. We pitched our tent a mile up the river, just a stone's throw away from the clear waters of the upper Thames. It was idyllic and nature wrapped us around. The town itself provided all that we needed and we spent lots of time sketching by the beautiful bridge and walking upstream to Eel Pie Island and the picturesque loch gates above. We wandered into the grounds of Ham House and then into Richmond Park itself where we were delighted to see the Royal Deer and some magnificent swans on the lake. Down river we found the back gate to Kew Gardens (hence, innocently, we didn't pay), where we were suitably gob-smacked by the exotic plants and the fabulous collection of botanical paintings. The weather smiled on us. It was perfect.

We didn't neglect London and duly used the Underground (although much of it was above ground); indulging ourselves in Tate Britain, (Tate Modern still being only a gleam in the architect's eye), and then the fabulous National Gallery. Sharing the experience with other young people, even sitting on the steps, I felt that I was now doing what I should be doing.

Our stay was far from incident free. One day we returned to the tent just in time to see a river rat disappearing with our loaf of bread. On another occasion, a rat of another kind, had removed the lid of one of our tins and disappeared with a pound of sausage! Then we were treated to a game of baseball in the next field, played by Americans from the nearby airfield, though I never discovered where exactly that was.

The other pastime that we observed being indulged in, by the miscreants of the nearby estate, was 'touting' on the courting couples that wandered into the fields nearby to do a spot of love making. What was just a bit extreme was that they had built up a signalling system between themselves and it was quite funny to see heads popping up in the surrounding hedges.

The idyll couldn't last. Our money would eventually run out.

We didn't discuss the possibility but we were all too aware of it.

Brian came up with his own very personal solution, as was his wont.

About a hundred yards from the tent there was a tap that we used as our water supply and for washing in turn. On this particular morning Brian left the tent with his soap and knapsack. He didn't come back!

I eventually began to wander and made my way over to the tap. No sign of Brian. We had become friends with one of the men designated to pick up litter in the early morning.

29

BRIAN

He was there going about his work. I asked him if he had seen Brian and he immediately pointed to the town!

Of course, I was nonplussed. Back at the tent, I checked that he had all his personal stuff with him, the only thing left being a few used socks and the like.

Why? I really didn't know. We hadn't had any argument and I could only assume that he had become bored with my company - or perhaps I snored and he was too sensitive to tell me. I really didn't have a clue. I was surprised, puzzled, and left feeling somewhat let down, but his method of departure, on reflection, seemed appropriate enough. I think he had made his mind up and he didn't want me to change it for him.

I admit that, for me, this had all been a great adventure and I was quite used to living in a tent. Not so Brian!

The only other cause that I could think of was my sometimes effusive reaction to my surroundings, together with my expletives and general chatter. My enquiring nature and my propensity to categorise and analyse things was perhaps a little too much for him as he only seemed to want to gaze and dream on.

I assumed, wrongly, that he had gone home. Not to be put off, I carried on with my adventure. I wasn't going to carry anything of his with me and so I posted it back to his parents!

Months later, I received a letter from him in which he apologised. He hadn't gone home but had gone to Chelsea where he rented a room and got a job at the corner café! This didn't last long and he soon returned to the sanctuary of his parent's home in Sheffield.

On The Thames

30

The next day found me on the far bank of the Thames. I was drawing. A voice behind me said "Aha! I must add you to my list of riverside painters and poets." It was the local bobby. "Have you read Masefield's 'Scholar Gypsy', he asked.

I admitted that I hadn't but if ever there was a prophetic remark thrown my way, that was one. I explored the left bank of the Thames, opposite the Kew Gardens area and later found to my delight and amazement that Van Gogh had actually taught at a nearby school! The signposts were there! It was time for me to go.

The next day I packed up, hoiked my tent and belongings onto my back and set off walking.

I remember drawing out £5 from my Post Office account at Kingston-on-Thames. The world was my oyster.

I had membership to the excellent Youth Hostels Association and on perusing the handbook, I conceived the idea of heading for the South Downs and Kent with the vague idea that I might use the hostels and get work in the fields. I reached a main road and caught a bus in the general direction.

Maidstone eventually hove into view and I thought it as likely a place as any to alight. I bought some food in the town and squatted to eat on the banks of the Medway. Fortunately this must have been a great year for good weather as the sun seemed to shine on me all the time!

I set off walking again and soon met up with gypsies and travellers. I assumed that they were also heading for the fields. I was attracted by the girls in their colourful skirts walking behind the traditional horse -drawn wagons. I had to cut into the countryside to seek out my hostel.

On arriving, I was disappointed to find that it was full but I was quickly found a spot in a nearby field where I could pitch my tent. I was happy with that, up to a point. As far as I could see, there didn't seem to be anybody working in the fields and I was getting a bit tired carrying the tent. The next morning I wandered into the sleepy village nearby. Whilst chewing on a pork pie from the nearby baker's, I noticed an advert in the Post Office window. 'Bicycle for Sale - £5.' Of course! Why not! The address was nearby and the genteel lady who answered the door was happy to sell me her bicycle - albeit a lady's one!

With my new treasure, I dropped out of the hills and began to explore the valley of the Medway. From my exalted position I had now a better view of what was going on over the hedges and soon spotted people working in the fields. I quickly came across the tiny village of Yalding, the pretty bridge spanning a small tributary of the Medway. From the bridge I could see that there was an assortment of gypsies and travellers living in a row of small huts provided by the nearby farm. I quickly learnt that the crop they were picking was strawberries. I enlisted, and returned to my original village to collect my tent and before long was setting up in Yalding.

Gypsy Life

It's unfortunate that at this time, away from the retirement of home life, I didn't keep a diary or a journal - I learnt that lesson later - but I did do some drawings.

The small stone hut that I was allotted was comfortable enough and a big improvement to the tent, although heavy rain did make an awful din on the galvanised roof. The ample pile of straw in the corner proved to be tolerably more comfortable than the bare ground. The row of huts were stationed by the river. Not all of them were occupied, as many of my fellow strawberry pickers were, indeed, travellers and gypsies, and one or two of the families had their ornate gypsy barrel-shaped caravans with them. Suddenly I was in the world of Augustus John and Alfred Munnings!

Gradually I came to know them all, although I was obviously very different from them and definitely on my own. I was respected and I suspect rather admired for the fact that I had ventured into their realm.

My beard by this time was quite substantial and had gone through one or two stylistic alterations in the past. As I didn't have sophisticated toiletries with me, let alone a mirror, and I wasn't given like Narcissus to gazing into pools of water, it did its own thing; I was usually mistaken for a University student trying to earn a little income.

Far from the truth! I was a bit of an adventurer and explorer and I suppose always had been. If I failed to come up with something useful in life I was well aware that I could just degenerate into a tramp. I had thrown myself into the lap of the Gods.

Picking strawberries wasn't what I called' work'. It was more of a holiday with pay, with the bonus of eating as many strawberries as you could afford not to get paid for. I was always first in the field - getting up early wasn't new to me. This didn't go unnoticed by the overseer who stalked the rows. I did long hours in the sun and I earnt respect.

Gypsies will be gypsies and, let's face it, some of them were too old to be doing back-breaking work which it certainly was, crunching along the rows on your knees. The family was the thing and most of them were attached, combining their efforts and their earnings. The overseer and the staff at the counting tables had to keep a sharp eye out for the odd stone that may have been lodged in the bottom of the punnets to make up the bulk. They soon got to know the culprits!

The best of the bunch, and I was pleased to be included, were occasionally asked to work Sundays and we were lorry-loaded over to nearby farms who were having a problem getting the harvest in.

I was soon to get on friendly terms with the little varied community by the river and evenings would see me being allowed to sit by their open fires and chat. I was soon christened 'The Professor' as they were largely uneducated and they took the opportunity to ask me things; I think they found me a curious animal. The gypsy-type barrel caravans were attractive and immaculate inside but access wasn't allowed, however I was invited on to the top step in order to do drawings of the interior. By now they had an idea of what I was good at and how I was different. I spent time drawing and some of them would sit for me. I must say that one or two of the girls were actually attracted to me but I was very careful not to respond - I was, after all, amongst aliens!

By the way - do Gypsies eat hedgehogs? Yes.

The river too was very attractive, especially when it was hot weather and brave souls would jump in and splash around. I was quick to point out that I couldn't swim, just in case some of the boys got ideas. The atmosphere was generally benign and I never saw any nastiness. One or two of the fellows were pointed out to me as not being 'travellers', but rather 'runners' - from the police. They kept to their space and caused no trouble.

I noticed that the local pub had a notice in the window saying - 'No Travellers' - so there was the usual social barrier. Not without cause; there were occasions when I witnessed petty pilfering, usually on farms where certain objects could easily be picked up and carried off with impunity.

I was briefly befriended by a smart young man and his very attractive girlfriend. They would sit in my little hut and we would chat. The surprise was that he admitted that he was a bit of a gangster (on the run?) and operated in the East End of London. He belonged to a gang which met in the Blue Parrot, which I assumed was some sort of night club.

"When I walk in, the 'Guvner' always lays on a dozen oysters and champagne". Respect! I didn't pursue that line of conversation much further!

Well there were no oysters or champagne to be had hereabouts. On the day they were due to leave, they popped in to say "Cheerio" and gave me a chicken pie that they had just bought in the village but then decided at the last minute not to take it home with them - they were on a motor bike.

Well, I didn't have an oven so I extracted the chicken bits and fried it in my little pan over an open fire.

There was a shop built into the parapet of the little bridge. It must have been quite ancient and I was attracted by the curious hooks arranged along the outside. It was a butcher's shop still and I assumed that at one time meat and poultry would have been displayed on the hooks.

I did a drawing and as I finished it, the butcher came out and was very taken with my effort.

"How much for it?" He enquired.

"Oh! Two bob's worth of steak", I offered.

"Done", he said

Later, he invited me to his home nearby. He showed me his fireplace which he claimed was by Adam. I was impressed. He asked if I would do a drawing of it and I was happy to oblige. More steak.

I was also drawing in the strawberry fields during the break period and I made many friends. One particular middle-aged woman never failed to chat me up. She was with her husband and a young boy. I had noticed that they had a motor car. In the evening, I was invited to their nearby hut -to sit on the step, that is. We exchanged life histories.

She was called Mary, and her husband was Lennie. The boy about ten years old was called Joey. He was as bright as the proverbial button. Mary claimed Romany blood and as she looked the part, I wasn't one to argue. She also claimed that Lennie, who I must say didn't speak a lot, had been a fairground fighter and I could well believe it as he was tall and looked strong, even though at this later age his feet were obviously giving him trouble. "My Lennie can use his mitts alright!" I had learnt to be discreet and only ask questions when invited. Lennie was largely unsmiling but obviously intelligent and not in any way threatening. Mary, on the other hand, just loved to talk.

"What are you going to do when the strawberries are finished, my Vic?"

"I really haven't a clue. I'll just get on my bike and see what turns up."

"Well, me and Lennie have been thinking. We have a home in Hertfordshire, where we do crop picking. If you're interested, you could come back to Manuden with us and we could show you how to go on. You would be good company for Joey. We could also let you live in our gypsy caravan - no charge!"

The moving finger having writ - moves on! How could I say no?

The day arrived when it was time to say goodbye to my fellow travellers and leave Yalding. We all piled into Lennie's large, old, sedate Austin, which he drove at a very sedate speed. My bike was tied on the back.

We had plenty to talk about as we gently motored along the back roads to Hertfordshire. They were very interested in the fact that I knew about Art and Mary was quick to point out that she had once lived on the Thames near Cookham and had encountered Stanley Spencer on more than one occasion. She added that he wasn't generally liked and I could well believe that. She had also known the Van Sittarts who lived in a mansion, I think below Windsor. I suspect that she may have been 'in service' to them at some point, though I didn't ask questions.

Eventually, we rolled into the benign market town of Bishop's Stortford and from there up into the low hills beyond.

Manuden was a pretty typical English village with a duck pond, a church and a Post

31

Office. The ground that Mary and Lennie owned lay just up the road by a copse and was guarded from the narrow road by raised hedgerows, a simple iron five barred gate, and two dogs. The dogs were very pleased to see us! A goat watched whilst chickens ran in and out of the undergrowth and a couple of rabbits scuttered around in their hutches. A rubber-wheeled wagon of good size stood in the middle of the ground. "There's your home" said Mary proudly. A young woman had just vacated and I assume that she had been looking after the animals.

Just beyond was a serviceable four-square tent, which was furnished with a bed and chairs. Later on, Lennie erected another tent by the gate. The dogs were lively and very friendly. I didn't know anything about rabbits or chickens - or goats!

I quickly settled into my caravan and found it comfortable. Oil heater and lamp provided the light and warmth. By now, it was autumn.

Mary and Joey moved into the big tent and Lennie meanwhile disappeared in his car intent on some job or other. This happened fairly frequently.

Mary and Joey busied themselves around the ground, which I suppose measured something like an acre or so. I was introduced to the friendly post office manager as Lennie's cousin as Mary assumed that this would be a simple explanation as to who I was suddenly appearing in their midst.

Before long Lennie would return and we were soon making sorties into nearby Bishop's Stortford, usually on market day when Mary seemed to know everybody and would busy herself around the stalls as they closed down - bargaining for the left-over fruit and veg. - and often getting it for free.

Later on, I made solo trips on my bike down to the town and visited the library where, I remember, I borrowed an autobiography of Alfred Munnings, and also another artist, who had travelled around in a horse drawn wagon and painted the gypsies. Another interest was the day of the Auction Sale, which would be well attended by local farmers and villagers. Coming from my city background, this was all very charming and rustic.

Lennie was friendly albeit somewhat taciturn. He gave me a brief lesson in driving along the quiet back lanes, saying how easy it was, but then quickly changing his mind as he realised how vulnerable his most expensive asset had suddenly become. He was always busy- and had to be. The copse and the surrounding woods provided him with logs that he cut into serviceable lengths by way of his circular saw, ready for retail to the local villages. He piled these into his very useful trailer, (which they called the 'whuppie'), and off they would go.

Mary had her own vocabulary of words, which seemed to be a mixture of Romany, expletives and spicy swearwords. 'Fuckin' tuppeny' was one of her favourite expressions of surprise and "You can pawn your life, my Vic" when she wanted to impress something on me. Little Joey seemed oblivious to much of this and was usually quite happy playing with his dogs or chasing the chickens.

We would often sit by the open fire, kettle on the 'kittle prop' and recount stories from two seemingly different cultures. Mary was always very interested in my background. We had, on travelling up from Kent, briefly called in at an encampment where many traditional caravans and trailers were permanently parked. We waited in the car whilst she said hello to old friends. There was generally an air of suspicion about strangers unless accompanied by someone they knew very well and as Mary revealed, feuds would sometimes spring up and their own form of justice would be applied, sometimes going as far as to burn out someone's wagon. It was all very family orientated and the more family you had, the stronger you were. I suppose that I was that sort of supplement, my main asset being that I was young and obviously a strong worker.

On another occasion, I got to meet Aunt Famie, a benign old gypsy lady, surrounded by her offspring. We spent an hour with them in their home which was, in fact, an old railway carriage. I think they saw me, with my scholar's beard, as being something unusual; being 'Lennie's cousin' was my protection.

It was soon time to be working the fields. Mary and Lennie were very experienced in knowing where to go to find work at any one time.

One memorable morning, I remember standing in a line of gypsies and travellers waiting for the overseer to blow his whistle. The line of workers was so long that it disappeared into the mist! We were about to pick peas! As the magic whistle sounded, a thousand fingers burst into frantic action. This crop was quite different, mainly because you had to pull, shove them into a sack, and then extricate yourself from the leaves and tendrils that were trying to trip you up as you worked your way, as it happened, up the hill. It was plain to see who the professionals were and they were soon racing ahead.

These arable fields were sometimes vast, there being no hedges to intrude on the working of the tractors involved in the sowing. Many years later, in my artistic career, I was honoured to have Professor Jim Lovelock as one of my clients, an important figure in the world of space research and survival of the human species. He revealed to me that the immense areas of uninterrupted arable land was largely due to his suggestion, that by uprooting the ancient system of hedgerows, an enormous amount of time and effort would be saved, rather than tractors laying down crops in small areas. This, of course was to do with the War Effort and the feeding of the Nation. He, however, very much regretted the loss of wild life habitat as a consequence. He also worked on the - unresolved- cure for the common cold, which was responsible for the loss of many man hours in the factories.

A favourite crop was the honourable potato.

Morning would find us standing at our stations in yet another vast field waiting for the tractor with its spinner to turn out the spuds, so that we could fill as many sacks as possible before it returned. Mary always advocated giving the last filled sack to the tractor driver in order to curry any favour that might be going. A good policy when work became a little scarce. When work was finished at day's end, I was expected to follow suit and walk off with a couple of empty sacks. These would later be sold back to the farmer for a few pence - it was all in the game. We needed work and they needed workers - and sometimes quickly, before the crop rotted. It would also have been churlish not to have secreted a few spuds about one's person for later consumption. After the spuds had finished Mary was quick to point out that the curious mounds, some being in the field across the road, were in fact potato clamps. "No need to go hungry in the land of plenty, my Vic." I admit I never bought a potato all the time I was there.

I had a chance to indulge in another crop, thanks to Mary's instigation. She introduced me to a farmer who needed an acre or two of sugar beet bringing in - at £5 an acre. I was quite familiar with just how big an acre was, having scythed my way through many a one for the Forestry Commission.

We met by the farm at yet another caravan. The farmer explained the procedure. Rows of beet had been spun out into lines. I had to work my way down each line using a short billhook, an instrument I was already familiar with at the FC. With a deft twist of the wrist I had to top and tail each beet and then smartly throw them behind me without stopping, the aim being to hit the pile accumulating behind one's back. As one advanced up the line one had blindly to judge how far you had travelled from the growing pile or else there would be more back-breaking work rounding up the strays. I was pleased with my accuracy and as I moved out of range, in my long yellow waterproof apron, I would then start another pile.

What I enjoyed was the rhythm of the work and I was reminded of Van Gogh's comment about the nobility of agricultural work and his admiration of Jean Françoise Millet's paintings of reaping and sowing.

Having been duly paid for the work and complimented by the farmer, I commented to Mary on how attractive and younger the farmer's wife was.

"That's not his wife, my Vic. The old lady feeding the chickens behind the wagon is his wife. He's took her in for his pleasure in exchange for helping the old lady". 'Hmmm' I mused.

"But the young woman doesn't look gypsy".

"No, she's a gorgie, my Vic. A house dweller".

Rather looked down on by the didicoy (another name for the gypsy) gorgies were boring workaday people who lived boring lives in boring houses.

Ah well - needs must when the devil drives. I hope no one thought that I had been offered the same deal!

I was interested in Mary as almost being part of another species but anything else never entered my head. Celibate since Beryl, I was still waiting for my dream girl to appear. As for Mary, I was a bit of extra company and, I suppose, security when Lennie wasn't there and likewise, a different species to study. It came as a complete surprise, therefore, when, one evening as winter approached and we were sitting very snugly in the bottom tent, Lennie sharpening his tools and Mary making pegs to sell to the Gorgies, that Joey suddenly popped his head up from behind his comic and blurted out …. "When you and Uncle Vic were in bed together in the big tent….." Mary quickly cut him short with an incredulous look.

"What the fuck are you talking about, boy? Have you gone mad or summink?" She gave him a withering look that pushed him back behind his comic. Lennie kept on sharpening his axe.

Nothing more was said - perhaps they had heard similar things before. I expected the worst-and absolutely nothing happened.

Joey was certainly a bright boy with a wayward imagination and apart from indulging in dangerous fantasies, Mary later revealed that he had a surprising talent i.e. - that he could snatch a bird in flight. Now, I thought - this has to be another flight of fancy, but the following week, finishing off a crop in a nearby field, I was watching Joey running around apparently at random when he jumped and incredibly plucked a small bird from the air.

"There you are, my Vic. What did I tell you?" I wouldn't have thought it possible, but I saw it happen right in front of me. Joey then released it with a celebratory - 'whoop'. Gypsies in tune with nature - I'll say.

I befriended the Postmaster at Manuden as he seemed to be the centre of attention in the village, and found him to be an educated, friendly chap. I had written to Brian's home in Sheffield and asked for a Poste Restante. I didn't have to struggle with a personal address as the Postmaster was well aware as to where I was residing. To write to Brian was a long shot but I didn't hold any grudge against him. Soon there was an answering letter in which he apologised profusely. He had gone to Chelsea where he had rented a flat and worked at a Lyons corner tea shop. A short while later having realised that this wouldn't work for very long he returned home. I was by now desperately missing some intellectual contact.

The seasons changed and it was explained to me that the 'great hop-picking time' was near - I think the bulk of this took place back down in Kent. This money-making event of the crop-picker's year was when swarms of gypsies and travellers flooded into the hop fields. They thought that I might just be a little out of my depth as I hadn't done any before and they asked if I would be good enough to stay and look after the ground and the animals. I explained that I knew nothing of animals. "It's OK, my Vic - they usually look after themselves. 'Fussy' the goat, however, needs milking from time to time so we'll get one of the village lads to take her in. If you follow the hens into the undergrowth, you'll see where they've laid their eggs - so you won't starve!"

I had carefully put cash away in my Post Office account. If they had asked for money, I would gladly have given them some - but they didn't. Their need was certainly greater than mine. I knew that I could 'cut out' at any time and get a job.

Mary, Lennie and Joey left for the hop fields and I had two or three weeks on my own. I was glad of the chance to do some exploring and more painting. I loved to wander along the deserted back lanes and then across the fields. There were no main roads for miles around and the sounds of nature were unaffected by a modern world. Birds singing, leaves rustling in the trees and far away, a vixen calling. I even managed to do a few small paintings.

Saffron Walden was about ten miles away and I set off on my bike to see if I could find it. It turned to out to be a pleasant, busy little town with plenty of old buildings to please the eye. I explored the shops and bought a few things. A woman and her daughter were showing some of their artwork in their front room, which overlooked the high street. They noticed my interest at the open door and invited me in to look further. They were delighted to meet an itinerant artist and I visited two or three times. We drew each other and I was glad of the tea and company. They were quite fascinated by the story of my current adventures.

On another occasion I stopped off at a hamlet where some half-timbered houses had attracted me. I sat and did a drawing. One of the occupants saw me and came over to look over my shoulder.

"I like that. How much do you want for it?"

Real money for a drawing!

"Er - half a crown", I offered.

"Done!" he said and after a brief conversation about my background - off he went.

This was my first picture sale and I was delighted - although my niece in Canada did, years later, remind me that one of my numerous aunties had bought a small scraperboard from me for 6d.

I knew that a few miles from Manuden the famous sculptor Henry Moore was selling his sculptures for thousands of pounds. He had a home and studio at Much Hadham, buried deep in the English countryside. I'm sure he wouldn't have turned away a fellow Yorkshireman but my inherent shyness wouldn't allow me to pay him a visit.

Interspersed with my rural wanderings was the occasional trip to the farmer's world of Bishop's Stortford; a town I liked but, apart from the library and the market, didn't have much else to offer me.

I quickly discovered that I had no talent whatsoever for husbandry and on the family's return the place had turned into something of a shambles. After a bit of moaning and groaning they forgave my oversights. At least 'Fussy' got milked - but not by me!

On one occasion, a film was to be shown at the village hall - an infrequent event apparently. Mary asked if I would take Joey to see it. I was happy to agree. This was just about the only outing that Joey and I had together.

No more field work - Lennie was busy cutting and loading his logs and delivering around the estates. Mary was making and selling her pegs to the Gorgies and coming up with any bright ideas on how to 'make a bit of bread'. Joey was making attempts at schooling. There would be no more crop picking for me and I would soon need to get a job. With Christmas approaching I think they also understood that my parents would want to see me back home again. I had to go and I discussed my intention to leave - they hoped that I would return. Brian was keen to continue our relationship.

I packed up my bit of gear. I left them my bike and my humble tent - I was sure that Joey would be spending some time in that! I also left a couple of oil paintings that I had done – one, a 'Monet' haystack.

Lennie dropped me off on the nearest A1 road. I was lucky in that I almost immediately got a lift in a lorry that took me all the way to Mansfield in Nottinghamshire. From there I got a bus and dropped off at Manor Top on the outskirts of Sheffield. A short walk in the dark and I was home.

I received a letter from Mary and Lennie assuring me that my home (i.e. caravan) would be there if and when I should return. By then I had realised that my gypsy days were over. I was culture-starved, and that sort of life would not sustain me financially in my aspirations to build a career of some sort out of my artistic talent. My funds had leaked away; I had to get a job.

Working - Sheffield Parks Department

It was the winter of 1957. I had just returned home to Handsworth from my wanderings in Kent and Hertfordshire and, having little money left, I had to get a job. On perusing the Sheffield Star, I saw that there was a vacancy with the Parks Department. I duly showed up at the Town Hall in the City Centre and presented myself, not knowing exactly what the job entailed. There seemed to be several applicants there for different jobs. The guy I was sitting next to appeared very friendly and chatty and I soon realised that we were after the same job, both of us assuming that it would be something to do with park keeping, which we were both familiar with from childhood. Park keepers were the ones who fielded the football when it got kicked into the local duck pond - easy. The fellow contender introduced himself as Ray. Little did I know that Ray Turner and I were to remain friends for what was left of our lives, although latterly, thousands of miles apart. He became instrumental in helping me further my career as an artist and I shall be eternally grateful for that.

On finally being interviewed I was quickly made aware that the job entailed a little gardening in summer but essentially was about something quite different, namely, cutting down dangerous trees, and keeping the shape of the trees that lined the sidewalks of many of the better class roads around the perimeter of the city.

I explained that I had recently been employed by the Forestry Commission at Wharncliffe and outlined some of the jobs that I was familiar with, which included felling trees of all shapes and sizes. I explained that I had left home to make my fortune but that this hadn't happened. He immediately offered me the job.

Ray was waiting for me outside and was delighted that we had both been taken on. The following Monday, we were picked up by lorry in the city centre and transported to what was to become our depot at Beauchief on the outskirts. Here we were kitted out with overalls and heavy topcoat. We also met the half dozen or so men who were destined to be our colleagues and I must say - they were a motley crew.

Our staple tools were a ladder and a hand saw and these we were soon to become very familiar with.

Although having become adept at several jobs, Ray wasn't used to dealing with wayward trees and this later became obvious as, together with the other odd naïve conscript, the error of using undue force would soon deplete the energy levels. As I pointed out in an earlier dialogue - rhythm was the key.

I was soon to find that the worst part of the job was actually getting to the depot. Having been shown where it was, we were now left to our own devices as to find our way there in the very early morning. In my case, I was about as far away as could be - Handsworth being on one side of the city boundary and not that far away from the Nottingham County boundary, and Beauchief being on the other city boundary and next to Derbyshire. I had to catch a tram at the end of the road, very early and often in freezing conditions, then change in town to catch the next one for Beauchief. Both trams were very near to their respective termini. The only good thing about all this was that I was given tram tokens, so I didn't have to pay. Meeting up with mates on the second tram did little to lighten my mood and I would pull my hat and collar over my face and refuse to speak. Ray would think this very funny and call me 'a miserable sod'. There were some very cold mornings on very cold trams.

The fellows who lived nearer to depot, or at least on that side of town, would fare better and would have the stove at the farm ready lit. Needless to say, I was the one who had to be dragged away to the lorry when the time came to go.

Many of the destinations were unknown to me as I hadn't been one to frequent the 'posher' areas of the city. I did enjoy this aspect of the job.

Other aspects, not so much, as for instance, accompanying the lorry driver, whom I did not at all like, to the burning dump to offload all the cut branches, which we called brash, and, if it was your misfortune, spending a few lonely hours burning it. Fortunately, my dexterity with a billhook and saw was quickly noticed by Eric, the ganger, one of the more enlightened souls in the group. I assume having reported to the, what could be called - Officer in Charge (who went by the name of Coleman), I was promoted to being a tree man! Having duly filled this function over a period of weeks, i.e. successfully managing to climb a double ladder, climb on into the tree and manage to saw off the wandering arms of said tree and make the whole thing look a reasonable shape, all without falling off, I was granted the coveted tree jacket!

This uniquely styled article of clothing was designed to provide warmth and protection from the elements whilst still offering freedom of movement. It was in the form of a corduroy waistcoat with sleeves and shirt lap length back made of black moleskin - very natty. I loved it and wore it many years later as a painting jacket. My dog, which I had for eighteen years, loved it too. I used to bed him down with it when I had to leave the house so that he wouldn't pine. He loved me that much that one day, on returning, I found that he had eaten quite a bit of it. I assumed this was because of his love for me - or perhaps he was just hungry. Anyway, I digress.

I mentioned Coleman. He was certainly approaching retirement and was our only contact with authority. He would appear unceremoniously in the small official van of the Sheffield Parks Department and tell us what we were expected to do for the day's work. I admit that we were never overworked and sometimes we wouldn't see him for the week - left alone to use what intelligence we had between us and work our way around the pavements of some expensive housing estate. We soon ascertained that Coleman's driving was nothing short of atrocious. He would pull away from the kerb at will without bothering to look. If he received a warning hoot, he would utter, "what the hell does he want?" or some such ridiculous remark.

Roundabouts were generally a nightmare. Occasionally, he would have to pick one of us up to help out in another area. This we dreaded most as we were well aware that we could meet with sudden death! Mates would give sympathetic looks as we slid in beside him.

His worst critic was Harry, who, as it happened I was often paired off with as we lived on the same side of the city, and he even nearer to the county boundary than I did.

"He's a disgrace to the uniform! I don't

32. Harry – Tree Felling Gang, Sheffield 1958

think he ever cleans it and I don't think he ever gets washed either. Have you seen the dandruff, when he scratches his poxy head? The weird thing is that his wife is a very nice lady." Harry never spared Coleman and there were many things said. I was quiet, reserved and careful not to make personal comments, that is except to Stan, the lorry driver, whom I grew to loathe. A nasty little piece of work.

I got on with everyone else absolutely splendidly. If we were paired off for a particular job, Harry would make sure that I came with him. He liked the way I worked and he was at ease in my company. I was twenty four at the time and he would have been somewhere in his thirties. He had served his time as a military conscript and much of his attitude to life seemed to be influenced by this. It had left its mark. Although married, the way that he appointed himself to the passing parade of women was far from circumspect and I think he thought that as a single man I should be perhaps showing more sex-orientated interest. I understood where he was coming from as both he and my brother had served in the Mediterranean and used the same language - some of it Arabic. I had learnt the sound of the words and could utter them but my brother never told me what they meant. - perhaps as well! "Have a shufti at that, Vic!" I knew what that meant! In Harry's case, however it only meant one thing. Then would often follow a series of quietly uttered commands to the object of his desire, willing her to do his bidding. "Up a bit - down a bit", whilst still deploying a rake around a rose bed by the roadside. Nothing particularly lewd - just rather naughty - and impossible, though I admit that he did seem to know quite a bit about certain ladies in particular houses. He had been on this same job for a few years now and local areas had been frequented by him more than once.

At lunchtime we sometimes had to eat by the road in any convenient spot. Harry would bring out the traditional worker's white enamelled billy-can containing the required quota of tea. This was very familiar to me as all the steel workers that I had known had one. I had a thermos flask - already made up. I never really classed myself as a dyed-in -the-wool worker! Wherever we were he seemed to know where to get his tea mashed but sometimes he would send me. "Go round the back door, Vic and see what you think to that one!" A clandestine affair with a housewife was really something I wasn't looking for! Anyway, he was in charge and I was happy to do his bidding.

He was a typical 'cheeky chappie'. Short, curly haired and heavy booted with a quick grin, he certainly seemed to know a lot of housewives. He loved to tell stories and I'm not sure I believed any of them, except perhaps the ones from foreign parts; how, for instance, being on sentry duty in some godforsaken Arabian town, young girls would be sent out into the night to earn a few shillings. But then I had other friends who had been conscripted and who eventually came home with some lurid stories to tell; the experience had changed their lives. Harry was nothing if not entertaining. He was also a good worker and we made a good team. The summertime job of looking after the flower beds, by the roadside, was when we were sent out together and Harry, who at one time had been in service to some grand house or other, certainly knew his plants and how to treat them. I quickly learnt how to prune roses under his guidance, for instance.

His predilection for seeking out ladies was not, however, restricted to our gardening sorties. Early mornings would sometimes find us high up in neighbouring trees and I would sometimes get a discreet whistle from Harry indicating that he wasn't particularly concentrating on taking out any branches. A nod in the right direction would sometimes reveal that a young lady getting ready for work hadn't yet put on her clothes in her bedroom and Harry by judicious means of climbing like a monkey had placed himself in a suitable position, whereby, obscured by a little vegetation, he was now on a level with the subject of his admiration. I suffered from a liberal share of embarrassment over such matters at that time, not Harry however, and if the lady in question happened to see the voyeur in such an unexpected and unusual situation, then curtains would be quickly drawn - but not always. If thus spotted Harry would give a cheery wave, a cheeky grin and saw off another branch, chuckling to himself the while. After all, he was the victim - he had to be up in a tree in the early morning.

"Did ya see that Vickie! What a shufti"

Eric was the ganger and he would keep an eye on us as we worked our away along tree-thronged streets in the sometimes beautiful areas of outer Sheffield. Occasionally he would discuss with us whether a certain bough should be extracted in order to balance the spread of the tree canopy. I always deferred to his experience although I felt that Harry could match him- none of us were afraid to request a second opinion. Bill was an older man from a country background. I suspect that he had been prised from his allotment in order to make more money! He too was beyond reproach. His secret talent was that he could imitate bird calls having reduced them to the spoken word, so to speak!

Ray, together with three or four of the gang, was yet to be trusted or regarded as agile enough to climb the ladder and enter the canopy, which, on occasion, could be tricky, to say the least. It was all about age and experience and, let's face it, you were putting your life at risk. The ground crew had the job of chopping up the lopped branches into a favourable size in order that they could be loaded into the lorry. Stan, the driver was expected to do his share of loading but was usually wanting in this respect. Eric would sometimes have to winkle him out of his cab where he would be having a crafty smoke. The other duty that the ground crew had to perform was to keep an eye out for the members of the public who might be passing under the trees. Again Health and Safety didn't seem too much of an issue in those days. There were no signs, for instance, to indicate that we might be working overhead. On one occasion Fred, my labourer- an older man who constantly got upset by all the swearing that took place- whilst chopping up the brash that I had dropped from above, had failed to keep a lookout for passers by. As I made the last cut on a substantially heavy bough, the canopy opened up beneath me and I could see that an elderly gentleman was walking directly under where the log was about to fall. It was already too late to shout a warning and I certainly didn't want him to stop and look up. I held my breath as I watched the bough, falling enough distance for the heavy end to reach the pavement first, heading straight for him. It thumped to the ground no more than a yard behind him. Amazingly, his stride never faltered (he may have been deaf) and he carried on not realising that he had just fractionally avoided having his head stoved in.

I now had time to be horrified. "Fred! Fred!" I shouted. "Where the fuck are you?" He eventually sauntered under the tree where I could see him. "What the fuck do you think you are doing, Fred? That old guy just escaped certain death, and it would have been your fault!"

"There's no need to swear - I was cutting up stuff and didn't notice him".

"Jesus, Fred, your prime job is to make sure no one walks under this fucking tree!"

"Now don't take the name of the Lord in vain, Victor".

Fred left shortly after saying that he didn't think he was suitable for the job. I thoroughly endorsed that one.

Then there was Steve, the friendly young chap who did as little as possible and actually got on well with Stan the driver and would volunteer to do the brash-burning. I suspect that they engineered the job to their particular requirements. He was of about twenty years and already overweight for his age. This didn't worry him whatsoever and he advocated a regime of sleep, little work, drinking a couple of pints of milk whilst on the job and pints of beer when not. He also, whilst proclaiming that he was a fitness advocate and attended a gym, had a philosophy of not standing when you can sit and not sitting when you can lie down. He would put this into operation when we had the relative good fortune of being near a Parks-run establishment, such as a cemetery or a horticultural establishment - or even a park- where we could enjoy our lunch hour in relative comfort. We might then find ourselves rubbing shoulders with a grave digger on the one hand and some aficionado of the plant world on the other, whilst having the benefit of eating our sandwiches while sitting on a bench, or in Steve's case, lying on it. Harry, of course, would be in his element talking to the gardeners in the glasshouses about the different plants, which were grown to decorate places like the Town Hall or for special occasions. In quieter areas, on more remote estates, we always carried our little hut with us. This had to be manhandled onto the lorry and then, on arrival, set up by the roadside. Cosy and warm with a small coke stove, it was a haven at lunch and when it rained. We were not, however, saved from all the wintry elements and some frosty mornings would find us climbing up into branches coated with ice or even snow. This required some skill with a ladder.

Occasionally we would have a really big tree to fell. This demanded working from the top down, as there were usually nearby houses to protect. Sawing the branches wasn't too difficult as you generally had something to hang on to but when they had gone, we were left with a bare pole of some considerable height. This then demanded the erection of a set of heavy ladders often on to a round uneven surface many feet above, and would engage the efforts of three or four men. Climbing this with no security could be a potentially heart stopping experience, especially if the ladder slipped. It certainly swayed and having a saw in one hand didn't add to one's confidence. The older guys had been here before but it was new to me and having reached the top segment, being faced with not much more than fresh air and a great view, I realised I had reached my limitations. Most of my energy was taken in making sure I didn't fall off. My inadequacy was noted and I was soon called down. I could then only stand back and admire the strength and attack of Harry, Eric and Bill – old seasoned campaigners. Down at the bole of the tree, it became a two-handed saw job and on occasion assisted by a wire pulley, which was tightened to a frightening degree - this to make sure the tree didn't land in someone's backyard.

At the time, I was getting £8 a week with an extra £1 if we had to finish the job on a Saturday.

Just occasionally, we would be approached by a house owner who happened to have a large unwanted tree in his garden and Harry or Eric would quote him a price for us to turn up at the weekend and do the job.

Coleman would turn a blind eye as well he might.

By now, Ray had been granted tree climbing status and we were to remain in this job for another year.

On one occasion we were working in adjacent trees and the rest of the gang had moved on. It had been snowing. Having been satisfied that his tree now

33. Big Bill and Eric

displayed a degree of symmetry, he came over to have a chat. As he approached my tree, he noticed blood in the snow.

"Have you cut yourself, mate?"

I thought that I had better explain where the blood had come from.

"No - I coughed it up!"

"What! How so?"

I had then to explain how I had a condition of the lung that, at this time, obliged me to cough up phlegm of a particularly unpleasant nature and sometimes blood.

"Well - surely you should be in hospital then?"

"I've done all that Ray, and been discharged. I don't want to go back there and I'm hoping that it'll just phase out. It has been a lot worse - believe me! It's not TB and it's not catching - so don't worry." "Well - what the hell is it then?"

"If you must know, it's called bronchiectasis - lung damage for short."

"How the bloody hell did you get that?"

"Nobody can say for sure, but I had a severe case of measles when I was young and I put it down to that. It's not bronchitis. I wish it were!"

The conversation continued. Ultimately Ray seemed to take up the position of a caring brother. He came to visit my parents -even debating about my welfare and future. He was worried about me, mainly I suppose because of my obvious discontent and the fact that I wasn't well. Ray had a sister whom he saw frequently, and a brother whom he was close to; he spoke little of his parents and I assumed that it wasn't a happy story. He was a young man who could well look after himself.

I chose to ignore my condition as much as possible. Hard work didn't seem to affect it and it was only my susceptibility to lung infection that tended to lay me low. Antibiotics were yet to arrive and it wasn't until I had access to these that my problem improved.

Meanwhile, I was still seeing Brian Robinson. The roof of his beautiful hut blew off in a gale one night and landed in a neighbour's garden. One of his many letters to me describes this and how he then immediately lost interest in it! He kept promising to repair it but it was apparently months later that it regained some of its, albeit rickety, presence. Brian was never one to chase a lost cause. We were still sustaining our common interest in the Arts and what we should be doing with our truncated artistic careers, but having chanced his arm in Chelsea, he didn't seem to want try again.

To St Ives

"Well - when are we goin' ter get arta this set up then?"

"Oh -shurrup. Ye've gorra job 'aven't ye?"

"Yeah. But surely there's gorra be summat more to life than this?"

"Well - what do ye suggest?"

"You know damn well what I mean."

"Oh - ye mean that St Ives thing you were on abart? Well, why don't you just piss off -ye've done it before. What's stopping you?"

"Well, I did have a mate to go with before but he's not budgin' at the moment."

"Well - what are you suggesting? As if I didn't know."

"I thought you might fancy a change."

"You're joking! What would I do in a place like St Ives?"

"Well you've done almost every job possible - perhaps you could go fishin'."

"You're a worrisome bugger, now you're upsetting me."

We were shouting at each other from the tops of trees that we were lopping, somewhere on the outskirts of Sheffield. The next day I was at it again.

"You're happy doing this 'till you're sixty then?"

"Oh! Bloody 'ell - shut up will ya?"

Ray was a real nice guy. Always encouraging and helpful and only getting 'near the edge' when he saw an injustice presenting itself.

In our job as tree loppers and fellers for the Sheffield Parks Dept. this wasn't an unknown phenomenon. Generally benign with a grin and a quip for everyone, he was one of the most genial people I had ever met and also very funny. He was about eight years older than me, I suppose about thirty-two at the time, with an ample backlog of job experience, which ranged from garage attendant to plastering and painting and any job that happened to come along.

We originally met in the Sheffield Town Hall, applying for the 'tree job', as it was called.

"OK" I said, peering through the leaves at him from across the road. "Let's go next week."

"It would bloody shake you if I said yes, wouldn't it!"

"I'm just thinking that if I have to find out whether I'm as good an artist as I might be, I really don't know where else to go to find out. I'm thinking that I might get swallowed up, if I go to London, and I'm not that confident."

"Well, how do you think that you could afford to get to St Ives and survive?"

"Well, I've saved about £200, and we could wash dishes in a hotel or summat'. It's a tourist town apart from being an art colony."

"Ok -ok-ok! If you're so convinced that you're a bloody artistic genius, there seems to be only one way to find out and that's certainly not by chopping down trees! Anyway, to be honest, I think I've had enough of Coleman (the boss), and two years on this job should be enough for any sod." "What you mean you'll do it?"

"Oh - anything to keep you sodding quiet. Give your notice in and we'll set off in a couple of weeks"

He really meant it and I then realised that it had to happen.

A couple of weeks later, we met early morning at the Midland Station. I couldn't believe that he had actually turned up - but then he was always a man of his word.

We were off to Cornwall.

I don't remember much of the journey, except the surprise of being offered, by the train attendant, biscuits straight from the tin - we suddenly felt a bit special. It was 1959 and we were still back in the days of steam and compartmentalised coaches with photos of holiday resorts mounted on the walls and it seemed as if we were the only people in England going to St Ives! As the train rushed on, I felt that we were entering a more sedate, relaxed world with a promise of a rather less aggressive lifestyle than the one experienced in Sheffield.

We probably couldn't have done it in a day and, in retrospect, I remember that we stopped off at Bernard's, one of my distant relatives who ran a boarding house, somewhere in North Cornwall. I also remember that the next day, Ray was mightily impressed by what seemed to us to be veritable forests around Bodmin; then that classic final run in to St Ives from St Erth left us wide-eyed and open-mouthed. The sun was out and the sky and sea were as blue as could be; as we rounded the headland at Carbis Bay we knew that we had not made any mistakes. Ray was as excited as I was and I finally felt justified in dragging him down from the trees.

We were not going to get rich but we had the fabulous freedom and beauty of St Ives - still a fishing town - to enjoy - and it was all on our doorstep.

No more waiting for trams and buses in the rain and snow at ungodly hours or being bounced about, huddled in the back of an open lorry; it had all been replaced with the reality of the blue sea and the golden sands. It was no illusion; it was a relative paradise. Walking down from the Malakoff and into the town, already replete with early holidaymakers, we must have looked fairly outlandish. We knew how to look smart, but we didn't know how to look relaxed.

In order to find ourselves, so to speak, we did the conventional thing and booked bed and breakfast, this at number 1 Carnellis Road at the top of the town. The elderly lady was sweet and looked after us like her own sons - eventually even washing Ray's shirts for him - at a price. Ray was far more conventional than I was and always kept himself immaculate. Looking after himself wasn't a new thing by any means and he was good at it. On the other hand I tended to throw things to the wind and hope that they would fall in a reasonably acceptable pattern. At first, we both wore suits as we thought this only proper if we were to go looking for a job, and certainly that would be the first requirement. We must have stood out like sore thumbs as hardly anybody walked around St Ives in a suit! Hotels were the obvious place to explore and we soon found employment at the largest establishment in the centre of town - Curnow's.

Whether the suits helped us to get the job, I sincerely doubt- St Ives was far too laid back to worry about things like that. We probably appeared as a gay couple from Up North, which we were definitely not!

How much does destiny really play in one's life?
Winston Churchill wrote that destiny is only the result of one's decisions - so I assume that he had thrown spiritual guidance out of the window, early on.
Choosing to apply for a job at Curnows was to begin a life for me that I feel would have been difficult to avoid even if I had wanted to.
Destiny? I have to say - absolutely.

We were invited to meet Treve Curnow, the owner, in his office at Street-an-Garrow. He was a decent enough man and he immediately took us on.

Perhaps it was the suits after all!

There were indeed two jobs available: hall porter and dish washer.

As Ray liked to be immaculate in ironed shirt and tie and I really didn't, it was an obvious choice. He made a very good hall porter and I made a good dishwasher! The work was seasonal. We were paid, I think £4 each but Ray would get tips from the visitors. We did however get free accommodation, as did all the itinerant staff - chambermaids usually -and free meals, which consisted mainly of leftovers from the kitchens and whatever you could scrounge. In winter, I went on the dole as the tourists diminished, whereas the hotel did have residents and jobs for Ray to do.

Curnow's Hotel stretched along the side of the Guildhall, situated in the side street of Street-an-Pol. Here was the main hotel entrance where Ray would field people's luggage and take them up to their bedrooms. The entrance to the Restaurant and Snack Bar was around the corner in Tregenna Place - the main road into the town. They were both very popular particularly at lunch time as I can well testify - I had to wash the breakfast service and later the dinner plates and cutlery!

Our accommodation was interesting. The Post Office dominated the end of Tregenna Place and behind it was Chapel Street. Opposite the rear of the Post Office was a short alley that had to be negotiated by the P.O. vans reversing into a garage. This I got to know intimately ten years later as I, in fact, drove a P.O. van.

For the moment, it was a small side door that drew our attention as this opened on to a flight of wooden stairs, which then landed us into a large loft, or garret. This had once been Curnow's bakery but now proving unprofitable had been abandoned to the dust and spiders.

There was an airy room at the end with two beds and windows overlooking Chapel St, which in summer thronged with tourists, many of them young girls on their way to the beach. Romantic and quite suitable for two Northern lads. Beneath us was another garage that had been used for the bakery vans but was again now unused - although it did contain a petrol pump.

I was then to meet Mrs. Curnow. Everybody called her Mrs. Treve. She was a large outgoing personality and considering the gaffers that I had had, was very personable and caring.

"We're all family here Victor, so make yourself at home as much as possible." I really couldn't believe my luck. All the staff were very friendly and helpful.

Treve Curnow took me along to the Still Room, where meals were dispensed into the restaurant, and dishes and cutlery emerged from another door to be washed and dried. I was introduced to the figure leaning against the washing-up machine. A short, stocky, unsmiling figure of some age with grizzly features and cropped thin grey hair, he was dressed in a yellow waterproof smock and smelt of sweat. Jack Binney had been there many moons and was a dyed-in-the-wool St Ives character. He had 'fisherman' written all over him, but now long past his sell-by date, he had been absorbed like so many others into the hotel industry, a catchall for budding artists, old fishermen and general layabouts who needed to earn the odd crust. Binney was as local as the limpets sticking to the rocks off by Smeatons Pier.

He grunted some sort of greeting, his yellow apron shedding drips on to the wooden floor. His truncated attempts at conversation were exacerbated by years spent at sea and little education. "You will not understand anything he says, Victor. I've known him since he was a boy and I can't. Just go along with what he does and you'll be fine." Jack didn't have any conversation so the problem never arose. I had worked with similar characters in the other jobs that I had done so it didn't really matter to me. The rest of the staff were generally very nice, particularly Polly, the oldest and most respected head of the waiting staff. Dressed in the traditional black dress and white cotton tiara and collar, she seemed to have been there forever. The kitchens were downstairs at floor level at the back of the hotel and were usually to be avoided in the 'rush hour' as busy chefs were inclined to lose their tempers. The upside of this however was that kitchen porters got more and better food as I was later to find out in other hotels.

Ray, who filled in as the night porter would often find himself there alone. He told how on opening the kitchen doors at midnight, a black sea of cockroaches would quickly rustle away under the metal benches and fittings. Food for thought; I suppose it kept the floor clean! Occasionally, I stood in for Ray as night porter, but I didn't bother going into the kitchens! The other night duty was to clean the shoes that had been put out in the corridors - how demeaning! And then the tiled floor of the snack bar had to be washed - this process usually being interrupted by the night 'bobby' stopping in for a chat and a free milkshake! Shades of Edward Hopper.

But now I was soon faced with piles of dirty dishes and, prompted by Jack, I plunged them, one by one, into a huge tank of hot soapy water in which two large brushes were furiously spinning. My delicate hands fortunately had been somewhat hardened off with knocking trees around for a few years; otherwise, they weren't really designed for guiding dishes of various shapes and sizes between the brushes. My fear was that one may disintegrate at high speed and take a few fingers with it, putting an end to my budding artistic career - but it didn't happen.

From there, the dishes, cups and saucers etc. were laid into wooden trays and immersed into another huge tank -this time of near boiling water, heated by gas jets beneath. Laid on the side bench to drain and dry - the end of the exercise was to put them in the required accommodation ready for the black-clad waitresses to pick them up and send on their way again via the chefs and staff in the next part of the room.

The restaurant was well appointed and very well frequented. I had glimpses of it through the swing doors, which opened and closed to the rhythm of the waitresses bringing out the leftovers.

I washed cutlery by hand in a nearby sink.

Occasionally Jack would shout a warning above the noise of the machine and general clamour. "Knives!" and he would plunge a tray of lethal missiles into my sink.

Cutlery had to be hand dried and I took a secret delight in noisily clattering them into the metal trays, ready for pick-up.

Lunch times were exceedingly busy and the dishes would pile up. Slowly Jack and I would be immersed in clouds of steam - not particularly good for my damaged lung but at least it wasn't a Sheffield smog. One onerous duty that the waitresses had to perform, in order to help us, was to knock any plates with remaining food on into a hole in the bench. This had a rubber surround that facilitated the release of the leftovers into a bin below, which was taken away every day by the 'pig man'. The waitresses hated that little procedure but Jack wasn't slow in calling them back if they opted out of it. There were moments of respite when the restaurant fell quiet and Jack would turn around, lean on the machine, peer at me through the steam and give me a look like one of Nelson's gunners having just sunk a Spanish galleon.

The saving grace of the Still Room was that it was on the first floor and was light and airy with wide windows on one side. In a quiet moment, I gazed out of the window into the small courtyard below. Something caught my eye in the window opposite, at ground level. Watching, I could see that a young woman of extraordinary beauty was combing her long dark hair over her right shoulder, whilst apparently talking to a parrot that was perched on her left shoulder. I had to metaphorically rub my eyes as this didn't seem quite real.

"Who is that Jack?"

Jack, peering - "Jacque".

"What - who?" I queried.

"Recepsh - receponist" he uttered.

Ah. I didn't think that I would understand anything else he might say so I intended to wait and see Ray.

I didn't have to wait that long. The side door opened and the same vision ducked under our counter with a swish of a coloured gypsy skirt and an intoxicating breath of perfume that I later learnt was Noa Noa - Gauguin lives! She flitted over to the serving counter to collect her dinner and exchange some bright repartee with the serving staff. It was very obvious that she was well liked and even loved.

She had a dark handsome beauty -her hair now back in a pony tail. A certain air of confidence and just a little sense of superiority pervaded her. She completely ignored my presence. I was smitten.

I had already made friends with some of the staff and one in particular made it clear that any interest I might show in 'our Jacque' might not meet with the negative reaction that I was already expecting.

I tackled Ray at the earliest opportunity.

"Who? Oh - Jacque - lovely -she's the receptionist. There's two - the other one is Kathy". I guess I had only been there a couple of days but I already felt that fate was beginning to sweep me along.

There were chambermaids, of course, and they lived in but I saw little of them, their hours not being coincident with mine, and their itinerary usually being getting sunburnt on the beach - never my thing. The exception was young Winnie, who by way of the hotel 'fixer' had been fixed with a date with me, as she purported to be lonely and, apparently, liked me. She had a boyfriend who was still working at home.

We walked together to Knill's Steeple Woods, one of my favourite escapes, overlooking the bay. Although a very nice Scots lassie, I thought a passing friendship would suffice. She was very young and I had bigger fish to fry i.e. a career in Art! The idea of having to look after someone emotionally and maybe financially didn't at that time appeal to me.

It had to be said that the whole place was full of character.

The other notable maid was Annie, who you couldn't avoid. Very attractive and from a good family, she floated in and out of the hotel. Long legged and lightly garbed for the beach, together with a rather 'couldn't care less' attitude, she was an obvious target for anyone wanting a holiday romance. She would trip in from the beach and leave a sand trail across Ray's entrance hall carpet. "Hey I've got to clean that lot up!"

A few days passed and Ray divulged that Jacque had a flat overlooking the bay and, what's more, he was in the process of doing some decorating for her! I was shocked! Where was I in all this?

"She cooks a dinner for me in lieu of money."

"Ray - mate - any chance of me -er - like - er -helping out?"

"Ask her, for Christ's sake - when she's on duty."

Plagued by shyness, I yet knew that I had to speak to her.

I eventually bucked up enough courage to go down to the little office and make my presence known.

"Oh. Hello! You're Ray's chum. Yes - bring a brush if you've got one. Ray says you're a bit of an artist; I'd like to see what you've done."

Not that again! I realised that I had unconsciously come up with an introduction and talking point despite myself.

I was awe-struck with her charm and beauty.

A couple of days later we were both three flights up in her Talland Road attic flat. I was painting the skirting boards at the top of the stairs and Ray was painting the landing.

A tall, handsome young man, casually dressed, came up the stairs.

"Don't get up" he said, stepping over me with long legs.

He disappeared into the front room that overlooked the bay. Being high up it had a wonderful view out to Godrevy lighthouse, Carn Brea and out along the North Coast.

He was chatting to Jacque.

"Who the fuck is that? I whispered, fearing the worst - some young Lothario.

"That's Phil, her brother. She's got a younger one, Paul. Great guys, they both spend time here.

"Well, why the fuck don't they do this job then?"

Ray suddenly saw the possibility that if I didn't shut up, his dinner might not appear. Food was number one on Ray's agenda - then sleep!

Whispering, "He's a ship's officer, drops his gear here and dosses until he finds the next bird and has a good time, which usually doesn't take long." "Well, bully for him" I thought, slapping on a bit more paint.

He left, throwing "Do a good job, lads" over his shoulder.

"Bloody cheek" thought I.

We were well fed and watered, but just to see her and hear her speak was thanks enough - for me, anyway. I thought it too obvious to show her my work at this time and I hoped that she would invite me for a private viewing. This, she later did.

I did have some time free from washing the dishes - but not a lot.

Sundays were the best days as the restaurant and café were closed and so I only had to contend with the residents' meals; then, Jack and I did alternate Sundays.

Meanwhile, I found the sensuality of St Ives quite overwhelming. It wasn't just the fact that young girls in bikinis littered the beautiful beaches but the sun, sometimes Mediterranean in intensity, the purity of colour, the sense of space over the sea, the sudden shower of rain pelting on the cobbled streets, the lapping of the tide against moored boats, sand trickling through toes and fingers, the slither and flop of fish being landed by the Sloop Inn, the smell of fresh pasties and bread wafting down Fore Street. Intoxicating!

Curnow's hotel became an anchor - somewhere to eat and sleep and a place I could call in any time. The hour I had off in the afternoons I usually spent on the Wharf, just soaking up the sun and the atmosphere. I soon realised how tense and uptight I was and even my normal walking pace appeared ridiculous in St Ives. I made a conscious effort to slow down!

If I was lucky, I might catch a glimpse of Jacque shopping, or in the lobby when she was on duty, but it was very difficult for me to speak to her. On initially meeting with anyone, I was usually excruciatingly shy.

I tried to concentrate on the dishes.

I'm sorry but this didn't always work. I was twentysix and hadn't had a girlfriend since my occasional truncated encounters with Jean and Doreen in the steelworks period in the middle fifties. I was definitely frustrated and seeing all the potential that lay around - mostly on the beach - I soon gave in.

The first event was a one night stand and not at my behest.

One of the waitresses was definitely not local and only deferred to the black outfit 'en passant.' Her shoes, I remember, were cute and colourful.

Very independently minded, she had definitely 'been around'. Lillian was, I suppose, around fifty. She was still very attractive and smart. Apparently she had rubbed shoulders with one or two English film stars of the period and told of how handsome they were. She also purported to like writing poetry and, given a lull in kitchen activity, she always took the chance to engage me in conversation about my artistic plans for the future. From then it was a case of 'can you show me your etchings!'

That evening, I sauntered up the Stennack to her flat where, after spending a while perusing some of my drawings and watercolours, we slipped into bed.

I had warned Ray not to expect me back before dawn. He did worry about me in a brotherly way, and having met my parents, he had sort of taken on the mantle of a discreet protector.

On my return, shortly after the golden light had spread across this golden town in the sea, he was awake and enquired as to where the hell I had been.

He groaned in disbelief, but always ready with a bit of North Country advice, he offered - "Wash under yer foreskin!"

Really! What did he think I had been doing?

"That won't take long Ray - I haven't got one." I washed anyway.

I slumped into my bed for a couple of hours sleep.

On arriving for duty at 9.00a.m., I could already feel eyes boring into me.

Ray and I were not the kind of people who traded amorous stories, but nevertheless, he had already spilled the beans and the story of my 'etching exposure' had travelled through the hotel like the proverbial wildfire.

Mrs.Treve appeared at the still room door looking somewhat like a dowager duchess.

"And how did you find Lillian last night, young man?" I was hiding behind a pile of steaming dishes.

"Fine thanks Ma'am"

"I'm just going down to see our Jacque - I wonder what she's going to say about the matter."

I was thinking that normally that would have been the end of any relationship between Jacque and myself but this was far from a normal place. Hard won Northern ethics didn't seem to exist here. People very rarely swore and the word 'fuck' was almost unheard - but yet they had a much broader outlook on the actual action.

Ray was the next to poke his head around the door.

"Jacque would like to see you when you've got a break" he grinned mischievously.

I arrived at the receptionist's window and sheepishly opened the hatch.

Jacque and Kathy were giggling.

"Oh - here's lover boy - did you have a nice time last night?"

"It was alright. I would rather have been with you."

"Oh really! Well you'll have to be a good boy in future won't you!" Blushing, I hurried back to my dumb dishes.

Lillian was asking me not to stay away. I had to tell her that by now, I was in love with Jacque. She understood and wished me good luck.

34. Jacque (c1966)

I confided in my mature lady friend on the staff.

"Why don't you just ask her? She doesn't have a boyfriend and I think she likes you."

I wasn't going to argue with that and bowing to her internal knowledge I decided that I had to make an effort.

My chance soon came.

The next day, the lobby was silent and I found Jacque standing looking through the window at the top of the main stairs.

"Er!" gauchely, "What are you thinking about?" Why I thought this a suitable opening gambit, I shall never know, but it seemed to work. Perhaps no one had ever asked her before.

She turned. "Oh. Hello. I was just watching the people going into the Guildhall. There's a ballet company on at the moment and I was wondering whether it would be worth seeing."

"I would like to take you" I blurted. I felt my cheeks getting hot and red, but I was still at the bottom of the stairs and so perhaps thought that the flush wouldn't be noticed.

She ignored the offer but supplanted, "You didn't bring any of your work to show me when you came to the flat. Why don't you do that?"

"Er - when?"

"This evening would be good. I'll make you some tea."

And so it happened. I was at last alone with this beautiful sophisticate, who had such charm the like of which I had never before encountered.

She seemed genuinely intrigued by my work.

"This is very good - you are a real artist. I know what I'm talking about. You should be doing this all the time, not washing dishes. It's better than much of the work on show in the town."

"Really?" Was I dreaming all this?

We had tea and talked about our backgrounds. They couldn't have been more different.

I was twenty-seven and still fairly naïve about relationships with the opposite sex, whereas she was thirty-six and worldly wise in such matters.

I was intrigued to hear that she had spent twelve years of her early life in India, her father being a Captain in the Indian Army. He went by the name of Moran and was of Irish stock.

As a young schoolgirl, she had experienced the Quetta earthquake where her school had been thereby demolished. Apparently she was the only white child attending at the time. When she finally left India with her mother and Desmond, her elder brother, it seemed natural that the boat, which left from Karachi, was caught up in nothing short of a typhoon!

Colourful? Absolutely! The family had Indian servants to call on, as was customary in the period of the great British Raj, and she and Desmond were tended by an Iya - an Indian nanny.

"I didn't like my brother much, I used to hide up in trees and jump on him!"

Like many people brought up abroad, she had a certain look of the people who had fostered her. She was not pretty - she was handsome, with dark eyes and long dark hair tied back. At five foot and six inches she was just under my height. She had a certain delicacy of movement and hand gesture and a distinctive flavour about her apparel. Tastefully colourful and worn with flair - almost - but not quite - a gypsy. I had spent a few months living and working with gypsies - so I knew what I was talking about. What became quickly obvious was her confidence and fearlessness. Absolutely nothing fazed her. "Why don't you leave the work with me? I'd like to spend more time looking at them." I'd never received that measure of attention before and I was happy to do so.

My heart was singing as I ran down the steps and on to Tregenna Hill, down Chapel Street and flopped onto my bed in the welcoming loft.

Ray had just finished his shift of duty. "What are you looking so cocky about? You're usually a miserable bugger."

When I told him what had happened, I sensed a mixed reaction. Although he never admitted it, I think he was just a little bit in love with Jacque himself.

Ray shared the hall porter job with one other. He was called Bert.

Older and very cynical, he didn't seem to like anybody and certainly couldn't be deemed to be an attractive person in any way. Obviously sexually frustrated, he would hang around the reception area and attempt to chat up Kathy and Jacque. They didn't like him, of course, and he paid them back by saying venomous things behind their back.

Sometime in her late twenties, Jacque had fallen into a relationship with Sven Berlin, a handsome St Ives sculptor/painter who fitted the drinking, womanising image of the Bohemian far better than most could. Sven could be said to have modelled himself on Augustus John whom he knew and who had connections in Cornwall. Certainly the similarities couldn't be discounted. John was already famous and Jacque recounts how she found herself sitting between Sven and Augustus John in the Ship Inn at Mousehole - both with a hand on each knee. In one of his books, Sven recounts how John was too interested in Jacque to notice him! There were no secrets in a place like St Ives, and the Jacque/Sven affair was no exception. Although it had happened years before when Jacque had fallen very ill, and Sven had left St Ives under a cloud, stories about local celebrities die hard!

I was very curious to know more.

"Huh! Seven Berlin!" spat Bert. (I learnt that many of the older locals, often uneducated, couldn't countenance the name Sven and replaced it with the more familiar 'seven' probably a memory of their 7 times table.)

"Unwashed dead-beat. Long greasy hair - God knows what she was doing with him!" I was convinced that this wasn't the real story and decided to avoid Bert wherever possible. Ray didn't like him either.

In my time off, I would set off for the woods surrounding Knill's Steeple above the town, to do some drawing and gouache work. Here I could confer with nature and commence to do what I had come here for. Alternatively, I would make off in the other direction, down the Digey and along beautiful Porthmeor Beach to Man's Head and Clodgy. All reached within the hour, it was a romantic paradise and my work quickly began to develop.

Back in the still room a short time later, I had a surprise coming to me.

Jacque suddenly entered holding a framed picture. I turned and she held it up for me to see. It was an ink drawing that I had done up at the Steeple Woods. I had called it 'Resurgam'. This was the inscription engraved at the base of the monument, and although I wasn't a Latin scholar, I thought it appropriate. I had left it with her up at the flat.

She had had it framed at Lanham's in the High Street at her own expense. I was absolutely lost for words and couldn't quite believe what I was seeing. It was one of my drawings that had suddenly been given status.

"It's for you. This is what you must do", she said, seriously.

I knew that this was a turning point in my life.

St Ives, of course, had been an Art Colony for decades but still had only two major galleries in the town. I feasted on these and began to learn the names of artists that had passed through and many of them who were still here working. I tried to figure out how, when and where I might fit in. Due to my crippling shyness, I knew this wouldn't be easy.

However, I soon became familiar with all the names, some of them now gone but their work not forgotten, and others of current fame and occasionally to be seen strolling around the town. I was still on the outside looking in and, this time, Ray couldn't help me.

Halfway down Fore Street was No.36. This had changed hands from time to time but had now settled into being the venue for art of a more abstract nature. Some of the most important abstract artists to have graced St Ives had split from the St Ives Society of Artists to form their own group and this was their venue. I could walk in and view work by Ben Nicholson, Barbara Hepworth, Johnny Wells, Peter Lanyon, Terry Frost, Patrick Heron, Roger Hilton, Bryan Winter, Willie Barns-Graham and many others, all appearing from time to time, and apart from Nicholson who had left just a few years before I arrived - they were all still here! Much of their work had already been shown in galleries around Britain and in Europe and one or two of them were challenging the powerful American artists, but there are many books written on the subject and I'm not a historian.

I was totally unknown, of course, and my only chance of bumping into celestial beings was if I happened to pass them in the town or on one occasion, when Peter Lanyon and I crossed the hotel entrance at the same time - and he acknowledged me! Apparently he was the art representative for the local Rotary Club, which held their meetings at the hotel. He was appropriately dressed in a suit and looked like a businessman! The impossible thing was that, in those days, particularly in winter, any newcomers on the Art Scene were soon identified and maybe assessed as a possible threat to sales and reputation or discarded as not to be considered further! I certainly wasn't either but I was a new kid on the block and couldn't believe it when I was actually recognised as such. Suddenly I found myself rubbing shoulders with Dame Barbara Hepworth - in Woolworths! And then finding myself alone with her looking at some of her sculpture which had been put on display in the local park and being asked how I was! Needless to say I didn't tell her how the dishes were piling up.

Whilst washing the plates one day, I was told that someone was at the back door to see me. Still garbed in my yellow apron and somewhat puzzled, I was met on the back step by a smiling Misome Piele, admittedly not one of the great artists in town but still someone to be reckoned with.

"I wanted to welcome you to the St Ives Art Colony and I'm sure that you will not be washing dishes for very long! I've just seen your work in No.36 and it's a pity that you've just missed Ben!"

Swallowing my shyness, I thanked her and glowed. I found that many of the artists were somewhat upper class, well educated, well spoken, and certainly didn't come from the back streets of Sheffield! I was still talking in a broad Yorkshire accent, which like other accents, didn't become fashionable until much later. Misome, like most of the women in the Art Colony was a lady, and most of the male artists- gentlemen. I had a long way to go.

I had submitted to the No.36 gallery two gouaches that I had done up in the woods. As it happened, they had turned out to have an abstract look about them, rather like Ivon Hitchens, whose work I admired. I hopefully thought they might just fit in at the 36. Fit in!! When I arrived breathless at the Gallery, I couldn't believe that one was displayed in the window! Vivian Nankervis was the curator (in those days this word still meant someone who sat there all day and not someone who chose the exhibits) and I found her to be so friendly to me that much of my shyness seeped out of my boots. A very nice young lady. I had arrived and in pole position!

"Your work is well thought of - you should send more in."

I did. My ink and charcoal drawings were particularly acceptable and when the 36 became a class restaurant, my work was deemed to be good enough to be hung around the walls and exclusive!

St Ives, of course, wasn't the only or the first Art Colony in West Cornwall. Indeed, Newlyn had attracted many well-known artists and Stanhope Forbes and his fellows were prominent at the turn of the 19th.century. All traditional and years before the incursion of modern abstract art, the Newlyn school were generally depicting the local fishing and farming scene in a very literal style. Newlyn Gallery eventually showed little of this and the space was given over to contemporary art, mainly by local painters, I'm happy to say, as I was now one of them. The old Newlyn paintings were eventually resurrected from the cellars and attics to find a new home in the Gallery in Penlee Park. Like much of Victorian art they had been out of fashion for many years but have now been given their true value.

Newlyn Gallery in the sixties became our out of town gallery; it was run and supported by local artists and enjoyed by all. Unfortunately, eventually being strapped for cash, John Halkes who had proved himself in Penzance as a successful entrepreneur gallery owner, was called in. He ultimately called for the marines in the shape of the Arts Council and that, in my humble opinion, was the beginning of the end to one of our free-thinking galleries of the period.

But back to St Ives.

The St Ives Society of Artists was the old original Society formed in 1927 and was always the flagship of what was known as traditional art. This was the stuff that had to show something that you could readily recognise in subject matter and skill in all the parameters of painting: such as colour, design, atmosphere etc. and if your work wasn't of a high standard in all those departments, there was little chance of you being made a member, or even getting over the threshold.

The Society is still going strong; I write this as 2013 dawns and I find myself, from being the second youngest member on my election in 1961 to now being the longest-serving member that the Society ever had!

It was originally conceived in one of the remarkable Porthmeor studios overlooking that fabulous beach, and exhibitions were regularly held there. Borlase Smart also had a studio there and this was combined to make further exhibition space. Together with the efforts of Commander Bradshaw and other founder member stalwarts such as Moffat Lindner, the Society went from strength to strength. Smart was extremely adept at promoting the Society and by 1936 exhibitions were being organised in cities and towns, among them Birmingham and Cheltenham. Painters such as Shearer Armstrong, Bernard Ninnes, Leonard Richmond, Laura Knight, were to join and many of them were to be successful at the Royal Academy and the Royal Society of Marine Artists in London. RA members such as Muncaster and Munnings were invited to show and even for a short period became presidents of the Society.

By 1938 Show Days had been promoted by Bradshaw, Smart and their colleagues and had become extremely popular with visitors, even from as far away as London.

Newlyn artists such as Stanhope Forbes, Lamorna Birch, Harold Harvey et al were invited to show and their work was accommodated at the Porthmeor Studios. Leonard Fuller, a well-respected gentleman and an excellent artist, ran the St Ives School of Painting in nearby Back Road West.

In the early days even trains were engaged to carry traditional work up to London and the Academy.

Wilhelmina Barnes-Graham (known as Willie) joined in 1940, and with the likes of Shearer Armstrong were being attracted to Modern Art so much so that together with Borlase Smart who, although fully immersed in his beautiful seascapes and local views was not, unlike Bradshaw, averse to 'The Abstract Boys' - and Girls becoming members of the Society. By 1943, none other than Ben Nicholson and Barbara Hepworth had joined. Bradshaw and others resented their inclusion; Munnings was also showing his disaffection for abstraction at the Academy in London.

It soon became clear that the studios could not hold all the members' work.

Modernists like the young Peter Lanyon, Bryan Wynter, Johnny Wells and Sven Berlin were also to join the Society.

As it happened, just across the road in Nor'way Square, the Mariners Church had not yet been consecrated and had been put up for sale. Many of the St Ives people were dedicated Methodists and I suspect that this had something to do with the church ultimately being abandoned.

The Mariners Church, in those early days, overlooked Pudding Bag Lane, which although being pictorially useful for the artist, was now regarded as something of a slum area.

Consequently, it was eventually demolished, and is now one of the ubiquitous car parks, this one being behind the famous Sloop Inn (on the harbour slipway), itself a popular meeting place for artists.

And so, in 1945 with the aid of a private grant, which was ultimately paid back, the Society became the owners of the church, (at that time called the New Gallery) and, in fact, still own it.

Other artists of both affiliations joined and were now accommodated. One such, Hyman Segal, joined in 1947 and became very popular with the locals, his work being easily accessible and much of it depicting portraits of the local fishermen. Many of these portraits were hung in the Sloop Inn. He also drew, often in pastel, native people, revelling in the quality of the dark skin. This work was certainly different from the accepted St Ives genres but certainly could not be termed as modern either. One or two sculptors were to join, notably Faust Lang and his son Wharton, whose wood sculpture was to grace the floor for many years to come. Barbara Tribe, a sculptress in stone, although nothing like Hepworth, also became a long-term member. Bernard Leach who was rapidly becoming the most famous studio potter in Britain also showed his wares.

Eventually the modernists closed ranks, took over a section of the lower part of the church and called themselves 'The Crypt Group'. Painters such as Lanyon, Wynter and Sven Berlin showed there. This move eventually led to the infamous split, and headed by Nicholson and Hepworth, they retired to a pub in Fore Street to form The Penwith Society of Arts.

One or two of them, notably Segal, didn't agree with the categorisation that was being recommended and, in his case, returned to the fold of the Society. A number of local artists and craftsmen joined neither the Penwith nor the Society, such as the potter, Anthony

Richards, who was busy plying his trade in the Digey. Small independent spaces, like Lanhams in the High Street, and Downings Bookshop in Fore Street, continued to give small exhibitions.

Soon enough the members of the new society went off to do their thing in their own inimitable way and took over No.36 Fore Street. This venue, in prime position, became very active and showed work by most of the abstract artists in the area, although Nicholson by now had left. In the early sixties I felt privileged to have shown there.

But the old Society carried on regardless, producing work that much of the public loved and wanted, and I wasn't averse to admiring much of it. Many of the abstract painters however were biased enough not to cross the threshold.

Eventually, the Penwith were able to gain grants from the Arts Council and the Gulbenkian Foundation, probably promoted by the increasing fame of some their number, and were thus able to purchase a pilchard cellar at the centre of Back Road West, which, after renovation, made an excellent modern gallery. This is still serving today, although not with anything like the élan of those former years.

One service it did provide was that of showing work which was difficult to fit into the concept of traditional art and therefore wasn't generally accepted by the St Ives Society. Neither being of abstract or of a modern nature and so differing from the work shown at the 36, or now at the new Penwith building, it was nevertheless not overlooked there. This was the area of Art that became known as naïve or primitive. St Ives had one particular example, notably Bryan Pearce, a son of St Ives who had an unfortunate condition of the brain, which restricted him socially but gave his efforts at painting an unusual slant. With the help of his mother and other well wishers in the community, his work developed over the years, became popular nationally, and ultimately attracted very large prices. This was certainly in part due to the encouragement of the Penwith. Alfred Wallis was another important St Ives painter, who never considered himself as such. Discovered painting ships and harbours on old scraps of board by Ben Nicholson and friends, he was labelled primitive. Although dying penniless in Madron workhouse in the 1940's, his work ultimately was regarded as important and of high value. The Penwith showed Bryan's work successfully from his early beginnings and Alfred's work posthumously.

Sven Berlin was also impossible to categorise. A well-known character and denizen of the Art Colony, he was good looking and muscular and he could be seen carving stone and wood figures outside his studio on the Island - that beautiful promontory of St Ives, that, in fact, was nearly an island, but not quite. Rather like Sven's studio that he called The Tower - but in fact, wasn't one.

As I have said, I'm not an historian - neither am I an Art critic but I felt that I had a fair judgement of much of the Art that was produced around me and which, you could say, I was ultimately competing with.

I felt that Sven's perhaps biggest contribution to the St Ives Story was his very presence. A larger than life figure that was perhaps his finest work!

Certainly a great tourist attraction, especially in the town pubs and probably judged to be the epitome of the St Ives artist, although I'm sure that the more reserved members of the Colony didn't think that.

There's no doubt that he worked at his image and his art; his sculpture being particularly difficult to handle physically, as I doubt that he had much assistance, unlike Hepworth, who employed a number of people, some of them fellow artists, such as newcomer Breon O'Casey and the more mature Denis Mitchell.

I thought, having recently seen a retrospective exhibition at Penlee Gallery in 2012, which enforced my view that although Sven's work was very variable and often unsuccessful, occasionally the strength and mythology revealed in the stone did win through. His paintings, I thought, were totally lacking in sensitivity and sometimes bordering on the brutal. This seemed to me to be about largely enforcing his personality on the viewer. His drawings on the other hand could be absolutely charming and show great spontaneity and sensitivity.

But to me his best work was his writing. He had several books published which I thought that at their best gave an insight on what living in the Colony was really like - not some glamourised version. However, he eventually came unstuck when he had Dark Monarch published. This book described the people and fellow artists of St Ives in a disguise that wasn't too difficult to unveil, the consequence being that Sven wasn't then perhaps the popular figure that he had been. Why he should have wanted to do this is not in my remit, but it seems that this was a feature of his leaving St Ives and going to live in the New Forest with his new lady Juanita Valasquez, also known as Mrs. Elsie Fisher. This occurred in 1953. His friend Guido Morris, who ran a printing service close by, also left, unable to sustain the business and probably the victim of his own extremely high aestheticism. He had printed exquisite catalogues for exhibitions and also small editions of up and coming poets - now highly collectible.

Jacque remembers seeing him working on the London tube, years later.

It's interesting to note that the banking that dropped down to Porthgwidden Beach, below Sven's and Guido's studios, was, at that time, nothing more than a tip for local rubbish and certainly nothing like the attraction it is today.

Shortly before this, Jacque had almost succumbed to a long battle with tuberculosis. After being very ill in St Ives- coughing up her life's blood in the Little House in Street an Pol- she had been saved by Doctor Hall who, on hearing about her dire condition had her shipped up to his sanatorium at Rosehill in Penzance. She underwent surgery to remove part of her right lung and an area of ribcage with Mr. Griffiths at Hawkmoor Hospital on Dartmoor, and later recuperation at Tehidy Hospital at Camborne. She was lucky to survive. In those days there were no antibiotics and it was largely down to streptomycin and surgery to promote a cure; Jacque eventually saw many of her friends and fellow sufferers fall to the disease.

One would have to say that her bright spirit and positive nature helped her survival and recovery.

Sven apparently wasn't the sort of person to wait and find out, and he abandoned Jacque to her fate.

People were attracted to her, and friends like Alex and Eddie Kalma (a Dutchman who was part of the St Ives Art Colony) who lived at Exeter at the time - later at Zennor - helped her recovery. She also found employment with the Hamburger family. She had domestic duties and care of their very young child called 'Guggles'. Michael was a published poet who seemed to spend much of his time lying under a tree in the orchard whilst his wife, Ann, delegated much of the household duties to Jacque - but she was happy there and was regaining her strength. Later Jacque found employment at D H Evans, a large store on Oxford Street in London, whilst living in a nearby hostel. Her mother had moved to Plymouth at the time; unfortunately this was the period when it got heavily bombed. Jacque came down to see her, only to find that the house was no more. She feared the worst but, in fact, her mother had been evacuated and eventually ended up in St Ives, where she spent the rest of her days and brought up her two other children, John James, known as Phil, and Paul.

Jacque decided to settle in St Ives, became a receptionist at the Chy an Albany Hotel, above Porthminster Beach and found a very nice top flat in Talland Road nearby. It was a few years later that she decided to apply for the same job at Curnow's in the town and it is there where we met, in 1959.

By this time many of the older members of the St Ives Society of Artists had died or left the area. The balmy days of exhibitions in other towns and cities, and plenty of exposure at the Royal Academy had gone. There was a closing of ranks and the Society wasn't to show any work of an abstract nature until a relaxing of policy around the year 2000. Twelve years later it took Limited Company status in order to gain grants for the upkeep of the building.
I was elected in 1961. Bradshaw had died in 1960 aged 72, but some of the older members were still showing their work. The gallery was tended by Hugh Ridge, the Secretary, and the curator, Mrs. Leddra, and headed by Claude Muncaster as President. The committee included Hyman Segal, Denys Law and Sybil Mullen Glover. Notable members were Charles Breaker, Stuart Armfield, Fred Whicker, Jack Merriott and the progressive Bill Redgrave.

Meanwhile, Ray was getting itchy feet. As he had no interest in the Art Colony and little talent finding a friend of the opposite sex, he felt that reading the daily paper on the Wharf had its limitations. We did go for walks, notably up the Belyars and across the fields to Halsetown or along Hain Walk to Carbis Bay, even on one notable day, taking Jacque with us - but he was already looking for wider horizons. "Canada, I think, mate, is the place for me! Can't think what I would be doing". "I could see you as a Mountie", I suggested.
"I doubt that and I suspect lumber jacking could prove to be too much like hard work. Anyway, I think I'm off soon."
He could see that my relationship with Jacque was taking a serious turn; I was beginning to spend more time with her than with him. Not that we had much time, anyway. This might have pushed him to make the move.
In fact, he spent the rest of his days in Vancouver working as a postman and where he did actually get married. He only returned once to see me in St Ives, on his way to meet up with his brother and sister in Sheffield.
I always thought that he was a born bachelor but I suspect he was ready for a more settled life. Sadly, many years later, his wife died of cancer; he said that he would never want to go through that again. We still exchange Christmas letters.

Jacque at that time was a very sociable person and well-loved in St Ives. She would invite friends up to her flat for a drink. I would usually sit in a corner, rather tongue-tied.
"Don't worry about it - it's not important."
I had arrived from another planet and I hadn't yet learnt the language.
I was doing my best at the hotel; the staff were generally kind, especially Polly, the elderly head waitress, and Johnny Williams, the head chef. The old lady in charge of the chamber maids and the linen was a bit of a nosy old trout but meant well and was always ready with a bit of advice. Treve Curnow would sometimes put in an appearance in order to cheer us along.
"Scrub the floor before you go off duty."
This would infuriate Jacque as fingers, having been well softened by a few hours of hot water treatment, would easily bleed by coming in contact with the wooden floor. As I had wielded axes and saws for the Forestry Commission and the Sheffield Parks Department, this wasn't exactly new to me.
"You mustn't be doing this! You must look after your hands."

That was new.

But for the moment there wasn't an alternative.

Winter in St Ives was different. There was little work as the visitors left and it became no discredit to pay a weekly visit to the Labour Exchange behind the Royal Cinema. Hotel workers, fishermen and labourers would congregate there as the weather became somewhat bleaker.

The seas could be awesome; it was exciting for me to watch huge waves breaking over Godrevy lighthouse or occasionally rushing up so high as to cover the lookout on the Island. On one occasion in an incredibly strong gale, I attempted to walk up the path to the lookout to view the tremendous rollers pounding across the Atlantic with little to stop them on their wild journey. After almost being blown over twice and then experimenting with a spate of crawling, I had to concede defeat.

The local legend was that you could fire a shotgun down Fore Street in winter and not hit anybody. Theoretically this was certainly sometimes true; an unbelievable contrast to the summer months when it would be jam packed with tourists. In later years, although St Ives became even more popular and the seasons began to merge, hotels and cafes would have to close down. Curnow's Hotel, restaurant and café, although the largest establishment of its kind in town, was no exception, and so eventually I found myself without accommodation.

I was desperate to stay. Jacque immediately came up with an answer.

"Kathy has a large house over in Primrose Valley. She says you can have the ground floor flat for a minimal rent". Needless to say, I was delighted.

The steep Primrose Valley ran from the main Tregenna Road down a steep track to Porthminster Beach. The house, Manderley, had a huge front room for me to work in; from the large windows I could see across the tennis courts to St Ives and the harbour.

My Shangri-la.

Ray had already returned to Sheffield in order to prepare for his trip to Canada. He called on my parents to give them the news on how I was and also helped Father to crate up some of my possessions that I had requested.

The crate duly arrived at Manderley; by now it was obvious that I wasn't coming home.

Having failed my Army medical in 1951 due to a severe bout of bronchiactesis and moderate short sightedness, it wasn't any surprise to me that, soon after, I didn't receive any further word from the Canadian Emigration Board after I had had a medical in Liverpool. I had thought to follow my brother to Canada. Resigned to fate I carried on and made my St Ives plans. What I didn't know was that I had, in fact, passed the medical - fit for Canada, but not for the British Army. I suppose that my father was relatively happy for me still to be in England, albeit incidentally as far away as I could go.

I was drawing a small amount of money from the dole office and I also had some money that I had saved from my work in Sheffield. Jacque had said that she would love to see a couple of friends in London as winter drew on but she really couldn't afford to do so. I was happy to give her a part of my savings as I was by now confident that she wouldn't let our broadening relationship wane.

I was left to work at Manderley, wander the fields above St Ives, and explore the coastline. I was lonely but it wasn't the first time, and I knew that, at last, I was doing what I had to do. If I failed, then at least I would also know that I had tried.

I had a large bedroom in the flat which, however, suffered from condensation and lack of sunshine, being in the lee of the narrow valley. My conservative brown suit left hanging in the wardrobe eventually gathered mildew; as I threw it in the bin I felt that I had shed my chrysalid skin and hopefully would now emerge as a rather more colourful object.

Kathy was always very kind but Len, her husband, wasn't. He was much older than Kathy and I would say that they were ill-matched, in my opinion. This was later born out as she ran off with an artist friend of mine and never returned to Manderley until Len had died. He once stomped into Curnow's and took Jacque to task for influencing Kathy. He wasn't wrong there. Things like that didn't bother Jacque - she had been through too much for that.

I wasn't the best housekeeper but as I was paying rent I assumed that I could go along at my own pace - er -no. He soon began to complain about this and that; I began to find it difficult to keep him happy, perhaps the only time being when he asked me to paint the house name on the front gate, which I did successfully.

Kathy was still working with the skeleton staff at Curnow's, which usually had a revamp at this time of year. I tried to avoid Len but he spent quite a time patching and painting around the large house - keeping up his very high standards. He was a tradesman and very good at what he did but I felt that he would never understand anyone who was artistically inclined.

I can't say that I did any significant work at Manderley. The best of it would have been my drawings as the painting side of it had not yet gelled.

Jacque returned as the spring arrived; I began to spend more time at her flat and our relationship became even more intimate.

She had a younger brother called Paul who would put in an appearance from time to time. He was a bright boy and would drop off a few jazz records, which I readily became acquainted with; these, together with an LP record of Buddy Holly, became iconic of the period and the place, and forever after I couldn't hear them without being transported back.

These were supplemented by my classic collection that had been sent down from Sheffield; Jacque and I had plenty of Sibelius, Mahler, Brahms etc. to choose from. Often it was enough for me to go there alone and listen to the sea in the Bay below and reflect on what I saw as my good fortune. The flat became a sanctuary.

On leaving Sheffield I had left behind a very good friend who had similar artistic aspirations to me. His name was Brian Robinson and I have already written about our meeting and the subsequent relationship.

I was keen for him to come to St Ives; as Ray had left and Jack Binney had retired, it seemed a perfect opportunity for him.

My fear had been that he would fritter away his talent in Sheffield, a place that I never saw as being particularly Art conscious.

He agreed to come down and as the season began we were back in Curnow's garret and together trying to further our artistic bent and washing dishes! There was a difference. I would talk about the idea of getting on whereas he would always reply that there was nowhere to get on to. He was a committed dreamer and this was reflected in his work, whereas I had a hard practical side to me: I felt protective towards him.

I suppose that I could be a little overbearing at times; this occasionally would evoke a rather petulant reaction in him. But at least he stuck at it for the time being.

He soon transformed the garret into something that would have graced a production of 'La Bohème'; the place started to exude atmosphere. We set up easels and work was soon starting to appear. He liked to fill up sketchbooks with dreamy landscapes gathered mainly from his long walks. It wasn't easy to go out together as our duties were often interdependent. I was still doing gouache and pen and ink drawings around St Ives, up in the Steeple Woods and over to Clodgy or Porthminster.

35. Victor and Brian dishwashing at Curnow's Hotel 1960.

We both submitted work to No.36 and Brian too was immediately accepted, both our work being displayed in the window. Brian quickly sold one for £42, which, at that time, was a good sum of money.

We spent time together with Jacque and her young intelligent friend, another Jacqui (Leafe), who was still at High School.

As I have written, Brian was sufficiently different and camp enough for one to assume that he was gay but up to that point there was no actual evidence of it, apart from how he appeared. Much later, Jacque swore that he was, having had time alone together; she thought me naïve to think otherwise. But then he also spent time with another of Jacque's friends, whom we christened 'mad Maggie from Helston'. She wasn't really mad, just a bit zany and unconventional. "

"I thought he could well be queer" offered Jacque, fishing.

"Well I couldn't say", offered Maggie, "but he did keep sticking something into my leg." "Oh! That would be one of his pencils", I said, trying to confuse the issue.

I had been closer to him than anyone and as I definitely wasn't gay it didn't really concern me. The women around us seemed more interested.

Things perhaps became a little clearer when he took up with Stephen Church. Phil, Jacque's brother, was convinced that Stephen was a 'closet Queen'; he certainly did have a penchant for taking in young fellows who were somewhat dead-beat and giving them a bed in his house by the harbour. At the time there were plenty around as this was the time of the hippy. Another clue was that Stephen made it obvious that his favourite artist was, with his 'Yellow Book', Aubrey Beardsley.

Later on Stephen took Brian on a trip to Spain and that seemed a bit significant. By then I was getting more and more involved with Jacque; Brian quite rightly was looking elsewhere for friendship. I felt that at least I had helped him to cut the Sheffield umbilical cord and broaden his artistic outlook.

Stephen was a friend of the family, so to speak; he was one of the few people that we knew who had a private income. He supplemented this by collecting insurance. He could afford to run a small car and being a generous person he would later on help me out if I had to deliver a painting or two to Newlyn Gallery. He knew that I had little money and would never baulk at buying me a pasty and a pint. Sometimes he would drive Jacque and me out to Cape Cornwall or other beauty spots. He was always happy for us to call in at his home on the harbour, which was part of Watch House Flats, which we believed he owned. Tall and thin with a Ronald Coleman moustache, he regarded himself as a bit of an aesthete, tending to write off my presence in St Ives as mere escapism - I assume he meant from Sheffield. His preferred Art on his walls were reproductions of Aubrey Beardsley's work.

Jacque and I were married in 1960; Steve said that he would give it five years. Well, he was out by about forty-eight years so far.

Eventually Steve went to live in Penzance at the bottom of New Street where, from his small garden, he had that lovely view across the bay to St.Michael's Mount.

Sadly for all of us, Stephen died shortly afterwards, still in his forties. He suffered from a lot of back pain and was found lying on his bed with whisky and tablets to hand. It was never established whether this combination brought about an accidental death or whether it was intended.

Brian went home for the winter. I thought that it might be the last time that I would see him - but not so. I had by now to introduce Jacque to my parents at Handsworth, only just a mile away from his parents' home in Frecheville, so we took the opportunity to visit him there. Oddly enough, his father was a butcher too, but didn't wear it on his sleeve, as my father often did. The house, like his parents and older sister was quite reserved and tidy - and boring. My parents liked Jacque very much but owing to the age gap of nine years my mother was quick to point out to the neighbours that there wasn't any scandal. By this we presumed that she meant that we hadn't left any babies behind in St Ives. Jacque had overheard the garden fence conversation and thought it very funny. I showed her around one or two Sheffield sights like Tinsley Canal and Burngreave Cemetery. Completely alien to her, she loved it.

The following season arrived and Brian, to my surprise, turned up! Whatever his fate had to be, I felt that I had played a large part in it; I still didn't believe living with his parents would prove to be an answer for him. But he was a dreamer.

We continued to walk and sometimes work together whenever possible. In those early days one of our haunts would be the Man Friday café run by Pat Griffiths and her husband. (I was happy to be asked to do charcoal portraits of their children.) This was directly by Porthmeor Beach and a great meeting place for beach bums, young bikini-clad girls and casually clad artists. Another café was the Daubers, as the brilliant name suggests, another artist's venue.

179

This one was at the top of Island Road. It was owned by Boots Redgrave, Bill's wife. Bill was an excellent artist with an independent approach of his own. Figurative but somewhat innovative and therefore often surprising. I remember a portrait he did, which had an eye floating in heavy varnish. A disturbing image. On one occasion he was sitting there reading his newspaper. Having finished, he offered it to Brian, who declined. I felt this tiny episode somehow encapsulated their different attitudes to the world. Brian could often turn the shoulder and even show a significant haughtiness- often, I thought, to his own detriment.

I would have loved to have known Bill better but that's where my affliction of shyness kicked in. It was too late - he left St Ives shortly after to further his career and love life in London. Boots on the other hand was prepared to be anyone's friend and wouldn't take 'No' for an answer. She was to go into business with Bernard Leach's wife Janet at a later date; I was to play a minor role in this undertaking.

Brian and I were still getting works hung in the 36 and at Newlyn Gallery, which were generally run by the artists, with independent curators. Michael Canney was the exception, the difference being that he was also a very good abstract painter in his own right. He also wrote the art criticism for the St Ives Times and Echo which always reviewed the local art exhibitions.

Brian and I usually got a mention in the also-rans but later, when I was elected to the St Ives Society of Artists, I was thrilled to be raised to the top rank. Brian had certainly viewed the Society but I think he felt his own work was too different. I would have agreed. I had much respect for the traditional.

At this time the lower part of the New Gallery, as it was now called, having been vacated by the abstract element, held the paraphernalia of the St Ives Operatic Society, together with its rehearsals. It wasn't until many years later that they left and the Crypt was once more taken over by the work of the Society and became known as the Mariners; largely a venue for one-man shows. A few years after the Millennium had dawned, the committee decided that it should once again be called The Crypt. Meanwhile the name 'New' had been dropped as it no longer was! Confused? So were many visitors. Curating my own exhibition one day, one such came in and wanted to know where the boats and things of a maritime nature were displayed!

Meanwhile, back at Curnows we were both washing our fingers to the bone. A particular incident happened that illustrated Brian's tenuous link to reality. I had stressed that we had to be a bit careful (as it had been made clear to me), because beneath our attic was the garage housing the delivery vans - together with a petrol pump.

Over at the hotel, one particular day, Treve burst in breathless, as I was into my tenth pile of dishes.

"Have you got the key to the loft?" He yelled.

"Yes".

"Then get over there right away - run! There's smoke coming from the attic window!" I ran, not stopping to take off my yellow apron.

Diving up the alley at the side of the Post Office, I was met with three members of the local Fire Service and a policeman who was trying to push back a gathering crowd. I was horrified. A pall of black smoke was pouring from the bedroom window. It was Brian's day off and I was already wondering what the hell he could have done.

I unlocked the door and ran up the wooden stairs and over to the bedroom door, clutching the other key.

A fireman's voice behind me yelled "Crouch down before you open it - any flames should shoot over your head!"

"Flames! - flames!" I'm thinking. "What the hell am I doing here? Jesus! If the pump goes up, I'm dead!"

Smoke belched out as I unlocked the door and pushed it open.

The kettle that Brian had left on our small electric stove had boiled dry and was in the process of melting. The fireman put out a gloved hand and after shouting a warning, dropped it into the alleyway to be tended to by the other firemen. The smoke dispersed. He grinned, "Lucky boy!"

Treve was furious but I managed to calm him down and promised to impress the seriousness of the matter onto Brian when he returned.

This I did but in his best haughty manner, he refused to be brought to task, saying that he really didn't care for my admonishment.

The bond between us, however, couldn't be broken by such a happening and we were soon looking over the work he had done, miles away in the fields over Lelant.

Treve that year wanted to refurbish our lovely garret and garage and turn it into flats; I'm not sure whether the incident had any bearing on his plans! Consequently, there would be no particular reason for us to stay at Curnow's, the free accommodation having been the main factor.

I now had a home at Jacque's flat. She thought that I shouldn't be having to do so much work anyway.

Nevertheless, Brian and I found work at a small café at Carrack Gladden, which was perched on top of the road high above Carbis Bay beach. Brian didn't stay long, but found work as a breakfast chef in a hotel nearby where he could live-in. He couldn't quite believe his role and I shuddered to think what might happen to the numerous eggs that he would have to fry every morning. However, he seemed to get by. The best part was that he was able to live in one of the huts provided.

I carried on at the café for a while, enjoying the happy-go-lucky style that it generated. The best feature was the brightly dressed girl waitresses who fluttered around the outdoor tables like butterflies. The patrons were passing tourists, usually coming up from the beach; if they had seen the often chaotic conditions that ensued in the tiny kitchen, they might not have bothered to stop. All the staff were young and inexperienced. The ageing owner would put time in, but much of that was taken up with him trying to date one of the girls, having got bored with his wife. It was late, usually 11p.m. by the time we had cleaned up. I found that the quickest way back to St Ives was to walk the railway line - in the dark! The last train had long gone; the awkward part was to adapt to the distance between the rail sleepers as they weren't designed to walk on. I enjoyed the sense of trespassing in the dark. There was always work in the Season and I certainly met a lot of young itinerant workers.

The café job soon folded - I didn't have to look far to replace it. The Karenza Hotel just across the way on Headland Road needed a kitchen porter. The owner was a really nice man as was the head chef. He made sure that in return for washing his pots and pans and 'rumbling' the spuds, I was well fed.

The Chy an Drea was another hotel that I washed-up for. This was newly owned by two Up Country families that had pooled their savings and bought this splendid hotel overlooking the bay. They had met Jacque at Curnow's and been charmed by her, and then intrigued by our relationship. Consequently, I was becoming rather spoilt. After my shift had finished one of the owners would like me to accompany him in his sumptuous car over to Penzance, where we would drop into the best café, and consume cream cakes. I fancy that this was a way of being naughty behind his wife's back as he wasn't in the best of health; he was probably banned from eating cream cakes. He was sympathetic to my artistic aspirations, and he would sometimes push a £5 note into my top pocket.

Unwittingly Jacque and I had engineered a combination that proved to be somewhat irresistible to visitors that came in contact with us and this certainly helped my budding career along. It seemed that we had innocently taken on an iconic status as far as the art colony was concerned.

I needed a studio for the winter months and again Jacque came up with the answer. Clair Knight was an old friend of the family. He lived with his sister in one of the large houses on Park Avenue, overlooking the town. On Jacque's enquiry, he was all too happy to let me have the basement as a rent-free studio. It had a window only just below street level and so was tolerable.

It was here that I began some serious indoor work and Still Life became my theme. In a way, I felt that it was just a bit too easy for me to produce outdoor work on paper or work that had an abstract slant to it.

36. Self-portrait 1962

I needed to look really hard at objects and try to extract the truth behind the visual. At this early period, I needed an honest approach. I didn't want to fool myself or anyone else.

Jacque had decided to leave Curnow's; she was offered a job in a shop in Fore Street, owned by a Falmouth business man - a cheery friendly fellow who was quick to appreciate Jacque's gifts and abilities. He gave her leave to manage, and choose the goods to display. These were mainly ladies' dresses, trendy tops and Italian needle cord suits, costume jewellery and bikinis. He had called the shop Hades and painted it black, which had the effect of showing off the goods to advantage and intriguing the visitors. The shops in St Ives at this time were largely owned by local people and could only be described as pedestrian. You could say that this shop was the beginning of modern St Ives and what you see today is partly our fault! People loved it and a small crowd would often gather at the window. I have to say that this was in some part down to me as I found that my artistic talents, such as they were, had a flair for window dressing! This was made interesting as we had rigged a fine black fishing net as a backdrop- this proved a brilliant way to show bikinis and jewellery!

One side of the shop had been franchised to West Country Cleaners and here jackets, suits and coats etc. were taken in, and later dispensed clean. It was an easy, albeit mind-numbing job, that at that time was done by another friend of Jacque's: a very attractive blonde girl, Angela from St. Erth. Not unnoticed by Phil, he added her to his tally.

37. In the Mill Studio Nancledra c.1966

Jacque suggested that a space above the dress rail might well be a good space to hang two of my recently framed still-lives. I agreed and they were duly hung.

It wasn't long before she had some interesting news.

"Mrs. Leddra, the curator at the St Ives Society of Artists came in with some cleaning, saw your paintings and was very impressed. She wants you to take them down to the gallery and let Hugh Ridge see them."

I was knocked sideways, even more so when I received the news that they would be happy to retain the paintings for the next show and - would I be interested in membership?

Would I be interested? I'll say so.

I became one of the few artists who had bridged the gap between the Penwith and the Society, having shown in both at the same time.

Newlyn had tightened up and my friend John Clark - later John Charles Clark- who was at that time on the Newlyn Committee, revealed that I had not succeeded in my application for membership as I was a Society member. And so I didn't complete the hat-trick.

That parameter didn't work the other way around as Ken Symonds, a highly respected artist and significant member of Newlyn, was accepted by the Society when he became disenchanted by the new policies that were being implemented in his own gallery- and he wasn't the only one to become disenchanted!

I didn't have to stay long at Clair Knight's as I learnt that a condemned cottage in Back Road West could be rented as studios. I acquired the top room and opened it on the next show day, selling one of my first oil paintings. From there I acquired the use of an airy space in the car park at the top of Tregenna Hill. This had windows all around and I really couldn't have wished for a better studio. There was a drawback in that I needed to be open to the public, but it was situated up a steep driveway from the main road. People don't generally like hills or steps! However, I had arrived and the next thing I knew is that a photo of me in my little paradise appeared in the Geographic magazine along with Bryan Wynter, Peter Lanyon and Patrick Heron. It was an article on the St Ives Art Colony; it also included a photo of Bernard Leach. I was labelled as a newcomer, but I must say - a happy one.

Brian, in the off season meanwhile, had rented a small house in Teetotal Street. This belonged to Willie Barns-Graham. Willie by now was a leading light in the Penwith. Brian's work had taken on a more abstract look and he had no difficulty in showing it at the Penwith, which had by now moved to its new home in Back Road West. I was seeing less and less of him and it soon came to my notice that he had moved to Halsetown, a village outside St Ives, where he had apparently been invited to share a home with another fellow. This was the last I heard of Brian.

Meanwhile, almost every still life that I produced sold very quickly at the Society. By this time Hughie Ridge was giving me pride of place in the middle of each wall. I had begun to do some really large paintings, mainly in egg tempera, and as they had to be framed under glass, they were quite heavy. He called me 'The Heavy Brigade.'

The Penwith particularly liked my large charcoal drawings and in 1968 I had a show there in the side gallery. I remember Bernard Leach stooping to peer at every exhibit and on leaving declaiming "Well, you can certainly draw!!"

This was the only interaction that I had with Bernard - not so his wife Janet, more later.

I sold two or three drawings from this exhibition.

I had by now become well acquainted with Jacque's three brothers; the eldest one Desmond was married with two fast-growing sons whom he tended to treat like soldiers. They stayed for holidays in a house by the harbour. On his whistle, they were expected to leave the beach, come running and report. He was very intelligent, being the head salesman for Bachelors.

I was pleased when he bought quite a large painting of a sunflower that I had done in Clair's basement.

Jacque also had a younger sister, Annie. She was married and lived in Bradford with Frank her husband, and three very young children. Jacque had never seen the family and asked me if I thought it reasonable to spend a few days in Bradford. It was OK by me so we caught the train and found ourselves eventually in a gloomy Northern town.

We located the street of back-to-back houses; the children that we saw playing in the back alley were indeed Deborah, Susan and Michael, Annie's kids. Jacque was immediately looking somewhat distressed at the condition of both the alley and the kids. I had been brought up in similar surroundings in Sheffield and so it wasn't so surprising to me. Children generally accept their surroundings, no matter how dismal, and they were playing happily enough. They were excited to see us as they had been told that we were on our way.

The house was ill-furnished and uncomfortable, with lino hardly covering the bare floor and the coal fire barely warming the interior - something I knew about all too well as a child.

As depressing as the situation appeared, it was to get worse. Annie, however, was like a breath of fresh air, and the place certainly needed it.

She was a tall, attractive brunette with a quick sense of humour and also not a little zany. I liked her very much; she was charming, as were the children. Frank, her husband worked at Fyffes in one of the warehouses where bananas and other imported fruit were unloaded and stored. Ostensibly there was little wrong with him. A Northern working-class man finding solace, when needed, in the nearest pub. A man in his own environment.

Annie just didn't fit in, and it soon became obvious to us that she was very unhappy there. We learnt how creative she was, making attractive cushions, and dolls and clothes for the children, from bits and pieces that she had collected. They were original and full of charm.

A real case of finding out who you are before committing yourself, they were heading for a divorce.

Michael being overloaded with energy was a real handful. I have a mental image of us waiting by the gate of the local Infant's School at Home time. All the children left normally, chatting away with their parents. "Where is he, Annie?" I enquired, worried.

"Wait -wait! This is what he does! Here he comes!" The last one out, he had waited until everyone had cleared, then burst from the doors and ran around the yard three times as fast as he could, a huge grin on his little face. Apparently, he did this every school day! He also spent some of his sleeping time banging his head against the wall! I treasure a drawing that he did of me where my moustache had migrated to the top of my nose!

I couldn't say that he was troubled - he was happy.

Jacque discussed Annie's plight with her at length, and soon volunteered that we should offer the girls a long holiday in St Ives, until the divorce was done with. Annie agreed and I agreed. A short time later found me meeting Annie on Bristol station and then taking the girls on to Cornwall.

Needless to say, not having seen a sandy beach or the sea before, they couldn't believe their luck. As Jacque was still employed in Fore Street, I found myself suddenly being turned into a father figure and showing them the things that you were supposed to do on a beach! Two beautiful little girls, they soon made friends. Jacqui Leafe and another friend, Angela, became very useful as 'foster parents'.

Later on, Annie having got her divorce, decided with Jacque's encouragement to come down and live in St Ives; we put her up in the flat, briefly. She soon made friends and found accommodation at the end of Island Road where she continued to make her beautiful dolls and cushions. Jacque showed them in the shop window, and they soon began to sell. Janet Leach, Bernard's wife, had recently opened The Craftsmen's Shop opposite Woolworth's. She showed Bernard's pots, and those of other potters working with Bernard, at the Stennack

Pottery, higher up the town. She also introduced into the town foreign wares by way of an agent in London. This was something entirely new in St Ives.

Such things as woven baskets and rush matting appeared and began to attract a lot of attention, especially with people who had bought second homes in the area and were already beginning to let out their property to the many visitors who were now starting to discover Cornwall and St Ives in particular.

Janet used to bring her cleaning into the shop and Jacque's flair, and my talent as a window dresser, didn't escape her notice. Her manager had recently left - Janet lost no time.

"I want you guys to come and work for me!", she one day offered in her Texan drawl. "I'll put you on commission and you can stay open in the evenings." Evening opening was becoming more common in St Ives at that time; even the Society did so, until in later years the occasional drunk would wander in and ruin things for everybody else. We needed the money and it seemed progressive. It also brought us more into the Art Colony and I must say Janet turned out to be a real eye-opener. A very progressive lady! She gave no heed to me as an artist, feeling that her role should be more aligned to Modern Art. Dame Barbara Hepworth became her friend and ultimately her drinking partner, albeit very private. No! I was quickly recognised as a useful tool to carry the foreign wares through the streets of the town from where they had been dropped by the lorry. Strictly speaking, I wasn't even on the payroll, but the more I fed the Craftsman's Shop, then the more money we made, and we did stay open until 11p.m.! Annie's dolls were sensational sitting in a basket ware chair in the window!

38. With Phil in the Digey.

Occasionally Phil would give me a hand with the baskets etc. and we would string them along a bamboo pole and bounce up Fore Street to the Craftsman's Shop, much to the delight of the camera- toting visitors. The baskets and mats etc. were dropped off by van at what was the backdoor to the boatyard which later became the Sloop Craft Market and which at that time had covered accommodation.

Later, Barbara Hepworth's garage was brought into service - she didn't have a car. Eventually Janet had Boots Redgrave join forces with her and the New Craftsman came into being, just a few doors away from the Craftsman's Shop.

Jacque and I agreed to get married in 1960; we were duly married in Penzance at the same registry (opposite the Acorn theatre) where Dylan Thomas married Caitlin.

Since a child I had suffered the effects of bronchiactesis- I think from a severe bout of childhood measles- that left me with scar tissue on my right lung; I was never often free from nasty mucous and occasional bleeding. Jacque having suffered years in a sanatorium with TB wasn't exactly unused to this and was always ready to allay my worries.

When I asked her why she had, as I saw it, deigned to marry me, she replied- "Well- I thought you were the most honest person that I had ever met- certainly in St Ives, and also I didn't think that you would last five minutes!"

Despite the charm and convenience of the flat, Jacque began to wonder whether we could find a place of our own. I soon detected that she didn't really want to stay in St Ives despite the fact that everyone loved her. I think that perhaps she felt that she and the events in her life had become too well-known locally. She wanted to slip out of the limelight - being the centre of attraction in Janet's popular shop in Fore Street wasn't easy.

I discussed the situation with my father; he agreed to stand me £1000 on a house and, after a little searching, we decided on Nancledra- its location on the bus route from Penzance to St Ives being important for us, as I didn't drive at the time. The house cost £3000 which seems a ridiculous amount of money now but in fact took us years to pay off on a mortgage.

Janet interceded: "I don't know why you guys bother going home - you're here until gone ten o'clock - you can have the flat over the New Craftsman for nothing and let out your house!" And this we did! Every Saturday I would go over and clean it out, and let new people in.

Janet was very good to us; she paid for me to have driving lessons - I only needed ten! Then we had a little van!

WAGGER

We also acquired a dog.

I spent a lot of time helping Jacque in the shop, especially helping bikini -clad girls, straight off the beach, to choose their necklaces. Believe me, there wasn't much room in that shop! Jacque would occasionally slip next door to see Beryl Segal, wife of my fellow artist Hyman. On this occasion she bounced back in: "You must see this charming dog that Beryl has!"

"I don't want a dog!" I said. But I went anyway.

As soon as I entered Beryl's shop, this brown bundle of energy jumped into my arms. "That's your dog, Victor!" exclaimed Beryl.

Hyman was the local officer for stray animals; people would turn up with abandoned pets etc. This particular animal had eventually, after one or two chases around Camborne, been picked up by the police and then rescued from the police station by a St Ives girl who had devoted herself to such operations. How she got it back to St Ives on the bus I shall never know. This was a tear-away dog! Very handsome, with a bobbed tail - so he had belonged to someone at one time - he was the Charlie Chaplin of the dog world. He occasionally broke into the high-stepping gait of the well-known Spanish horses and this immediately caught people's attention. He was good at that!

People would ask about his pedigree and I would answer that he only had a police record. I did meet a man in Fore Street who said that he had bred Basenjis - he was adamant that Wagger was one. I later found out that Basenjis didn't bark and Wagger certainly did. I had him for eighteen years - he was a wonderful but naughty companion.

Having bought the house at Nancledra and moved out of Jacque's beautiful flat at Talland Road, we were now set up in Janet's flat in Fore Street. Wagger wasn't sure. The first thing he did, whilst we were working in the shop, was to proclaim his territory by digging a hole in the mattress.

Jacque had a lovely yellow canary that she kept in a golden domed cage. She would talk to it - she called it Little Bird - and it would sing and jump up and down in delight. This didn't go unnoticed by Wagger; I suspect that he found it quite annoying. Either that, or he was jealous. I did my usual morning check on him to see that he was alright. Alright?!

He had shredded one or two of Jacque's sanitary towels and deposited the cotton wool on top of Little Bird's cage. Understandably, Little Bird wasn't pleased and was jumping up and down on his perch -shrieking, not singing!

When admonished Wagger would wriggle under a convenient bed or settee and keep out of the way for a while. On this occasion he had other ideas. Grabbing a sanitary towel in his mouth, he shot between my legs, down the stairs, and ran through Fore Street, with me chasing him - much to the delight of the tourists.

On another occasion, taking him for his early morning walk, I let him loose on the harbour beach where at that time there was no dog restriction.

The beach at the Porthminster end had been beautifully flattened by the early tide, and claimed by Wagger as his own. Unfortunately for the very early small groups of sun bathers etc. they didn't know that this was Wagger's beach; they were quickly informed by his cocking-of-the-leg. Just a little drop- it had to go around. Further on, a small group had gathered by a pool which held a small dead shark. "My shark", said Wagger. Anyone pressing too close to have a look was quickly reminded by a low growl.

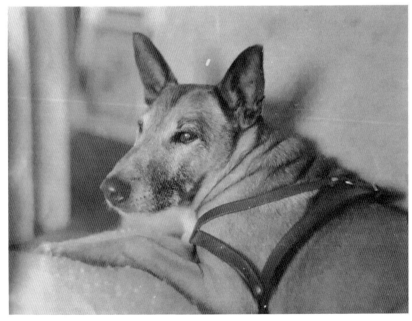

39. Wagger

Bernard Leach, of course, was by now famous for his pots, his Japanese connections, and his wonderful pottery at the top of the Stennack. Many of the senior artists were already 'giving it large' in America, sometimes noticeably making sure that they weren't usurped by incomers. Hardly 'feet of clay', but sometimes I thought that there was occasionally a hint of that. Hard-won ground, I suppose.

On one occasion, Janet and Bernard came into the shop with a person of some import. No introduction. Janet scribbled his name on our sales pad.

Bernard was showing off his pots, however the man turned to us and asked me what I did. I was happy to respond but Bernard obviously didn't like it. The gentleman in question was Mark Tobey, a well-known American Tachiste painter of the time. Unfortunately, my shyness and inability to mix well precluded me from going to private views and the parties that were often held in the town - one exception being in Janet's new flat overlooking Porthmeor beach.. These modern flats had been built after the old wooden Piazza and neighbouring studios had disintegrated with years of constant battering by the sea. Years later the Porthmeor studios were also refurbished.

But I did have friends in the Art World - notably Jeff Harris, whom I regarded as the best abstact artist at the time, and Roy Conn with whom Jacque and I spent many happy hours at Nancledra. They both later spent some time teaching at Falmouth Art School.

The Penwith had opened its gallery doors in the old pilchard lofts on Back Road West and needed a secretary. Kathy Watkins, who had been with Jacque as co-receptionist at Curnow's Hotel, was a very good secretary, albeit rather old-fashioned in that she for many years eschewed a computer and still banged out the necessary stuff on her old typewriter!

Having now left Curnow's, she was out of a job. We suggested that she apply to the Penwith. "I don't know anything about Art" she responded.

I suggested cheekily that perhaps they didn't know that much about it either.

She got the job and ran the Penwith almost with the proverbial rod of iron for over fifty years. On her demise in 2014, she received more reviews than many artists ever did! She had left her dreary husband at Manderley in Primrose Valley, Porthminster, and had taken up with Roy Conn, having both acquired the terraced house by the Penwith, probably at minimal rent. Roy had been favoured with one of the huge Porthmeor studios overlooking the beach, where I suspect he may have been guilty of watching the girls behind their sunscreens slipping into their bikinis.

Roy was at the head of the wave in those days, I suspect heading for the top with his finely painted hard-edge abstracts, but fashions change in the Art World and ultimately his wave passed over.

The building at the bottom of Barnoon Hill was the local dance hall in the war; Jacque was often danced around by American soldiers, billeted nearby and awaiting D-Day. It had now become Barbara Hepworth's studio and workplace for some of the very large sculptures that she was becoming famous for. Janet's flat overlooked the yard where Barbara's workers would be chipping away. The flat, and later another display and work area -preserved after her death- were just across the road.

The Art Colony was generally stunned when it was discovered that Barbara Hepworth had burnt to death in her bed in 1975; a smoker, it wasn't difficult to see what had happened. An earlier tragedy was the death of Peter Lanyon in 1964.

40. Victor with his self-portrait in 2005 (Painted in 1962)

Postscript

"I am living faster than I can write and can never hope to finish it".

Victor died in 2014, having been diagnosed with cancer in 2012. He was unable to complete his memoirs and was never to see them published.

In the late 1970s Jacque chose to withdraw from the world and live as a recluse. Victor felt he owed Jacque a great debt. Though he created a new life with Bernadette in Penzance in 1979, he continued to care for Jacque and regale her with stories of his adventures, until her death in March 2014. In April 2014 Victor and Bernadette married. Victor died shortly after in June.

Victor had planned an 80th birthday retrospective exhibition at the St Ives Society of Artists, to take place in September 2014. With typical good humour he said it may well be posthumous. With the help of members of the Society and friends, Bernadette presented the exhibition as planned.

Victor was very proud to be acknowledged as the longest serving member of the Society. In the weeks before his death he instructed Bernadette to donate a painting to Penlee House Gallery and Museum in Penzance. Since then, "A Dream of Fishes" has been part of its exhibition on the first floor.

To quote John Watson, the chairman of the St Ives Society of Artists:

"Beaming smile, Yorkshire twang, warm handshake. Victor Bramley, a proper man".

Appendix 1:

School Certificate July 1950

UNIVERSITIES OF MANCHESTER LIVERPOOL LEEDS SHEFFIELD AND BIRMINGHAM

JOINT MATRICULATION BOARD

SCHOOL CERTIFICATE

VICTOR OLIVER   BORN 16 NOVEMBER 1933

ATTENDED   FIRTH PARK GRAMMAR SCHOOL FOR BOYS, SHEFFIELD
AND WAS AWARDED THE SCHOOL CERTIFICATE OF THE JOINT MATRICULATION BOARD
IN JULY, 1950, HAVING SATISFIED THE EXAMINERS IN THE EXAMINATION AS A WHOLE AND
HAVING ATTAINED THE STANDARD SHOWN IN THE FOLLOWING   EIGHT   SUBJECTS:

ENGLISH LANGUAGE	VERY GOOD
ENGLISH LITERATURE	PASS
GEOGRAPHY	CREDIT
FRENCH	VERY GOOD
ITALIAN	VERY GOOD
MATHEMATICS	PASS
PHYSICS	PASS
ART	CREDIT

(The standards of award in individual subjects are Very Good, Credit, Pass)

SIGNED ON BEHALF OF THE JOINT MATRICULATION BOARD

Chairman

Secretary to the Board

THE MINISTRY OF EDUCATION ACCEPT THE EXAMINATION AS REACHING THE APPROVED STANDARD

SIGNED ON BEHALF OF THE MINISTRY OF EDUCATION

Under-Secretary

Appendix 2:
Reference Letter from the Headmaster 21st July 1950

TELEPHONE No. 36184

W. R. C. CHAPMAN, M.A., PH.D.
HEADMASTER

FIRTH PARK GRAMMAR SCHOOL,
THE BRUSHES,
BARNSLEY ROAD,
SHEFFIELD. 5

21st July, 1950.

VICTOR OLIVER entered this School in September, 1945, and followed a five year course to the School Certificate examination, which he has just taken.

Although he had rather a long period of absence during his third year, he has worked hard and is now above the average of School Certificate candidates in ability, and he possesses distinct aptitude for language work and Art. During the past year he has applied himself very diligently to his studies.

He is a very pleasant fellow, quiet, sensible, willing and thoroughly reliable. He has never given us any trouble whatsoever, and his manners are excellent.

He has participated in the normal School athletics and has played for his House at football.

I know that he will be happy if he has a post which will give scope to his interest in Art, but I am equally sure that he will do his very best for any employer even if his artistic bent cannot find any gratification.

Headmaster.